The Six Sigma Leader

How Top Executives Will Prevail in the 21st Century

Peter S. Pande

Foreword by
W. James McNerney, Jr.
Chairman, President, and Chief Executive Officer
The Boeing Company

McGraw·Hill

New York   Chicago   San Francisco   Lisbon   London   Madrid   Mexico City
Milan   New Delhi   San Juan   Seoul   Singapore   Sydney   Toronto

The **McGraw·Hill** Companies

To Olga, with love.

1 2 3 4 5 6 7 8 9 0   DOC/DOC   0 9 8 7 6

ISBN-13: 978-0-07-145408-7
ISBN-10: 0-07-145408-X

This publication is designed to provide accurate and authoritative information in regard to the subject matter covered. It is sold with the understanding that the publisher is not engaged in rendering legal, accounting, or other professional service. If legal advice or other expert assistance is required, the services of a competent professional person should be sought.

—From a declaration of principles jointly adopted by a committee of the American Bar Association and a committee of publishers.

McGraw-Hill books are available at special quantity discounts to use as premiums and sales promotions, or for use in corporate training programs. For more information, please write to the Director of Special Sales, Professional Publishing, McGraw-Hill, Two Penn Plaza, New York, NY 10121-2298. Or contact your local bookstore.

Contents

Foreword

FINDING AND DEVELOPING leaders is one of the greatest challenges faced by organizations throughout the world today. The importance of leadership is not new, of course. But what is becoming increasingly critical is the role and impact that every leader can have—be it on a large organization or a small department.

The best, most inspiring leaders I've had the pleasure of working with and learning from in my career are those who were relentlessly striving to improve themselves and those around them. They never let their own success lead them to the assumption that they had all the answers or were ready to stop growing as leaders or as individuals. Limited perspectives—for example, the attitude that "I've gotten this far so I must be pretty darn good," or the excuse that "I don't have time to work on my own effectiveness"—make it hard to fill the growing need for great leaders in many environments.

What is compelling to me about the concept of the "Six Sigma Leader" is that it borrows from ideas that have helped companies become more customer focused, use facts and analysis more effectively, break down barriers, and drive innovation. I've seen and felt the impact of Six Sigma and Lean methods in my past roles at GE and 3M, as well as at Boeing. These are goals that should be foremost priorities for any leader.

But beyond that, the message of this book is that the impact of Six Sigma shouldn't just be confined to projects and processes; instead, it must be broadened to include building *better leadership*. What Pete Pande makes clear is that "Six Sigma" as applied to leaders means two primary things: first, that a higher standard for leadership performance is essential (just as 3.4 defects per million operations set a new standard for business processes); and second, that the real lesson and value of Six Sigma—to those who truly understand it—is not about analytical tools, or about figuring out customer needs, or about improving teamwork. It's about *all of that* and more.

Six Sigma Leadership addresses the importance not just of personal values such as integrity—which should be a given—but also of leadership fundamentals such as adaptability, versatility, and nonstop learning.

I can apply some of my own leadership observations to illustrate these ideas.

In talks I give on the challenges of global innovation, one of my most important messages is that the myths that hamper innovation are based on a one-dimensional view. For example, *discipline* is often assumed to inhibit innovation, squelch creativity, and dampen enthusiasm. In reality, however, discipline is an essential ingredient of innovation; it provides focus to creative efforts and enables new ideas to become reality. To promote innovation in their organizations, successful leaders must be active champions of *both* creativity and discipline—and never favor one at the expense of the other.

One of the things I'm proud of about my tenure at 3M was how strongly our Six Sigma initiative was tied to the importance of challenging assumptions about what was possible, about breaking through the limits of "entitlement" (the designed capacity of the business) to reach new levels of performance. The leaders who made the most progress in their businesses, and their own development, were those most ready to challenge entitlement—which could happen only by embracing both discipline and creativity.

Another lesson echoed in *The Six Sigma Leader* is the importance of teamwork as an ingredient of outstanding leadership. Go-it-alone stories seem to pervade a lot of writing on leadership, when the message should be exactly the opposite. The development of any one of Boeing's many successful commercial airplanes or military systems is a classic example of how the dedicated efforts of many people, with their leaders coordinating their efforts, have resulted in breakthroughs of enormous benefit to the world.

I suspect those who have seen Six Sigma as a corporate program may have difficulty making the connection among tools, projects, and the essential elements of outstanding leadership. But I would encourage you to explore how the essential ideas of a Six Sigma Leader can help you explore and strengthen your own capability as a leader, and to take more active responsibility to continually improve your own efforts. The concepts in this book can be of significant benefit in supporting your success and helping us meet the growing need for great leaders in every organization and at every level.

W. James McNerney, Jr.
Chairman, President, and Chief Executive Officer
The Boeing Company
Chicago, Illinois

Acknowledgments

THE MOST important part of any book, I believe, is the support an author receives from others. This is where the real credit lies for this book, and it's an honor and privilege to be associated with the people who've made such a huge contribution to these pages.

A great deal of credit and huge thanks goes to John Kador, whose advice and enthusiasm helped get the writing process moving after a lot of deliberation (but not much speed), and whose ideas, examples, and words of wisdom have kept it going. John's influence and his challenging of the principles of Six Sigma Leadership—helping test the concepts and their validity—have been invaluable.

The support, experience, and eyes and ears of my outstanding colleagues at Pivotal Resources have added an enormous amount to defining the challenges of leadership as well as validating the suggestions presented here on how to meet those challenges. Rowland Hayler, Brett Cooper, Greg Gibbs, and others looked at early drafts and made gentle but smart suggestions for streamlining the message and finding the right tone for the book. Very helpful examples came from Ross Buckwalter, Mo Cayer, Bob Neuman, Elisabeth Swan, and Carolyn Talasek. Ramya Venkataraman also contributed her experiences in dealing with leadership tunnel-vision as well as the "lean management" diagram.

Special thanks goes to Cheralynn Abbott, who not only provided encouragement in the early stages and drafts, but who also read every word and provided extensive and perceptive suggestions in the final manuscript. There's hardly a sentence I've written that a visit from Cheralynn couldn't improve, and *The Six Sigma Leader* greatly benefited from her input.

A huge thank-you goes to all the Pivotal Resources team for continually challenging ourselves and our clients to raise the standard of leadership and success, for advocating the ideals of Six Sigma Leadership, and for allowing me the time to devote to this rewarding project.

To so many clients and leaders that I've had the pleasure—and occasionally, frustration—of working with through a lengthening career go the most important acknowledgment. Unfortunately, to list them would take pages and still not be complete. Special thanks, though, is due to: Kevin Kelleher, President and CEO of global relocation leader Cartus, who provided insight and inspiration at the early stages of the book; Craig Long, Senior Vice President at Milliken and Company, for asking some very pointed questions about the future of Six Sigma, and then providing feedback on my notion about the need for a new standard of leadership; Glenn Bennett, global head of operations for Adidas, who modeled the 10-Second Rule and helped convince me it deserved some prominence in the "toolkit" for leaders; Jeanne O'Connell at 3M for helping to arrange some important interviews in the early stages of the writing process; and particularly Jim McNerney, Chairman of The Boeing Company, for his time and insightful words in the foreword.

At McGraw-Hill, a great partner whose confidence in my role as an author is much appreciated, thanks to editor Jeanne Glasser for advice, patience, and persistence in this somewhat extended process, and to Philip Ruppel, Vice President and Group Publisher, for his continued support of my writing endeavors.

Final special thanks and love to my wonderful kids, Brian and Stephanie, for their interest, support, and inspiration—not to mention helping keep the critical role of organizational leadership in perspective. As important as it is, there are certainly plenty of other things that deserve our attention and commitment.

A New Standard for 21st-Century Leaders

*L*EADERSHIP IS a key determiner of organizational success. Although it's not the only factor, outstanding businesses—and mediocre ones as well—are often best defined by their leadership. The culture, personality, and performance of a business are determined by its leaders throughout the organization—at various levels, in different business units, in locations around the country or the world.

Six Sigma—or the development and continual reinvention/ improvement of customer-focused products, services, and business processes—has also been defined as a key method for organizational success. Many business leaders throughout the world have invested time and energy in learning about and supporting Six Sigma efforts. These efforts have enabled organizations to significantly "raise the bar" in terms of profitability, customer satisfaction, cycle time and waste, and associate empowerment. [1]

This book brings together these two elements of business performance—leadership and Six Sigma—into a compelling and

1. Many companies now describe their initiatives as "Lean Six Sigma," recognizing the merging of Six Sigma (methods credited to Motorola, Allied Signal, and GE, among others) and Lean (derived from the "Toyota Production System") into a more robust change methodology. I'll stick with the simpler and better known term *Six Sigma* throughout this book, though the concepts here will draw from *both* Lean and Six Sigma ideas/principles.

practical approach to improving leadership performance. *The Six Sigma Leader* is based on two premises:

1. Greater focus and attention needs to be paid to the caliber of leadership as a driver of organizational performance.
2. Six Sigma principles and methods, adapted to challenges of leadership, offer a robust set of best practices critical to any leader hoping to succeed in the 21st-century.

As we'll see, this means establishing a *new standard* of performance—one that can and should be demanded of leaders in today's highly competitive, fast-changing environment. The ability of leaders to get away with being "okay" is no longer acceptable if you expect your organization not just to be competitive but to *stay* competitive. London Business School professor and strategy guru Gary Hamel puts the challenge this way:

> **The ultimate test of any management team is not how fast it can grow the company in the short term, but how consistently it can grow it over the long term. . . . In recent years we have witnessed adaptation failures by incumbents across a wide variety of industries: airlines, pharmaceuticals, automobiles, newspapers, and recorded music. . . . What the laggards have failed to grasp is that what matters today is not a company's competitive advantage at a point in time, but its evolutionary advantage over time.[2]**

The same challenge of adaptation and skill at a *strategic* level is reflected in the skills and actions of leaders throughout an organization. The new standard that will be outlined in this book will apply to any leader in any role.

To be clear, this book is *not* about how to lead, plan, or implement a Six Sigma "program." There are plenty of other books on that topic. In fact, the more familiar you are with "leading Six

---

2. Gary Hamel, "Management á la Google," *Wall Street Journal*, April 26, 2006.

Sigma," the greater the challenge you may have in understanding Six Sigma *Leadership*. That's because, to get the most value from these pages, you'll need to concentrate on the work you do every day as a leader—regardless of your role in or view of Six Sigma programs. (This book could be described as an upgrade of what I call the Six Sigma "brand," surpassing what's on the market today.)

Fortunately, though, if you do have experience with Six Sigma, many of the concepts and ideas that comprise Six Sigma Leadership will be familiar, so you have an advantage going in. At the same time, if you have *no* prior exposure to Six Sigma—or just know a little from what you've read or heard—you won't be far behind and may even be able to "get it" more quickly. So you have an advantage *too*.

In the remainder of this Introduction, we'll explore why the time is right to bring Leadership and Six Sigma together into a more powerful vision and standard for 21st-century leaders. I'll also lay out the plan for presenting that vision and the practical skills that bring it to life in the following chapters.

SIX SIGMA: FROM COUNTING TO IMPROVING TO LEADING

Throughout this book you'll find the terms *Six Sigma Leader* and *smart leader* used interchangeably. That reflects the fact that even if Six Sigma had never come along, the vision and skills of leadership presented here would be just as relevant and powerful. (Really, *Smart Leadership* or *Leadership for the 21st-Century Business* would also have been very appropriate titles for this book.) There is a reason, of course, why Six Sigma is a foundation and inspiration for building better leadership. But there is also a risk, noted earlier, that your preconceived notions about Six Sigma will get in the way of unlocking the value of Six Sigma *Leadership*. So let's do a bit of "level setting" around what "Six Sigma" means and how we will be linking it to great leadership. Even if you've been exposed to Six Sigma before—in fact, *especially* if you have—please take a moment to review these next few paragraphs.

There are a variety of "definitions" of Six Sigma—and many interpretations of those definitions. For our purposes, a quick review will suffice.

Six Sigma Definition I: A Measure of Performance

One of the key benefits of Six Sigma has been its emphasis on metrics. The Sigma *measure* was developed and popularized by Motorola in the 1980s as a method for measurement and a goal for improvement. *Six Sigma* refers to the statistical level of variation where problems impacting customers are extremely rare, signifying "almost perfect" quality. A key theme is to understand and quantify the defects delivered to customers.

Six Sigma Definition 2: Models/Tools for Driving Improvement Projects

Six Sigma is commonly associated with a set of project-based methods to design, improve, and measure a company's products, services, or processes. This is where most of the *activity* around Six Sigma has been focused and is the subject of most Six Sigma training.[3] These methods are important to Six Sigma Leaders because: (*a*) they provide a testing ground for many core principles we'll apply at a leadership level; and (*b*) the ability to change (innovate, design, improve, fix, etc.) your business is an essential skill of 21st-century leadership—and these methods offer you resources for that continual reinvention.

Six Sigma Definition 3: A Program/Initiative for Business Improvement

The most commonly understood meaning for *Six Sigma* (or *Lean Six Sigma*) today describes an organizational *program* combining

---

3. The "lingua franca" of Six Sigma at the project level is the DMAIC process—Define, Measure, Analyze, Improve, and Control—which has become a widely adopted roadmap for process change projects. It has proven very valuable as a common framework for change efforts within and between companies trying to address tough, cause-unknown problems. But there are other models for other types of projects as well in the most ambitious initiatives.

project selection, training, and change execution (using the methods referred to in Definition 2). Today, many if not most major corporations worldwide have some form of Six Sigma program. Some of these—like GE, Raytheon, Bank of America, Xerox, and quite a few others—are full-scale, top-down corporate initiatives. Others are not so all-encompassing—limited to certain business units or functions (though these may be very committed efforts)—or are less intensive (a limited number of people working on fairly specialized projects).[4]

Some common features of Six Sigma *programs* include special roles or levels of competence in leading projects (e.g., *Green Belts*, *Black Belts*), assignment of management-level *Champions* to guide and provide leadership-level support, and the use of cross-functional teams to provide a robust set of skills and perspectives to the issue at hand.

Six Sigma Definition 4: Skills for Improved Thinking and Business Leadership

As you might guess, this is the definition that's the focus of *The Six Sigma Leader*. We'll be looking closely at both what they are and how these principles/skills can dramatically enhance leadership effectiveness. Two points to emphasize now:

1. These leadership skills are *already* part of most Six Sigma programs. As noted above, they are integrated into the *project* methods that have helped achieve billions of dollars in savings and revenue gains. Many companies note this reality, describing people engaged in Six Sigma as candidates for the "next generation" of organizational leaders, based on the experience and skill set they gain from their efforts.

---

4. The variation between these different programs is one big reason why there are so many differing views of what *Six Sigma* means. For example, in some companies Six Sigma is the program for the "Improve" strategy, while in others it includes "Design" and "Manage." (See Chapter 6.)

2. Despite that nod to leadership, this last definition of Six Sigma is the *most important*, the least understood, and the *least consistently* applied. This gap hampers the impact of Six Sigma programs—which is disappointing. But more importantly, it ignores the reality that sustained improvement of a business at the *process* level will never be sustained until *leadership* processes and abilities are also improved.

If you have thought of Six Sigma as just a program or a method, for this book you will need to enlarge your definition. Connecting it with set of capabilities by which a leader can more effectively think through challenges, define goals, and guide an organization is the key to unlocking the true power of Six Sigma *Leadership*.

LEADERS AND SIX SIGMA: WHAT NOW AND WHAT'S NEXT?

The fact that leaders are not applying Six Sigma concepts consistently to *how they lead* does not mean they are not supportive or enthusiastic about it. To the contrary, some of the most admired executives in business worldwide have celebrated Six Sigma programs as a key to their organizations' current and future success. A look at a list of adopters will reveal companies in every imaginable industry and function, from hotels to high tech and banking to heavy manufacturing. Six Sigma efforts have been credited with billions of dollars in savings and new revenues, while whole new career paths have opened up for people with Six Sigma experience and expertise.

And it's become a truly global phenomenon. The experience of my own company is an example: In 10 years we've provided consulting and training in Six Sigma to firms on six continents. We're seeing an explosion of interest in Asia, where China, Vietnam, Indonesia, Thailand, and India are growing adopters alongside Korea, Japan, Taiwan, and Singapore. The first book I coauthored in 2000, *The Six Sigma Way*, has been translated into languages as diverse as Estonian, German, Turkish, Thai, Bahasa, Spanish, and Chinese, just to name a few. There's a "Sigma 6" brand of gasoline in South Korea, and even a hard rock band in the United States that calls itself 6Sigma.

And leaders, at all levels, have invested personal time in learning about and guiding Six Sigma. Among the many executive workshops I've conducted, one of the more memorable, because of the setting, was with a group of programming executives from NBC television—the people who brought you *Seinfeld, Friends,* and *ER*—watching them literally run around under the lights and backdrops of a giant TV production studio, trying to cut time and errors out of a fictitious business process.[5] Activities that demand leadership involvement include identifying project leaders and selecting and reviewing projects, as well as defining and communicating the Six Sigma "vision."

I've heard quite a few managers and executives, from company presidents to department managers, comment on how they've looked at problems in new ways, discovered incorrect assumptions about customers, used facts and data more effectively, and set better priorities, thanks to the methods and discipline of Six Sigma. I recall Tom Cole, vice chairman for operations, systems, and logistics at Federated Department Stores commenting that "These projects are important, but the big benefit is that we're starting to ask a whole new set of questions."

But, as noted, this good story is not the whole story. There's plenty of evidence that, despite results and accolades, Six Sigma has not yet infiltrated the leadership thinking processes. Some examples follow.

In that vast majority of businesses using it, Six Sigma is primarily a "program." Certain types of opportunities are *assigned* to Six Sigma, people either "do Six Sigma" or don't. The integration of Six Sigma principles into the DNA of the business is pretty weak.

5. This was held in the Burbank facility where for years late night TV legend Johnny Carson taped *The Tonight Show.*

Outside the project efforts, few adopters are applying many of the "infrastructure" elements of the Six Sigma system: for example, more effective "Voice of the Customer" listening systems or strong cross-functional measures. These happen to be the aspects of Six Sigma that most reflect, and impact, leadership skills and behaviors.

Another clue is that I'm often asked—including by some people who might be considered "experts" in the matter: "So, what's next after Six Sigma?" The answer I give is not what they seem to be looking for. The question implies that Six Sigma will eventually be replaced in favor of some as yet unknown "great new thing." I guess that's understandable; waves of programs and "great new things" indeed seem to have come along regularly. (In a wry attempt to deal with resistance to yet another perceived flash-in-the-pan initiative, one executive we worked with considered calling his company's Six Sigma effort *program du jour*)

But I'm not prepared to accept that companies worldwide who are now learning, applying, and benefiting from Six Sigma—some of whom have been at it for 10 years or more—will or should be expected to abandon it for the new *program du jour*. For one, that suggests a high degree of fickleness, not to mention a lot of wasted effort and investment. Second, it assumes there has to be something so new it will replace Six Sigma. It reminds me of the *Dilbert* cartoon making fun of Six Sigma where Dogbert claimed "I know it sounds familiar, but let me assure you this has a totally, totally different name."

Funny thing is, in some ways Dogbert is not that far off. One of the reasons for Six Sigma's value and staying power is that it's a synthesis and more effective application of many methods that have been around for a while. There are new ideas as well, and the whole system is being applied more consistently to more critical business issues, and with greater commitment—hence the huge results. There's a timelessness, really, to most of the fundamental principles of Six Sigma. So if there ever were a "next fad," I have a pretty strong suspicion it would be extremely similar to what Six

Sigma offers now, dressed up with some new features, and with a totally, totally different name.

So to the question, "What's next?" the best answer is not to replace but to leverage Six Sigma principles to enhance the standard for *how leaders lead*. It's the most logical, most effective, and most powerful way to build on what's already been achieved. And you or anyone willing to make the effort can become a Six Sigma Leader, whether or not you have a "program" in your organization.

ENCOURAGING WORDS: THE "10-SECOND RULE"

Before describing our path through the thrills of Six Sigma Leadership, I'd like to introduce one of the few "tools" included in this book.

Being a good leader *does* require a time investment, but it is not as onerous as you might expect. In fact, I've realized in my years of helping managers apply these skills that the difference between asking the right questions and just *acting* (i.e., failing to ask the right questions) involves somewhere around 10 seconds of additional thought. In those 10 seconds, you can ask a whole variety of critical questions—ones you often *should* ask, but fail to because of the extra moment of reflection it would take.

This is especially important because one of the more common complaints about Six Sigma is: "It takes too long!" That's a bit unfair: Six Sigma projects often tackle some of the toughest issues in a business, so of course it takes time to understand and resolve them. Nevertheless, I know *any* hint that adopting Six Sigma Leadership might take a lot of time is liable to scare you off.

So, as you're exposed to different suggestions throughout this book on upgrading your leadership to a Six Sigma standard, I'd ask you to remember and apply the "10-Second Rule":

Invest just 10 seconds of extra thought, once or twice a day, and you can be on your journey to becoming a Six Sigma Leader.

That's enough to get started and to help you begin to test and improve your own thinking skills. From there, it won't always be easy, and you will need to learn to hold yourself to a higher standard. I'll remind you of the 10-Second Rule at key points throughout the book to help you see where you can apply this simple tool. As challenging as better leadership can be, a small step can make a big difference.

ROADMAP FOR THE BOOK

Here's a brief overview of the chapters to follow and what you can expect in each. You'll note that the theme for many chapters is a kind of paradox—the attempt to align or master some seemingly contradictory concepts. As we'll see in Chapter 1, that's a foundational skill of Six Sigma Leadership.

Chapter 1—What Is *Six Sigma Leadership?*

Introduces the definition and core principles. Describes the challenge of balance and flexibility and the *Genius of the And*. Puts the need for Six Sigma Leadership in the context of the growing challenges of the 21st-century business. Defines the Vision of a Six Sigma Leader.

Chapter 2—Change and Constancy

Describes the role of change in leadership and the need to balance change with stability. Provides an overview and guidelines for managing change as an *investment*. Addresses questions around setting priorities, allocating your "portfolio," and executing sustainable improvement. Exposes the common misallocation of business change portfolios and how to rebalance them.

Chapter 3—Certainty and Doubt

Debunks the myth of leader infallibility. Examines ways to improve access to *usable* facts and data. Describes the value of and process for challenging assumptions as a key to smart leadership. Outlines steps to balance gut thinking and data by testing hypotheses. Exposes the weakness of risk management thinking in many leaders.

Chapter 4—Speed and Deliberateness

Explores the benefits and perils of "speed at all costs." Presents a set of key disciplines that actually *enable* greater speed. Emphasizes the importance of perception and clarity of terms to guide the right pace. Outlines scenarios for a "fail fast" strategy. Introduces concepts of lean thinking and the need for "lean leadership."

Chapter 5—Teamwork and Independence

Reviews the principle of leader success tied to organizational success. Describes the shortcomings of teamwork at leadership levels and provides steps to build greater collaboration. Reviews the challenge of encouraging, yet managing, individual initiative by leaders and followers. Encourages leaders to reach "Up and Out" to leverage their efforts and talents.

Chapter 6—Now, Tomorrow, and Next Year

Explores various aspects of defining and managing business change by different time horizons: short-, mid-, and long-term. Describes three core change strategies and why leaders must better understand and select the right ones. Presents options for accelerating and coordinating efforts over time. Offers tips on how to select and lead initiatives in each time horizon.

Chapter 7—Customer First . . . and Last

Identifies why customers are so critical, yet can also be a detriment to long-term business health. Introduces the "Law of the Ignorant Customer." Describes how a more thorough understanding of the customer's environment can provide critical insights. Presents a process for creating more thorough understanding of customer needs and ways to avoid insulation from customers. Examines situations where saying no and dismissing customer input are good choices.

Chapter 8—Selling People, Telling People

Presents "followers" as the real vehicle for a Six Sigma Leader's achievements. Reviews methods for creating aligned goals and activities. Describes the shared responsibilities of Leaders and followers in achieving greater balance and flexibility. Outlines key elements and leader skills needed to drive acceptance of change. Offers tips for balancing consensus (selling) and enforcement (telling).

Chapter 9—Bringing Six Sigma Leadership to Life

Outlines the factors likely to favor and inhibit successful adoption of Six Sigma Leadership. Advises leaders to take more direct responsibility for upgrading their businesses. Presents recommended steps to support *personal* and *organizational* adoption of Six Sigma Leader skills and results. Reviews the nature of the Six Sigma Leader vision: a constant effort to be a better leader.

Afterword—Life under Six Sigma Leadership

The story of a leader and an organization that go through a transformation thanks to the adoption of Six Sigma Leader principles and practices.

CHAPTER

What Is *Six Sigma* Leadership?

A foolish consistency is the hobgoblin of little minds.
—Ralph Waldo Emerson

DEFINING SIX SIGMA LEADERSHIP

Six Sigma Leadership is at once hard to define, yet simple to understand. Challenging to master, but easy to apply to what you do as a leader every day.

The simple part is: Six Sigma Leadership is about practicing principles that most of us would agree make up a *better* way of leading than what we often encounter. It's what I call a "new standard," but little of what makes up Six Sigma Leadership is likely to be controversial. The concepts we'll be exploring could appropriately be called "applied common sense"—neither earthshaking nor mind-bending, just smart and practical guidelines for being a better leader.[1]

The difficult part is: Six Sigma Leadership is not about absolutes or a defined set of steps. There's no formula; I can't say "Do

1. Can't avoid mentioning one of my favorite sayings, however: "Common sense is the least common of the senses."

this and you'll be a Six Sigma Leader!" With few hard-and-fast rules, the definition of a Six Sigma Leader can appear a bit squishy at first.

But don't lose faith! Just because it defies narrow definition does not mean Six Sigma Leadership is touchy-feely or a vain attempt to make you into some legendary leader like Gandhi, or Abraham Lincoln, or Darth Vader. Rather than focusing on traits like charisma or brilliant intellect (which usually we're either born with or not—most of us not), the core of Six Sigma Leadership is about practical skills that tie directly to how well you help your business succeed. These are skills nearly any individual can apply. They help you build on, not abandon, your existing strengths and talents.

The essence of Six Sigma Leadership can be described in two words: *balance* and *flexibility*. It's this combination of stability (balance) and responsiveness (flexibility) that gives Six Sigma Leadership its power. It argues against those who favor a particular leadership "style," or who excuse their own leadership approach—even when it's not working—by saying, "That's just how I am!" (To those of you thinking, "Well, a real leader *never* waivers!" I'd ask you to withhold judgment for a few moments and remember that flexibility does not mean "flutter like a weathervane.")

Throughout this book, we'll be seeing how *lack* of leadership balance and flexibility leads to poor decisions, misguided efforts, and millions, if not billions, of dollars wasted each year. We'll also see how it creates skepticism from followers about your ability to lead and failure of businesses to coordinate their activities to the best advantage of customers and shareholders. On the positive side, we'll also see how understanding balance and flexibility can make you a significantly *better* leader—and help you foster better leadership throughout your organization.

So, returning to the big question of defining *Six Sigma Leadership*, here's a starting point that will be built on as we continue to explore the what, why, and how of an effective, or even *excellent*, leader in this book.

> **Six Sigma Leadership is a set of principles that can be applied to create greater success and sustained results for an organization. It's based on the idea that outstanding leadership is an artful, but learnable, combination of skills that combine balance and flexibility to drive goals and performance.**

That's a starting point, but there's still more detail to fill in. Let's start by looking at the competition around some basic approaches to leadership.

LEADERSHIP TUG-OF-WAR

I've had the pleasure—and sometimes frustration—of spending a lot of time over the past 20 years studying the actions and impacts of leaders and managers. In every company I've worked with, every department and function, home or branch office, senior executive to hourly wage-earner, the same patterns emerge. Over time I've come to see this as something like an epic struggle—a tug-of-war between opposing forces of how leaders operate. It's not *quite* that black and white, but looking at that struggle will help us get to the heart of Six Sigma Leadership.

The tug-of-war is depicted in Figure 1.1. On the left are examples of leadership behavior that most people describe as the *right* way to work. These Good Habits, as I've labeled them, are not very controversial. For example, few would say that to "Make decisions based on facts" is a bad idea. Nor would concern for customers, teamwork, or doing things right the first time typically lead to a big debate. Asked to choose which is better, just about everyone says, the "Good Habits."

On the right, another set of behaviors tug at the leaders. These "forces of evil"—Bad Habits—are done out of expediency, under pressure, sometimes from laziness, or just to get something done so you can move on to the next problem. Similarly, most everyone agrees these leadership behaviors are the poorer choice compared to the "good side."

Make decisions based on facts
Pay close attention to customers
Take the time to do it right

I know what I need to know
Customer? That's my boss!
Get it done fast and we'll clean up later

Collaborate, coordinate, communicate
Avoid ruts and complacency
Set clear priorities for action
Etc. . . .

I got my act togther,
why don't the other guys?
This system is timeless!
Etc. . . .

Good Habits

Bad Habits

Figure 1.1   Leadership Tug-of-War

Which force, the good or the bad, is stronger? The nearly unanimous answer is: "The Bad Habits!"[2] Leaders by and large recognize a contradiction between what they know they *ought* to do and how they often *actually* fulfill their role. Of course, we all tend to see the mistakes, the Bad Habits, more readily in our bosses and colleagues. VPs complain about CEOs, plant shift workers complain about their supervisors. Department heads whine about other department heads. But in moments of honesty, most leaders I talk to recognize the prevalence of the Bad Habits in *themselves.*

Is it *really* that bad? It's certainly possible to exaggerate, and people can be hard on themselves at times. After all, businesses accomplish great work and achieve remarkable success every day. Products and services find their way to customers pretty regularly, perhaps not as smoothly as we'd like, but not too badly either. Dedicated, hard-working people who care about their jobs, their customers, and their organizations put forth tremendous efforts all the time.

But the ease with which people acknowledge the prevalence of the Bad Habits ought to raise an alarm. Even in the places or on

2. Note that the phrases used to describe the Bad Habits are really quotes—comments you might have overheard from time to time in your own office or plant. That was kind of an accident, actually, but it's indicative of the challenge we're examining here: There are a lot more examples out there of the Bad Habits in action, compared to the Good Habits.

the days when you're leading in the *right* way, you are vulnerable to those "forces of evil." We'll see many examples of the insidiousness of the Bad Habits throughout this book—as well as some showing the power of the Good. The story of Ford Motor Company is one that dramatically illustrates what happens when leaders lose the tug-of-war.

Back in the 1980s, Ford had a successful marketing effort with the theme, "Quality is Job 1." There was an internal audience for that slogan. To people inside Ford, "Job 1" meant the first unit of a new model. In other words, success and quality were not just a priority, but really a shared responsibility, "Don't count on the plant folks to fix the problems you created in design, tooling, procurement, etc."

Around this time Ford used some Six Sigma-type methods to conceive, design, and market a new car, the Taurus, which became a legendary success story. It was well made, had features motorists loved, was a good size, looked great—and sold extremely well. You might have expected, based on that successful experience and the message of Job 1, that Ford would have applied the same approach to a succession of other products and been on a steady upward trajectory. Instead, the opposite happened. As people at Ford described to me years later, the Taurus itself fell victim to old leader/manager habits. Over subsequent model years, saving-pennies-per-vehicle often became Job 1—and the features that made it attractive, the quality that made it reliable, declined dramatically. For members of the Taurus team that I spoke with, the rest of the story was not a success at all, but rather a sad failure.

By 1999, when Ford initiated its own "Consumer-Driven Six Sigma" effort, it had fallen to the *lowest* ranking of all major auto manufacturers in initial quality. Whatever lessons had been learned about smart leadership in the early 1980s had failed to be accepted as a new standard and were overwhelmed by old behaviors. Ford is just a representative example here, by the way. If you look behind why many past business "fads" have failed, you'll find a common denominator has been that the improved skills and habits were never truly embraced, or made a fundamentally expected aspect of leadership.

STRIKING A BALANCE: SMART LEADERSHIP

Why *aren't* the Good Habits able to prevail, even when people admit they're a better way to work? Why do successful organization improvement efforts—including, perhaps, Six Sigma—tend to stall and end up being replaced by something different by degrees, but not in substance? Examining these questions we can see both the need for and the essence of Six Sigma Leadership.

Much as I like the analogy of the tug-of-war, in reality it over-sells the so-called Good Habits and unrealistically denigrates the Bad. I'll still refer to them as "Good" and "Bad," but the truth is more complicated. It's like the extremely well behaved kid in school who constantly reminds you of the rules, until you just tune them out. While being a Six Sigma Leader means being *more* proactive, using *better* facts, paying *closer* attention to customers, etc. it would be annoying—and wrong—to tell you to always pull on the left end of the rope.[3]

To be a Six Sigma Leader you *must* apply the Good Habits frequently and consistently. That's essential, and on that score I may sound like that annoying kid at times. But *always* pushing the Good side would run counter to those themes already used to describe Six Sigma Leadership: *balance* and *flexibility*.

In Figure 1.2, the rope has been replaced with a scale, and the "Good" and "Bad" reorganized into a more reasonable set of *balanced* "Smart Habits." This image portrays the *true* essence of Six Sigma Leadership: the ability to choose the right approach at the right time—to keep in reasonable balance—and to avoid putting

---

3. Absolutism in favor of a cause or idea has its role, but in a business environment in particular it usually ends up working against you. I think one of the reasons Six Sigma (the program) has lasted and is still thriving in many organizations is that it has *not* been taken over by the ideologues. And the people who are most skeptical of Six Sigma seem to think it's inflexible and dogmatic. Six Sigma Leadership is neither.

Facts and data	Intuition
Customer focus	Ignore the customer
Do it right the first time	Make mistakes at a high rate of speed
Work cross-functionally	Optimize our own operation
Focused change priorities	Hedge our bets, respond to new issues

Smart Habits
(aka Six Sigma Leadership)

Figure 1.2   The Balanced Habits of Six Sigma Leadership

too much weight on *either* side of the scale. When people talk about building Six Sigma into an organization's *culture*, this is the critical objective (whether they realize it or not): to make "better balance" a standard for leaders and then to apply that ability to driving consistent and effective performance, change, and innovation.

Since the Good Habits (the left side of the scale) *are* usually the underweighted skill set, let's return to the question of why—at Ford and most every other company—they have so long failed to be applied in sufficient balance.

1. *Good habits generally take more work.* This is probably the most obvious answer. Getting facts and data, taking time to

define and reevaluate priorities, having to deal with those strange people in other departments—these are all activities that can be accurately described as a pain and are certainly hard to stick with when time and other pressures are upon you. (That "more work" equation is often a miscalculation, however, when you consider item 2.)

2. *Failure to recognize the costs.* If you have a dog that's chewed a prize possession and you scold him for it the day after, you *know* it's unlikely the dog will connect that punishment with the bad behavior. In business, the consequences of "bad behavior"—things like narrow decisions, rushed solutions, misunderstanding of the customer, etc.—are often totally disconnected from the behavior itself. For example, the people who cut features from the Taurus just to save money were probably never held accountable when the car's sales declined. It's not even clear whether the connection between those decisions and the drop in sales was even understood by leaders. So the bad behavior continues.

3. *There's a skill gap.* Just because people recognize that the left side is more often the better side doesn't mean they know how to do it well. The ability to, for example, set good priorities or interpret customer comments are not innate. Six Sigma "Green Belt" training, for example, teaches the "how to" for many of these good habits—which suggests why those enhanced skills have helped produce major breakthroughs in business costs and revenues. But here's a clue that will suggest why you should think of this book as very important to you as a leader: Most of the people who have learned these skills through Six Sigma would say that their *leaders* "still don't get it." And in many companies, there's still strong evidence that they don't. (More in the discussion later in this chapter on Competence.)

4. *Inability to be balanced and flexible.* To practice smart leadership you have to accept the fact that *inconsistency* has its virtue. But I see many instances where people, including

leaders, demand or seem to need *absolute* answers. The choice between Good and Bad Habits is not absolute, it is a balance, but you have to learn how to move along the spectrum to be optimally effective. We'll look more into this fundamental concept in a moment.

These points help explain why so many companies have failed in their attempts to adopt and sustain "smarter management." The key missing ingredient has always been leadership. Not "commitment," however, or "support"—but leaders actually changing *their own* behavior and skills, doing their part to improve the balance in how their organizations operate. Until that becomes an accepted standard for excellent leadership, the string of quasi-successes that fade away will continue. Six Sigma Leadership is an attempt to break that string for you, and hopefully for your organization.

AND VERSUS OR

I opened this chapter by stating that Six Sigma Leadership is hard to define. Hopefully, you're now starting to get a better idea of what it's all about—but also why it's hard to define. As we'll see repeatedly throughout this book, the key to smart leadership is about living with or managing contradiction, what I often call "tolerance for ambiguity." In fact, using ambiguity is a key to success for companies as well as leaders.

Unfortunately, as noted above, the need for a simple answer seems more pervasive than tolerance for ambiguity. A term that well describes this is found in the outstanding book *Built to Last: Successful Habits of Visionary Companies* by Jim Collins and Gerald Porras. They call it the "Tyranny of the Or": an inability or unwillingness to deal with two or more seemingly contradictory forces or ideas at the same time.[4] The Tyranny of the Or means forcing a

4. James Collins, *Built to Last: Successful Habits of Visionary Companies*, New York: HarperCollins, 1994, p. 43.

one-sided choice and accepting limitations. In organizations, this would mean choosing only one of the each of following:

- Bold or conservative
- Flexible or stable
- Formal or informal
- Short-term or long-term focused
- Price-driven or innovation-driven
- Hire from within or hire from outside
- Hierarchical or flattened
- High-quality or low-cost
- Profit-driven or values-driven

If you pay attention, you'll notice examples of the The Tyranny of the Or in many environments—but often it's just accepted. As an example, when my daughter started elementary school, reading instruction was in the grips of a heated battle between proponents of the "whole language" approach—which favored having kids learn to read by reasoning out words based on their meaning and context—and "phonics"—the more traditional method of using letter combinations so children could "sound out" words they had never seen before. But it became an all-or-nothing argument for many educators. For a time, while "whole language" held sway, teachers were forbidden from using *any* phonics instruction at all! (My daughter's school principal told me she had to *hide* the fact some teachers were still using phonics.)

I've seen this same tyranny grip clients as well. A business services company we worked with had prided itself on being extremely responsive to clients in order to win business and provide great service. Unfortunately, the company realized that to stay financially healthy it would have to be more careful in making commitments that imposed high costs. As that more careful decision process began to be communicated around the company, a number of people leapt to the conclusion that "We're abandoning customer intimacy"—as if the idea of providing profitable services and making customers happy could not coexist.

Keep in mind that the "Or" mentality is not about balance at all, it's about absolutes. And it can be a common, though unfortunate, theme in what I'd call cult-based leadership theories. This is expressed in the view that a true leader makes a choice and moves on, with no "escape route" or alternate plan. Followers tend to accept the "Tyranny of the Or" when they talk about the styles of their Leaders. I hear comments like these all the time:

> **"He's all about strategy and ideas. Execution or operations just bore him."**
> **"Our CEO came out of Finance, so she just wants to see the balance sheet."**
> **"Once a decision is made, there's no turning him back."**
> **"Never go there with problems, only solutions."**

We all have our strengths and preferences, but if you're a leader whose approach is that inflexible, I'd suggest you *especially* need to read ahead in this book! Unfortunately, if you look around I think you'll see many cases where people assume the answer is black or white, one or the other. It's a bad habit, as noted, and one that hampers leaders at all levels.

Fortunately, there's an opposing force: the "Genius of the And." This is the ability to pursue *multiple*, even seemingly opposite, goals or actions at the same time. Collins and Porras discovered this genius to be a focus and passion ingrained in the culture of consistently "great" companies. The Genius of the And became a pervasive theme of their exploration of how great companies are formed and nurtured: They use the "yin and yang" symbol—representing opposite forces united—throughout their book to reflect the power of that two-sided perspective.

The "And" so often turns out to be the right answer I'm sometimes shocked at how long it takes people to get there. Table 1.1 presents some examples of ongoing "Or" debates where "And" is (at least it seems to me) so clearly correct.

One the one hand . . .	On the other hand . . .
Kids learn to read and boost vocabulary using context/meaning.	Kids learn to read by being able to sound out words.
Offense wins games.	Defense wins games.
Companies need to execute.	Companies need to innovate.
Lose weight by reducing fats.	Lose weight by reducing carbohydrates.
Web-based companies are the future.	Bricks-and-mortar companies will prevail.
Consistency is critical.	Flexibility is critical.
Success is based on your people.	Success is based on your processes.

Table 1.1   *Or* Arguments that Are Really *Ands*

The Genius of the And will be a critical factor and recurring theme in enabling you to be a Six Sigma leader.

COMPETENCE AND CONSCIOUSNESS

This is a good time to share a lesson and reminder about levels of competence and incompetence—which will become another key theme of Six Sigma Leadership. Many of the things we do every day demand a level of skill that is instinctive. I learned this lesson the hard way in my first job, while still in college, as a weekend disk jockey at a radio station in Riverside, California. I'd worked at my college station, but it was a *thrill* to have a real job in radio!

For my training, I sat in the booth for several hours and watched other DJs do the job. Tasks included playing records, airing commercials, keeping a log, reading weather forecasts, and giving hourly local news updates. I took copious notes, asked a lot of questions, studied hard. I showed up for my first Saturday shift, all ready to go, and sat down at the controls.

The rest is pretty much a nightmare. I was nervous, which did not help, but the problem was simple: I had to *think about everything*. If you had to carefully look through the racks to find the commercials on the schedule, you couldn't get your spots lined up on time. If you couldn't "cue up" a record in a few seconds, it wouldn't be ready when the previous song ended. When the time came to announce the weather forecast . . . well, who had time to *write* the forecast? When I did manage to squawk out the weather—usually after several seconds of dead air—it was already way out of date.[5]

The problem was, my training had given me only what's called "Conscious Competence." It was like *reading a book* on how to fly a plane and then trying to solo in a real aircraft. What I needed was "Unconscious Competence": the ability to do the task swiftly and without hesitation. The only thing that saved my broadcasting career (besides being willing to work for minimum wage) was a huge storm pounding Southern California that first day that *knocked the station off the air*. I managed to recuperate, learn the right way, and before too long I could do most of those tasks automatically. I worked in radio for almost five years and had a lot of fun.

Unconscious Competence is what we strive for in many of the activities we consider important. We need, literally and figuratively, to be able to walk and chew gum at the same time. So a lot of the tasks accomplished every day at home, at work, even at play, are executed unconsciously. That includes much of what *you* do as a leader. You've been working for a while and earned your position, you're good at what you do, so you can achieve a high level of competence almost automatically.

5. *You* may think this is funny, and it is, but through my life the only recurring bad dream I've had involves sitting in front of a radio booth not knowing what to do. The parents of my girlfriend at the time happened to be driving through Riverside that day (they lived in Los Angeles, far beyond our signal) and heard me on the air. She told me they heard me—*they never mentioned it.*

There's a higher risk of mistakes, though, when you're operating in Unconscious Competence. On-air people in radio and TV know this; they frequently review "air checks," or recordings of their work, to watch for bad habits, "crutch" phrases, odd facial expressions, and so forth. Similarly, airline pilots (whose job is a lot riskier than broadcasting) are required to go through refresher training every year to maintain their certification. The underlying reason: there's a very thin line separating Unconscious Competence from Unconscious *Incompetence*. Over time, unconscious skills—including any bad habits you may have picked up—can become so ingrained that it's difficult even to describe what you do. Unconscious Competence is both essential to be a productive person *and* a pathway to failure. (See Figure 1.3.)

A Six Sigma Leader must be committed to a kind of leadership "air check"—to assess your own balance and flexibility continually, to reduce unconscious mistakes and constantly build your skills. Of course, as a confident, take-charge individual you may not feel comfortable admitting that you're prone to bad habits just like everyone else. And as noted, a lot of the principles of Six Sigma Leadership will make obvious sense—so much that you may say "I already do that." But from the examples of many businesses, and many leaders, it's clear there's still a lot of Unconscious Incompetence out there. You may be better than the crowd, but I suspect you can *always* do better.[6]

What does getting better mean? We'll explore a different dimension in each chapter, but generally it means:

1. Making clear decisions, but being willing and able to adapt your approach based on the needs of the situation. Applying greater discipline and smarter thinking skills to evaluate

---

6. This is a major reason why you won't find any profiles of a real-world "Six Sigma Leader" in this book. Even a leader with an outstanding track record can cross the line to incompetence or get out of balance. Fortunately, the goal for any leader is not zero defects, but rather to be the best leader you can.

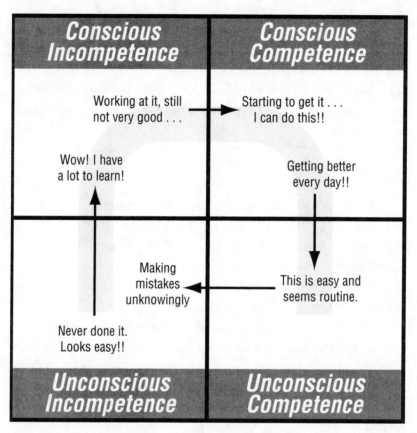

Figure 1.3 Levels of Competence and Incompetence

your choices, test assumptions, and avoid unconscious mistakes.

2. Evaluating and tracking your effectiveness based on the results, both short- and long-term, you achieve for your organization. As I'll discuss in more depth in Chapter 5, Six Sigma Leadership is about putting the business first—not to the detriment of your career, but as the best way to have a truly successful career.

To wrap up this chapter, let's take one more look at why a new vision and standard for leaders is so important.

A VISION FOR BETTER LEADERSHIP

Despite offering the 10-Second Rule as a starting point, practicing Six Sigma Leadership consistently and well will not be easy. So you may raise a legitimate question: *Why should I care?* Only you can really answer that question, but I'd offer three sources of motivation.

Yourself

I would suspect you, like most people, aspire to achieve and be the best you can be. That doesn't mean you should want to be CEO; being an excellent department head is a leadership achievement to be proud of. But a commitment to doing an excellent job and making a meaningful contribution is likely a big part of why you've become a leader.

Over time, faced with the challenges and frustrations of complexity, competition, change, etc., a lot of leaders I've observed start to surrender to the status quo. In fact, the most successful leaders in particular can become dangerously *fond* of the status quo and unable to see when it may need to be challenged, or overturned (an example of Unconscious Incompetence). So that internal flame that drove you to improve earlier in your career starts to die down. You may even lose connection with the reasons why you enjoy *being* a leader

Six Sigma Leadership can help you rekindle and intensify the flame that prompts you to strive for greater achievements. My vision for this book actually is to *inspire* you and other leaders to set a new personal standard, to gain new energy—and of course to support your endeavors with practical ways of being an outstanding leader. But the ultimate motivation must come from you.

Leadership as a Discipline

The state of leadership as a whole seems due for an "upgrade"—particularly in the willingness to review and build better thinking skills.[7] This is not to say that leaders are all incompetent or that good leadership is nowhere to be found. But I haven't seen any signs that the overall caliber of leadership thought and action is much improved today from 20 years ago. I would even venture that the dependence on information technologies, mergers to drive growth, and compensation systems with more upside than downside signal that complacency about leadership thinking is on the rise.

I'm certainly not alone in feeling there's a significant need for leaders to focus energy on raising their overall level of capability and performance, focused in particular on thinking skills. For example, in the book *Executive Intelligence*, author Justin Menkes cites numerous studies and instances of failures of leader and executive thinking and inflated perception by leaders of their own abilities. Menkes comments: "Unfortunately, all too often individuals are given tremendous authority over large amounts of human and capital resources even when they lack the cognitive skills to run a company well."[8] I'd question whether many leaders really *lack* the skills; my hypothesis is that leaders don't *use* those skills as well as they could—hence this book.

A broader, but no less strident, condemnation is found in the book *Think!: Why Crucial Decisions Can't Be Made in the Blink of an Eye*. Writer Michael LeGault suggests that business is too driven by what he calls "task-driven thinking," a step-by-step approach that tends toward rote action, and is failing to apply "critical thinking," which is focused on reviewing and using knowledge and information to make more informed judgments *and* boost creativity.[9]

---

7. I'm not going to challenge the integrity level of leadership for two reasons: (1) I think that recent highly publicized scandals are a tiny minority and not representative of the true honesty of most leaders (though those incidents are a warning to be careful not to rationalize your actions); (2) integrity is a trait rather than a skill, and our focus here is on skills you can develop and hone.

8. Justin Menkes, *Executive Intelligence: What All Great Leaders Have*, New York: Collins, 2005, pp. 85–88.

9. Michael LeGault, *Think!: Why Crucial Decisions Can't Be Made in the Blink of an Eye*, New York: Threshold Editions, 2006, pp. 35–51. Six Sigma Leadership includes elements of *both* task-driven and critical thinking, but the critical piece is definitely the most important.

It would be easy to dismiss this type of criticism. In fact, Menkes notes that leaders in surveys clearly feel they are pretty good in their thought processes, though they're much more skeptical of *other* leaders' ability. But I hope you would be willing to consider the possibility that you could become a better, more balanced thinker. That judging yourself as "good" in comparison to other leaders may be precisely what's holding you back!

Your Organization

I probably get as tired of hearing it as you do, but the fact remains that the business world today is a much more challenging place than ever before. The caliber of leadership skill that worked in the past just won't work as the margin for error gets thinner and thinner. Yet, as we can see every day from the ups and downs of so many companies, leaders are having a tough time keeping things on a steady path of success. Using the argument that "external factors" create these swings is a sorry excuse. If leaders today are playing a more challenging game, they can either prepare to lose, or learn to become better players. The vision of a Six Sigma Leader is about becoming a better player!

The importance of leadership to organizational success is clear. In studies of the major issues confronting companies, having effective, adaptive leadership has been ranked by executives in North America as the single most critical factor—out of 120 listed—in contributing to positive organizational performance.[10]

Organizations need leaders with better *thinking* skills for three big reasons:

1. *Thought is the essence of leadership.* Leadership is not brain surgery, or auto mechanics, or statistics—it's not about technical skill or proficiency in a particular discipline. Knowl-

---

10. *Major Issues Impacting People Management Survey: North America vs. Europe*, St. Petersburg, FL: Human Resource Institute, 2004.

edge is essential, of course, and the ability to get the information needed to make decisions and set direction is a key part of the skill set. But generally it's the thoroughness of the logic, intuition, and inspiration—which begin in the head of the leader—that will guide your organization to success.

2. *Growing complexity and increased specialization make it ever harder to be an effective leader.* We see this right at the so-called "C-level" of organizations: Where there used to be one "Chief" (Executive Officer), there are now many: Chief Financial Officer, Chief Operating Officer, Chief Information Officer, Chief Learning Officer, Chief Security Officer, and probably more Chiefs being created as you read this page. The same specialization is reflected at levels of leadership throughout the organizational hierarchy. The trends are working in opposite directions, putting a squeeze on leadership: roles with ever-narrower perspectives, but with complex problems that demand an understanding of the big picture.

3. *Growth as a leader demands constantly improving skills.* Studies have repeatedly shown that the high failure rate of many promising leaders is largely due to an over-reliance on a limited set of capabilities. Many times leaders are promoted because of a strong record of achievement, only to derail later because of their inability to adapt. For example, an individual may be good at demanding high performance from his or her followers, or have strong technical ability. However, those strengths are not sufficient when, for example, big-picture thinking or relationship building are also essential to success. To prepare yourself and others for growing challenges, you need the clarity of thought and flexibility to understand your own weaknesses and develop new talents.[11]

11. See W.M. McCall and M.M. Lombardo, *Off Track: Why and How Successful Executives Get Derailed*, Greensboro, NC: Center for Creative Leadership, 1983; E. Van Velsor and J.B. Leslie, "Why Executives Derail: Perspectives Across Time and Cultures," *Academy of Management Executive*, 9 (4), 1995, pp 62–72; M. McCall, *High Flyers: Developing the Next Generation of Leaders*, Boston: Harvard Business School Press, 1999.

Whatever your motivation, the concepts and skills of Six Sigma Leadership offer a vision that you and others can strive for, one that's based in fundamentals, yet that will challenge your abilities every day. As a smart, Six Sigma Leader, you'll learn to value balance and flexibility—and if you stick with it, very possibly have a lot more fun as a leader than you've ever had before!

Change and Constancy

The art of progress is to preserve order amid change and to preserve change amid order.

—Alfred North Whitehead

CHANGE IS the essence of leadership. The verb *lead* itself describes *movement*—guiding others on a path or journey to a desired new destination. Many of the most important ideas and skills we'll explore will focus on building your capability to define and lead productive change efforts, to stay ahead of the curve, to set a vision and achieve it. Six Sigma is really about helping leaders and their organizations *make change a core competency.*

At the same time, to be effective at change, a leader must also value constancy and stability. One of the best ways to undermine change efforts, or squander their benefits, is to try to change *too much.* Therefore, one of the first and most important responsibilities of a Six Sigma Leader is defining a vision for change (the objective or destination) at the same time as establishing boundaries and limits (like the border of the path). Without that focus—without a balance between change and constancy—your efforts become confused and the power of change is dissipated.

With so many things *needing* to change, and so much pressure from the outside, it becomes increasingly difficult for leaders to balance change and stability. This adds to the problem of leaders becoming disconnected from the day-to-day operations that are the foundation of any successful enterprise. So both suffer from a lack of focus.

With these issues in mind, we'll start our exploration of Six Sigma Leadership in this chapter by looking at how to better define and focus your change efforts and become more effective at using constancy as a balancing element in your organization's success. I'll use a financial analogy as a theme for many of these concepts.

PORTFOLIO MANAGEMENT

From a financial perspective, a business is a lot like a household. In a home, there are two types of financial activities to manage: One is the "operating budget," or the ongoing expenditures like food, rent, education, entertainment, transportation, utilities. The second is our "investment budget," the additional savings or other assets we accumulate (if we're careful and/or lucky) and apply to special things like buying a new house, major repairs, vacations, and retirement. The challenges businesses and households face are parallel, too: keeping ongoing expenses from exceeding income, deciding how much to save or spend, achieving a good return on the funds available for investment.

Which is better at managing these two dimensions, households or businesses? Well, of course there's a huge amount of variation, but this is my observation: On the operating side, while both can certainly waste a lot of money, businesses tend to at least *monitor* the situation better than the typical household. On the *investment* side, however, businesses are generally much *worse*. The problem in businesses is not with how they handle their cash; it's how their investments in *change* are managed.

I talk to leaders all the time about their efforts to change or improve their businesses, and while they all seem sincere about wanting to do the right thing, it's clear many are struggling. For example, the senior vice president of operations for one of our clients, a leading technology company, once remarked in exasperation to a group of his colleagues: "We've got 10,000 change projects going on out there, but no one knows what they are."

While the numbers may vary, I hear similar comments from many leaders. To achieve balance and flexibility, the Six Sigma Leader needs to adopt a common sense *portfolio management* approach to guiding change: think of your efforts as an investment you are responsible for managing and optimizing. This portfolio approach will be a theme connecting many of the skills of Six Sigma Leadership as it applies to driving effective change.

Among the features/benefits of a portfolio approach:

- *Improved awareness of your investments.* As the "10,000 projects" comment indicates, there's rarely any clear picture of exactly what's being invested and how. There are new product efforts, IT initiatives, departmental projects, etc., but little collective information on the complete portfolio. Even at a department or smaller unit level, senior leaders often are unable to describe what the full slate of activities/investments is.
- *Better "asset allocation."* Greater understanding of your investments gives you the power to improve the balance of your portfolio—shifting, diversifying, or concentrating as needed. For example, are you "over-invested" in IT projects? Where can those resources be used more effectively, or reduce our risk? Good questions for any investor!
- *Performance tracking and rebalancing.* Not every investment is a winner. Different types require different levels of scrutiny. As needs change, your allocation may need to be reevaluated. All these analogies apply to your effort to keep your organization effective, profitable, and competitive. You probably don't want to behave like a day trader, but a leader needs to be an active shepherd of his or her investments and to understand how they fit into the larger organizational portfolio.

The vision of the portfolio management approach I'm suggesting—which will take time to build and refine—is to more effectively connect your "strategic goals" and your "project list" to a cohesive *investment strategy* leading to greater returns and fewer losses for your business.

Reducing losses, by the way, is a very important point here. There's a sharp contrast between how a typical individual handles a portfolio and how leaders allocate their organizations' change resources. Let's take one of the biggest areas of investment today: information technologies.

Research firm The Standish Group, which tracks IT project performance in its "Chaos Reports," has found that a staggering 31 percent of projects will be canceled before they ever get completed, and only 16 percent of software projects are completed on time and on budget. The research suggests that American companies and government agencies spent $81 billion for canceled software projects. About $59 billion was spent on software projects that were completed, but came in late. What's the trend? Well, almost half of the IT executives in the research sample felt that there are *more* failures today than just five years ago.[1]

Risk and failure are an important and necessary part of business. The freedom to operate with an innovative, entrepreneurial spirit requires the ability to take chances and absorb mistakes. Fortunately for many successful companies, the return they achieve from ongoing operations is usually enough to cover their investments in change efforts. But I'm not sure we wouldn't see some panicked looks if, instead of quarterly sales or net profit figures, leaders were asked to present the return

---

1. Ryan Nelson, "Evaluating Project Success, Failure—and Everything in Between," *Computerworld*, March 6, 2006. www.computerworld.com/management-topics/.

on their IT, new product, process improvement, and other projects.[2]

Jim McNerney, who was CEO of 3M Corporation and is now at the helm of Boeing, recalled an "ah-ha" he had while running GE's Lighting business. McNerney told me:

> **Every year we had our productivity goals, with projects to achieve those goals. Every year we'd aim to boost our efficiency by 2 percent, 4 percent—and we'd usually declare victory based on successful projects. After a few years it occurred to me that if we'd *really* achieved those returns, by then we should have been getting 50 percent profit margins!**

A partial justification for the phenomenon McNerney notes is that an active effort to improve the business is necessary *just to avoid deterioration.* We're all, in a sense, swimming against the tide: part of our energy is expended to avoid getting washed away. But that kind of investment is just "loss avoidance." It does not provide any positive return. You need to improve your stroke, expend more energy perhaps, but use it more efficiently as well, to really make progress against the tide.

In this chapter we're going to focus on how a Six Sigma Leader can build a better portfolio, and in subsequent chapters we'll look at various aspects of achieving return on both the change investment *and* your operating funds. But first, I'll let you take a brief organizational assessment. Rate your company (or yourself, if you're that brave) on a 1–5 scale in the following situations. *Scoring:* Mark a 5 for every Agree Strongly; a 4 for every Agree; a 3 if

---

2. At Pivotal Resources we ask our clients to beware of OPM—pronounced "opium," for Other People's Money—a drug that tends to lead to warped investment choices.

you're mixed; a 2 for every Disagree; and a 1 for every Disagree Strongly. Then add up your total score.

1	2	3	4	5
Strongly Disagree	Disgree	Neither Agree nor Disagree	Agree	Strongly Agree

_____ 1. At any one time we have more projects or initiatives going on around here than we can really handle well.

_____ 2. A good proportion of the projects under way don't seem to have any real, clear potential benefit.

_____ 3. The idea of stopping or "killing" a project mid-stream is not very popular, or easy.

_____ 4. The people working on projects focus mostly on getting their assigned tasks done rather than on the actual value of the effort to the business or customers.

_____ 5. There is little to no overall management or coordination of the various projects around the organization.

Total Score: _____

20–25 Your organization seems to excel at flushing money down the drain. You may need to rein in your investments and start over.

15–19 This is a typical score for many organizations that are struggling to manage a large number of change initiatives.

10–14 Your organization seems to be displaying some reasonably good practices in directing its portfolio. Some improvement is needed, but it's not bad.

5–9 Congratulations. Your organization practices excellent portfolio management; hopefully what you read here will strengthen your "conscious competence."

1-4 There's little this chapter can teach you. Stop reading now and move on to Chapter 3.

By the way, if you're thinking "I just lead a small department and don't get to decide where to invest *my* portfolio"—well, think again. In fact, you do have at least partial control of where and how the assets at your discretion are deployed. You can tell people, "Drop that for now and work on this." You can initiate your own (local) efforts.

Anytime you start to think all these change investment decisions are made "on high," just ask the senior executives, who can find it very challenging to make anything happen in the face of passive resistance, priority overload, or just plain obstinacy on the part of what some of our clients have called the "frozen middle." Achieving the best possible return on your portfolio demands leader engagement at all levels of an organization. Your initiative can make a difference.

Our first priority in starting to refine your portfolio is to begin getting smarter about *how much* you're trying to get done.

BUSY PEOPLE

For a lot of organizations, your value is determined as much by the *amount* of activity you exhibit as it is by the value or quality of what you accomplish. It's natural, for both leaders and employees, to want to be able to show a long list of activities they have going on. More must be better. Here's some evidence:

- While ad campaigns suggest the initials BP stand for "Beyond Petroleum," a senior manager at the global energy company confided in me that it's better known internally to stand for "Busy People."
- A very successful retail firm that has grabbed a big chunk of market share over the past decade is governed by a key phrase: "Bias for action." Meanwhile, company leaders are also getting frustrated that a lot of that action is not directed at things that will make a difference.

- At one of our high-tech clients, a common method of validating your worth to the company is what's acknowledged as the "Check the Box" approach. This means a lot of people focus on getting *something* done so they can show progress—regardless of its actual impact on profits, costs, or customers.

That's our habit, but is it right? Well, I suspect you realize the answer is "No." While it can create the illusion of busyness, an overload of activity has a lot of negative impacts:

1. *Diffusion of resources.* People's time and focus are divided among an array of assignments, and progress slows.
2. *Unclear priorities.* The more balls you have in play, the harder it is for people to know which are the right ones to concentrate on. If priorities need to shift, it's harder to adjust.
3. *Management overload.* Too many initiatives turns you from a leader shepherding your investments to a frazzled herder of cats. The typical results (as noted, many leaders have confessed to me through the years) is that they simply lose track of all the things going on.

One of the first actions to consider in your path to Six Sigma Leadership is to review and very likely *reduce* your number of active change efforts. This should not be seen as backing down from a challenge or not encouraging your people to "push the envelope." It's simply adopting a more focused and realistic set of priorities. Remember that the root of the word *priority* means *first*—when you limit the number of projects at any one time, you are not saying "These others aren't important" or "We're never going to touch that."

By striking a better balance, you give yourself and your colleagues the opportunity to build a more appropriate "mix" in your portfolio. This means the right amount of change investment to meet your business goals, but without overtaxing your resources. The best way to achieve and maintain that kind of balanced portfolio—and ultimately boost your return—is through an ongoing allocation and review process. We'll look at how that process might work for you, but first let's review some basic issues to consider in preparing to take better control of your change assets.

HOW MUCH CHANGE?

It's a good idea to have some sense of the scale of resources you have "in play" and do a reality check against what your organization can really afford. There is no right or final answer to this question. Your estimation of how much effort you can expend and how much uncertainty your organization can absorb will always be affected by your needs (the size, urgency and risk profile of what you might invest in), the current competitive climate, how easily you can redirect resources, etc.

In a company with unconstrained resources, or where constant innovation is critical (e.g., high-tech, pharmaceuticals) you may have the means and/or the need for a large ongoing change portfolio. More stable industries or companies with less "excess capital" will want to, or have to, aim lower. In defining a rough size of your portfolio, don't feel you need to be locked in. The flexibility principle of Six Sigma Leadership should be a reminder that the comment, "We don't have the resources" should never be accepted without question. Yes, there are always constraints. However, a smart leader who recognizes a critical need will look for ways to *get* the people, money, and talent needed if the problem or opportunity warrant.[3]

One other caveat: There's a pronounced tendency among leaders to pull back on new initiatives when times are tight. This may be excellent and prudent resource management, but may also be exactly what *not* to do if your goal is to prepare your organization to handle a new wave of growth.

---

3. One of the first tasks for leaders launching a Six Sigma initiative is "project selection," where critical opportunities for improvement are prioritized for action. Interestingly, in these cases leaders usually *are* able to find resources for these projects even though their organizations would usually claim they are already "fully invested."

Here are some tips, then, on questions to pose when assessing the scale of resources you would want to invest in change:

What Is Our Current Level of Resources Dedicated to Change Efforts?

At a corporate level, my recommendation is that this inventory should include a thorough array of investments: new product development and introduction, new systems and technology upgrades, process enhancements, strategic initiatives, quality improvement, measurement development (e.g., balanced score-cards), best practice sharing, reengineering, acquisition integra-tion, supply chain streamlining, etc. The list of your own initiatives may be narrower, of course, but the point is to capture the true scale and impact on your business of both the "known" and "hidden" change efforts. Even your best inventory of projects will probably not capture all the current efforts, and there will be some debate on what really is a "change investment," so don't worry about getting it *perfect*.

Here's an example of why this broad inventory can be so impor-tant. I did some consulting work back in the mid-1990s with a Sil-icon Valley company that for a while was one of the most touted success stories in the world. I'd been asked to help improve "proj-ect management" for a team working on a major new hardware development effort that was one-and-a-half years behind schedule. As I interviewed project managers and team members, I discovered something none of the leaders had mentioned: a resource conflict between two initiatives. The company had recently introduced new software for which customers were demanding significant support. The same engineers assigned to work on the delayed hardware project were also expected to handle customer support for the software.

I tried without much success to get the company's leadership to recognize that their problem was not project management, but rather their own *portfolio* management. Instead, they were making major acquisitions while making threats to the people in charge of the delayed new hardware effort. I would describe this as the antithesis of Six Sigma Leadership. I guess the fact the company is pretty much a goner today is validation for my point. Failure to manage and to take responsibility for shepherding your change investments can lead you down a dead-end path.

What Are the Critical Change Demands on Our Business (and/or in Our Department, Region, Etc.)?

This question can lead to a long drawn-out debate that can delay action so I suggest the conversation be kept at a high level. There will always be more than you can handle and a lot of it will look alarmingly urgent (if it doesn't, well, we'll talk about complacency later). Focus on the more general question of the scale and importance of major critical gaps in, for example, operational capability, product offering, ability to meet customer needs, and financial performance. Ideally, existing strategic plans and competitive assessments will help in developing this list.

Generally, Are We Over- or Under-Investing in Change Efforts, or Does It Seem Pretty Much on Target?

Your answer to this question will give you a sense of whether you will be likely to want to: (*a*) live with the current level of change-focused resources; (*b*) reduce that investment; or (c) allocate more people and money to driving change. Remember, that through this process the goal is to improve your "change ROI," so, no matter what you dedicate, we're aiming for greater *impact* from these efforts.

Incidentally, all the steps for defining and managing a change portfolio will be more effective to the degree you can collaborate with others and align your efforts. That will be a major theme we'll explore in Chapter 5.

BIGGER—OR SMALLER—IS NOT BETTER

Watching how organizations direct their change investment, I've noticed the typical tendency to focus on the extreme ends of the size spectrum. Most fall into one of two categories:

1. Broad, ambitious, enterprise-level initiatives, usually sponsored at the most senior levels of the organization, with large budgets and staffs and typically widespread impact on the business. Examples of these would be major systems projects, reorganizations, strategic realignments, or even efforts like implementation of Lean Six Sigma!

2. Functionally or locally generated efforts, smaller in scale and aimed at fixing issues or addressing challenges at the departmental or regional level. They tend not to have much organization-wide visibility; even when they do, these smaller projects tend to be viewed by others as "their project." This category includes any attempt to eliminate the pain or improve performance within a specified group. For example, the finance department's project to reduce unapplied cash, the sales department's project to better track leads, HR's project to eliminate payroll errors. In reality, these efforts are often sliced too thin: four different business units' sales groups have their own *separate* lead tracking projects—often unaware or unconcerned about what the other guys are doing.

What is often *lacking*, as shown in Figure 2.1, is the middle range of projects that don't quite take the organization by storm, but that address issues and opportunities linking two or more functions or processes.

As indicated by the labels under each of the bars in the diagram, my suggestion is that this general approach to resource allocation has some significant downside. It's to be expected that organizations push large-scale change, and that individual leaders launch initiatives in their own areas of control. But the tall-bar categories of projects do have some inherent risks.

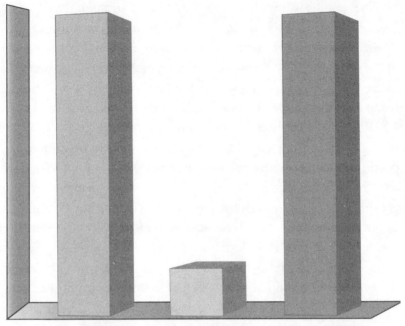

Figure 2.1   Common Distribution of Change Project Resources

Enterprisewide projects are more resource-intensive (i.e., expensive), complex, long in duration, require constancy of commitment on the part of leadership, and pose greater change management challenges. In other words, they can tend to die of their own weight or get bogged down by confusion, loss of enthusiasm, or changes in leadership.

Locally generated projects can consume a lot of resources (one or two per department or location across the business can add up—leading to the "10,000 projects" complaint from our client). Moreover, these localized efforts tend to address pieces of bigger problems in an isolated way and to unknowingly promote duplicate efforts. These isolated solutions may conflict, overlap, or just create redundancy.

The middle category—cross-functional, strategic change, or "the sweet spot," as I've called it—has some distinct advantages. These efforts tend to better balance complexity and cohesiveness of the solutions. They avoid both the massive scale and greater risk of the enterprisewide campaigns (though managing scope is still an issue) and the disconnectedness of locally spawned projects.

Whenever I've shared this diagram with groups of leaders they immediately acknowledge how well it fits their own organizations' portfolios and recognize the problems this kind of allocation creates. Because assessment of the whole enterprise change portfolio is usually not on anyone's list of responsibilities, I'd describe this as an example of "unconscious incompetence." Rebalancing the portfolio—that is, redirecting the resources to fill the middle category—actually takes more coordination and alignment *up front* than the very big and very small efforts. But it's one of the more important priorities for your success as a Six Sigma Leader.

PLANNING YOUR PORTFOLIO

How then does a Six Sigma Leader create a balanced, manageable, and high-potential-return change investment plan for his or her business, or segment thereof? The Six Sigma Leader will apply some smart ideas to help achieve that goal, while recognizing some important realities:

- Real "project definition"—creating a clear goal or assignment on which the business can carry forward—is an iterative process that goes well beyond the broad portfolio planning we're exploring here.
- Ongoing portfolio management requires revisiting and "rebalancing" the investment as needs change, efforts encounter challenges, new opportunities arise, etc.
- Portfolio management is not just about deciding *what* to invest, it's about achieving a return. We'll have a lot more to discuss about optimizing your portfolio and enhancing your operational results in this and in coming chapters.

Figure 2.2 displays a simplified but realistic view of that *front end* for portfolio planning. We can break it into four steps. I'm not going to get into an exhaustive how-to at this point, but rather note some of the key success factors and considerations for each.

Step 1: Identify Needs/Opportunities

The starting point is simply a list of concerns, pet projects, stunningly brilliant ideas that need development; major threats on the horizon, etc., described in some succinct way. We often call this a "business case," but it may also be a long-range product evolution plan or just a list of problems.

As shown in the top part of Figure 2.2, the "opportunity identification" can and usually should take place at each of these levels. Generally, enterprise-level areas of opportunity will address more fundamental competitiveness or critical performance issues. Cross-functional opportunities often involve key process "disconnects" or inefficiencies that add to costs, increase variability, or create obstacles to implementing needed change. Local issues can be described in most cases as "pain in the butt" problems or ideas that the department head or plant manager thinks need attention.

There will be a fair amount of overlap to the degree these ideas are generated separately, but one of the goals of enhancing your portfolio management capability is to identify and reduce redundancy or conflicting efforts early on.

Step 2: Describe Specific Projects/Initiatives

Based on each need/opportunity, a set of possible projects can then be identified. Some folks call this a "job jar" or a "project hopper," and it can get pretty big if you include *all* the potential investments. Those projects *not* selected are not necessarily eliminated from consideration—the choice is around *priorities*. Of course, items that remain in the "hopper" for a long time could be removed.

Note that as these specific investments/projects are clarified, you will have varying degrees of data and intuition to support the

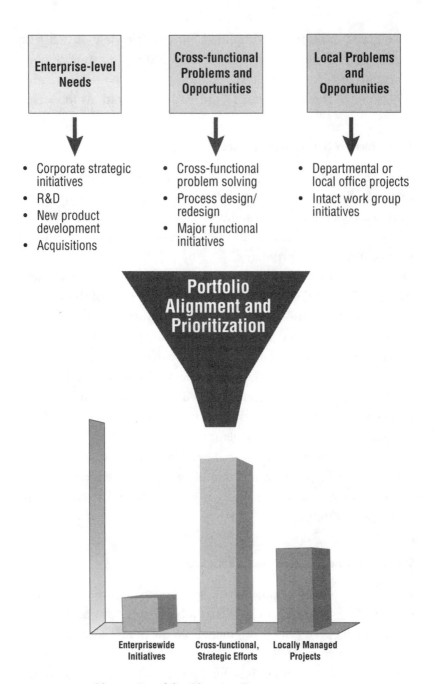

Figure 2.2 Change Portfolio Planning Process

need and value behind them. We'll examine how to apply critical thinking to the review and validation of possible opportunities in the next chapter.

Step 3: Establish Priorities and Resource Commitment

The degree to which your business already has some mechanism in place for project prioritization and budgeting will determine how big a change this approach will require. Fundamentally, selection of specific opportunities should balance two criteria: *meaningful* (high potential return) and *manageable* (complexity, achievability, and low risks). Across your *overall* portfolio you will also want diversity in your "asset allocation"—for example, a mix of long- and short-term projects; strategic and tactical, etc.

At the bottom of Figure 2.2, the distribution of projects by scope—enterprise, strategic, and local—shows my suggestion for a more appropriate mix, favoring the "sweet spot" of cross-functional initiatives.

Step 4: Assign Responsibility to Each Investment

Your change portfolio is not like putting money into a savings account and then collecting interest. Even the simplest project at the local level needs to be managed. Six Sigma Leadership demands taking an *active* role in ensuring that these investments pay off and, if they do not, then taking action to get them on track or cut your losses.

A key early activity will be to refine the goals, vision, and scope or sizing for each effort. Nearly always, a leader's view of a project is overly optimistic about the degree of complexity and effort required, at least in part because he or she sees things at a high level and misses some of the critical details.

It takes time and commitment to develop and refine this type of process. The example of one of our clients, global hospitality giant

Starwood Hotels and Resorts, illustrates one approach that worked well for their business. Starwood developed a top-to-bottom "give and take" process for setting priorities and optimizing change investments. The objectives and process included:

- *Provide "high-level" direction to local unit managers on high-priority areas for improvement.* These were tied to corporate goals and consistent issues identified in customer and industry research.
- *Allow "local autonomy" with localized guidelines.* The leadership team of each hotel was responsible for developing its own list of priority projects. However, the criteria used to choose the projects were weighted depending on the specific strengths and weaknesses of the local operation. For example, if the property had strong sales but, say, a higher cost of sale, the selection process would skew them toward cost-reduction efforts.
- *Maintain "high-level" review and control of the overall portfolio.* Priorities selected by the local executive team were passed "up the ladder" for approval in the context of all the various projects being identified. If too many efforts were being focused on one area of the business, some might be put on the back burner—or, a "strategic level" project team would be formed to address bigger, more holistic challenges.

This approach worked fairly well, but tended to be a little complex in its first iterations. Now, company-wide priorities are still defined at the Starwood corporate and brand levels—which include Sheraton, Westin, St. Regis, and LeMeridien—while local and many strategic projects are prioritized by Divisions (e.g., North America, Europe/Middle East, and Asia Pacific) and regions. In other words, the process has been enhanced and has become a standard practice over the several years since it was first applied.

To support the ability to manage the large portfolio, Starwood uses a Web-based project tracking application that lets people document their work while allowing "roll-up" reports and other features for leaders to keep an eye on their investments.

The trend around change portfolio management is somewhat encouraging. We see a growing group of companies doing some form of investment inventory and tracking; for example, around IT or capital projects, as well as some other improvement efforts (like Six Sigma projects). Unfortunately, this oversight is rarely integrated into an overall *business* change investment portfolio. So you have overlapping and redundant investment, and often a lot more under way than the organization can effectively handle.

Building a complete understanding of your overall change investment landscape is not a quick task. But you can still make some early progress by reviewing your current priorities, and perhaps taking some easy "reallocation" steps to get started on the path to a more balanced investment.

EXECUTING CHANGE

One of the most popular business books of the past few years is *Execution: The Discipline of Getting Things Done* by Larry Bossidy (former head of Honeywell) and consultant Ram Charan. As they note: "Leadership without the discipline of execution is incomplete and ineffective. Without the ability to execute, all other attributes of leadership become hollow."[4]

As Bossidy and Charan note, concern for getting things done is appallingly weak among far too many business leaders. My hypothesis is that aversion to doing the "heavy lifting" of making change *work* just aggravates the challenge of an over-burdened portfolio. Initiatives are launched; execution is poor; people lose interest; leaders get bored or impatient; *new* initiatives are

---

4. Larry Bossidy and Ram Charan, *Execution, The Discipline of Getting Things Done*, New York: Crown Business, 2002, p. 34.

launched on top of the existing ones; resources are spread even thinner. A dismal cycle!

The genius of the "And" here should sound like this:

> An outstanding Six Sigma Leader can inspire and establish the direction for change and can effectively guide that change to execution.

By "guiding to execution," I don't mean staying hands-on every step of the way. This genius does *not* require that every sales executive now become an Ops expert. Nor should we expect IT-types to take over launching your marketing campaigns. But Six Sigma Leadership demands people on both sides of the divide between ideas/direction-setting and execution to stop behaving as if the world ends where their span of interest and aptitude leaves off.

We'll be looking at other critical aspects of "execution" throughout this book—and for anyone really committed to being a Six Sigma Leader, it's highly recommended you read *Execution*. The main point for now is that you can't start working on your change portfolio management without also addressing the question: How are we going to make this happen?

THE BEAUTY OF CONSTANCY

This chapter began by defining change as the *essence* of Leadership. For that to be true, however, *not* changing is also essential to Leadership. In a business, change is like motion. If everything is changing, we have no effective reference point to understand or measure the change. If there is no constancy anywhere, if there is no predictability in the day-to-day operations, you lose the foundation on which to build effective change—whether it's a new product, streamlined process, new benefits plan—and to sustain it.

No leader can control all the change that impacts his or her organization, as we've noted. What a Six Sigma Leader *should* do is put value on "standing pat" or taking a patient attitude when that's the best choice. From an investment perspective, constancy in a business is a little like leaving your money in the bank for a while before you decide what to do with it. You can use that "downtime" for research, reflection, learning—and for executing the change efforts and ongoing operations you have to take care of anyway. There are some keys to "managing constancy" that we can explore in coming chapters, but for now, and in concluding this chapter, the message is: Learn to love and respect constancy just as you do change; concentrate on balancing the two.

Certainty and Doubt

There are two ways to slide easily through life: To believe everything or to doubt everything. Both ways save us from thinking.
—Alfred Korzybski (1879–1950)

THE INFALLIBLE LEADER

The title of this chapter sets up an age-old argument on the nature of leadership. This is deliberate. The conventional wisdom suggests that any leader who does not project absolute certainty in his or her decisions or convictions is doomed. "Never blink, never waiver," is one of those powerful, inspiring phrases that many people would say defines a great leader.

But both common sense and a basic knowledge of history (political and business) should remind us that *smart* leadership in reality demands a dynamic balance of certainty *and* doubt. The literature is filled with stories of leaders who made full-steam-ahead choices and ran smack into icebergs. Conviction *is* critical. Trepidation *can* show weakness. But unwavering, foolhardy conviction is not the path to successful leadership either.

In *The Seven Habits of Highly Effective People*, Steven Covey tells a story illustrating that certainty in leaders is not always a virtue. Two battleships were at sea on maneuvers in heavy weather. The captain of the lead battleship was on watch as night fell. The ships were traveling through patchy fog that made visibility poor. Then, the lookout on the wing of the bridge reported, "Light, bearing on the starboard bow."

"Is it steady or moving astern?" the captain called out.

"Steady, Captain," came the answer, confirming that they were on a dangerous course.

The captain called to the signalman, "Signal that ship, tell them we are on a collision course, advise you change course 20 degrees."

"Advise you change course 20 degrees," came the reply.

The captain said. "Send this message: 'I am a captain. You change course 20 degrees.'"

"I'm a seaman second class," was the reply. "Advise you change course 20 degrees."

Now furious, the captain spat out, "Send this message: 'Change course 20 degrees. I'm a battleship.'"

Back came word from the flashing light, "I'm a lighthouse."

The question for a Six Sigma Leader must be: *How do I balance the type of strength and certainty needed to inspire followers, while allowing the seeds of doubt necessary to avoid disaster?*

In fact, the theme of this chapter may be the most important in developing the habits of a true Six Sigma Leader. Fortunately the answer to striking the right balance between certainty and doubt is not found in being "weaker"—it's actually found in being smarter and stronger. First, though, let's look at the initial part of the problem, which I'll call the "culture of the infallible leader."

In observing our clients and hearing dozens of stories of leadership hubris, several factors emerge that seem to drive the "never blink" attitude of many executives and managers:

- *Equating success with one's own brilliance.* As people take on greater and greater leadership responsibilities, they gain greater confidence in their judgment and decision making. This is a natural reaction and often has some merit, but is dangerous when taken too far. It's good to have pride in your accomplishments, but take care that the pride doesn't overwhelm the accomplishment. None of us succeeds purely on our own talent: We all rely on the support of others, on overcoming obstacles, and on plain luck. As Benjamin Disraeli wisely remarked, "Every leader has the right to be conceited—until he is successful."

- *Overemphasis on independence.* As we all have heard hundreds of times, "It's lonely at the top." This view of the isolated leader has some glamour and, unfortunately, reality tied to it. Leadership is inherently isolating. Many organizations' structures and governance policies reinforce this image by cultivating a larger-than-life image of the CEO who has all the answers. This patriarchal attitude serves neither their CEO nor the organization well. At its worst, this culture prevents leaders from receiving the accurate information they need to make informed decisions. The go-it-alone attitude is counterproductive in the context of today's complex, interdependent organizations.

- *The perils of power.* Let me borrow from my own experience on this: As my consulting company has grown, I've had to make a special effort to ensure that people around don't grow reluctant to tell me when *I'm* wrong. At times they seem concerned that I might think less of them if they object to my views. Obviously it's important that the people around me feel empowered to disagree, and it would be a big risk to our business if they were to bite their tongues. My company is fairly small, so if the peril of power affects me as it does, it's not hard to project what the impacts can be on leaders in a medium to large business. I've observed direct effects of this "fear factor" phenomenon in meetings or workshops with a mix of people in the room. On more than a few occasions, when observing that people seem to be very quiet, someone has explained to me that "Folks are afraid to talk because *so and so*, the VP, is in the room." And these are usually cases where discussion is *encouraged*. For a leader, the cumulative detrimental effect of people's reluctance to speak up is this: If no one ever tells you you're wrong, eventually you start to think you're always *right*.

- *Leading into the unknown.* Especially at the more senior levels of an organization, the leader's responsibility involves taking followers into "uncharted territory." In those circumstances, the ability to *ignore* doubts and forge ahead undaunted is indeed extremely important. The notion of "certainty" in the ambitious efforts to stay ahead of the competition, develop new products and technologies, or boost organizational capabilities is unrealistic: there is no set of facts to prove or guarantee those "large bets." Certainty has to come from the conviction of the leader that the course set is the right one now. So for reasons both worthwhile and regrettable, the tendency is to see a "real leader" as one who is 100 percent certain, who must make decisions and have them carried out with little room for second guesses. Certainly very few leaders really view themselves as perfect, at least consciously. But an inordinate number present that attitude, or at least are perceived to by their followers.

How to counter the infallibility problem without undermining the strength and confidence any good leader needs? How to recognize *uncertainty*, fill gaps with facts, and make more informed choices without bringing progress to a halt?[1] That's our agenda for the remainder of this chapter.

LEADING WITH FACTS AND DATA

"Management by fact" or "data-based decision making" are phrases that describe some of the most recognized good habits— and are important characteristics of Six Sigma Leadership. Your goal should be to become a leader who values and uses relevant

---

1. More specific focus on encouraging communication and open exchange of issues will come in Chapters 5 and 8.

knowledge, information, and measures to set direction, guide and set expectations for others, and evaluate performance. By seeking—and relying on—facts and data, a leader can better clarify goals and priorities, reduce guesswork and limit risks, change opinion-charged arguments into a reasoned discussion, and more accurately quantify results. By contrast, the hallmark of "seat of the pants" leadership is an individual who pays scant attention to facts, until his or her luck runs out.

But it's also true that a Six Sigma Leader does not get overly enamored with data! Here's a "Good Habit" where getting out of balance can turn into analysis paralysis. The trick is to know when and how to demand or rely on facts and data, but also when to let things move forward based on gut and guesswork. (Intuition should never be removed from your "toolkit.")

The technical side of fact-based management, including topics like sampling, database design, surveying techniques, or statistical analysis, is important but outside the scope of our discussion here. And in reality, none of these techniques is as critical as having the right *leadership habits* to target and use facts, data, and knowledge well.

Here are some of the most important guidelines to enhance your own and your organization's effectiveness in managing and using facts and data.

Guideline I: Less Is Better

One of the biggest obstacles to using data and facts more effectively is the sheer volume of data to short through and/or things to be measured. The downside of the information age, as often noted, is the explosion of data we have to sort through to find anything relevant. In businesses, the growth of information technologies presents the same challenge: there's so much stuff in the database, so many transactions to examine, so many ways to slice the data that it becomes increasingly difficult to know what to look at. Information becomes an obstacle to knowledge.

This overload is worsened by "trial and error" reporting systems, where different stakeholders—executives, managers, regulators, IT people, and so forth—dream up and demand various packages of data. Their intentions may be good, but the majority of these reports end up being of little long-term value. Think of the reports you see in your organization and ask how many of the following phrases accurately describe them:

- Hard to read and/or understand
- Not relevant to your responsibilities
- Redundant (you can get the same information elsewhere)
- Too dated to be of any value
- Not believable (you don't trust it)

Efforts to kill the reports are rare, but revealing. A team at one of our clients did an inventory of data being generated on a regular basis and came up with a list of reports (I believe it numbered about 200) that did not seem to be of any benefit. So they just *stopped* issuing them. You might expect the managers on the distribution lists would have noticed when all those reports stopped arriving. But, in fact, only two people raised any question at all! The lesson is clear: Many legacy reports live on like zombies, emerging every week, month, quarter, consuming resources, and rarely being used. How many of the reports generated in your organization actually add value to the enterprise?

To say "less is better" as a starting point for more fact-oriented Six Sigma Leadership may seem counter-intuitive, but when you're sitting at the bottom of a deep hole of data, you first have to stop, climb out, and then determine where you really *should* be digging. Questions to help you get out of the hole include:

- *What are we going to do with this data?* If you can't describe a discovery that will lead to some action, a decision, or some specific "next step," then it may not be worth it. Apply the "So what?" test. Try to look at data out of curiosity only when you have a meaningful question—and beware of its becoming another monthly report.

- *Is there a simpler way to get the facts?* This question gets at the relative cost, value, and reliability of the data you hope to receive. In our high-tech world there's a common knee-jerk assumption that the database is the best source of facts. However, it may well be quicker, simpler, cheaper, more accurate, and more *meaningful* just to use "low tech" methods, such as talking to people, reading your intranet, looking through your past correspondence, etc. If you can use those approaches more often (and kudos if you already do) you're less likely to find yourself the recipient of a lot of pointless charts, graphs, and printouts. As an advantage, through these methods you are also likely to be more *connected* with your business, too. The story told to me by the head of an internal IT group from the old TRW (now part of Northrop Grumman) is a good example. A department contacted the IT team requesting it to develop a database for some information that groups in two different parts of the country needed to access. Rather than just jumping on the project, the IT folks asked a few probing questions. The final solution: a copy was made of a binder full of information being kept in one office, which was then sent to the other office. Certainly not all data requests are so easy to resolve, but the key point is that this team *asked* about the supposed need—which in my observation is a pretty uncommon approach.

- *Is there already another source for the same data?* A lot of redundancy in reporting occurs because a Leader or group wants a "new" report that is already being produced for someone else. But without checking, that new report (that isn't *really* new) gets added to the "to do" list. In fact, even data *sources* are often duplicated, such as when the marketing department and the order fulfillment group have duplicate customer purchase records—the kind of problem you can almost *count on* finding in a company of any size. What looked smart at the time—develop "our own" database that will help us keep track of things—ends up creating greater cost, confusion, and conflicting information. When the need arises, a Six Sigma Leader would look first to find an existing source or creative way to get answers *before* initiating another report or adding another database.

- *Is this a short-term or long-term need?* Well-meaning people tend to want to anticipate their boss's needs. If you ask for a report or piece of information one time, you may start getting it regularly even if you never asked. Or you may think, "We ought to look at this every month," but then rarely have time to take a peek. So the pile of unneeded bundles of facts and data grows.

The questions we've seen so far are aimed at damming the flood of data that can drown your ability to get to the facts. However, applying the "less is more" principle won't get you focused on the *right* facts. Now let's explore how to identify the facts you *should* be concerned with.

Guideline 2: Clarify the Goal

When we consultants arrive to work with a leadership group or project team, one of our favorite techniques for shaking things up is to ask: "What's really the goal here?" It's almost guaranteed to stop people in their tracks (usually each person has a different interpretation of the goal). For a Six Sigma Leader, the ability to check and refine goals is critical, while it's one of the more prevalent areas of "unconscious incompetence" for leadership at all levels.

Even as you're starting to crawl out of the hole of information overload, you can begin to assess what information *is* needed by focusing on your goals. What's the situation? What are you trying to manage? What's the problem you're trying to understand? These are the kinds of objective-focused questions that can help prioritize and target your search for relevant facts. Because each situation is different and no predesigned data system can feed you exactly the information you need every time, your focus should be on a simple, generic question:

> In this circumstance, what information will be most helpful in ensuring that we achieve the goal at hand or have a successful resolution?

With greater awareness of the context and purpose, it's possible to set clearer guidelines and priorities so you and your people can find and use facts more effectively. Table 3.1 presents examples of some of the data you might seek in different situations.

It will be important, especially if you are not prone to ask a lot of fact-focused questions now, that you make clear to your people, and yourself, why taking the time and effort to gather more facts will be worthwhile. We'll look at that aspect of being fact-based at several points in the remainder of the book. But it all starts with understanding your goal.

Guideline 3: Adopt a Systems View

Over the past few decades, the concept of a "system" in business has evolved to where it's applied almost exclusively to information technology. Reading the words systems view, you're liable to think: "Oh, yeah—computers, ERP, Web, database, CRM—all that stuff."

But what I'm referring to is actually much more fundamental and vastly more important: the *business* system. This is the system that connects all the pieces of your organization—customers, employees, suppliers (even those IT systems)—and enables you to meet your goals, make money, create new products and services, etc. The *business* system is what you lead. The systems view may in reality be one of the most important perspectives, not just for "management by fact," but for *all* the critical skills of a Six Sigma Leader.

Situation	Typical Goal	Facts/Data Needed
Make a decision (hiring, purchasing, selecting a location, etc.)	Select the best alternative to optimize results	• Criteria that will determine a successful outcome • Limiting factors or other constraints • Data relevant to the available options on each key criterion
Execute a project	Implement a solution or build a new offering	• Benefits of the solution • Potential risks or unknowns • Budgets and resources (and their current status) • Interdependencies among tasks • Schedule and deadlines
Run an "ongoing operation"	Optimize customer satisfaction and profits	• Key customer requirements (stated and implicit) • Current performance against customer requirements • Costs of running the operation • Leading indicator data to alert you to issues, opportunities

Table 3.1 Data You Might Seek

As shown in Figure 3.1, the basic systems view is simple—which is one of the reasons it's so powerful. The Input-Process-Output components describe the "value chain," indicate key customer interfaces (the little people in the circles), and describe the feedback loop that at least *should* inform the "upstream" activities of what's happening "downstream."

In this diagram, beyond the Output, there's an additional "result" component—the *Outcome*—that represents the things that occur beyond the immediate delivery of a product or service to a customer. Most business systems are more meaningful if you include *both* an Output *and* an Outcome, or "final" result.

That's the generic view. We can apply a systems view to pretty much any activity, at any level. For example, in Figure 3.2 the model describes a single event: the handling of a question by a Customer Service representative. Note that the feedback connection from the Outcome phase (Customer Action(s)) is faint, since often there *is* no real feedback! But those actions may impact the broader "market" depending on the nature of the communication, whom the customer talks to, their subsequent purchase decisions, etc.

Figure 3.3, on the other hand, takes a *very* high-level view of the business system, from developing a strategy to meeting shareholder goals. A lot of detail is hidden here, but the same "flow" and feedback loops apply.

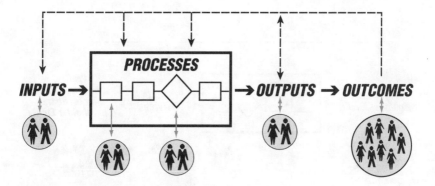

Figure 3.1   Basic "Business Sysem"

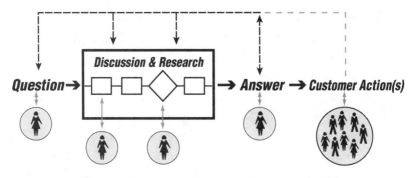

Figure 3.2 Business System Applied to a Customer Inquiry

The value of the systems view lies in its ability to convey *both* the simplicity and complexity of the business simultaneously, and to remind us of the tight interconnectedness of all the events that happen every day. One of the biggest challenges in leading an organization is keeping an eye on the "big picture" while managing the small pieces well. This is a theme—a Genius of the And concept—that will arise several times as we map out the skills of a Six Sigma Leader. The system view takes you away from the "org chart" to the real cause-and-effect chain of events that make up any organization. Rather than seeing just the parts, we can see an engine at work.

Connecting the systems view back to "management by fact" is the best way I've seen to help leaders begin to define and prioritize

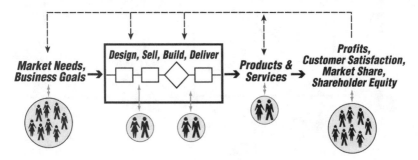

Figure 3.3 Business System at the "Whole-Business" Level

the information needed to understand and run the business. Without it, you tend to get a lot of data points, but no real picture of how the points connect.

The benefit of a systems view is evident in how it's helped businesses leverage their application of the Balanced Scorecard tool/method. Introduced in the early 1990s by Robert Kaplan and David Norton, the Balanced Scorecard (BSC) provides guidelines for developing a more robust set of measures to support operating and improving a business—much the same objective as the one we're addressing here.[2] But despite its popularity, a lot of companies have struggled to apply the BSC effectively. The Hackett Group, an Ohio-based business advisory company, recently concluded that more than 70 percent of U.S. and European BSC implementations are failing to provide "concise, predictive, and actionable information about how a company is performing and may perform in the future."[3]

A big part of the problem is putting too many items on the scorecard—more evidence for the need to get out of the data hole. But perhaps the bigger concern is that most Balanced Scorecards are, well, not balanced. Hackett found that half the metrics in a typical BCS concern internal financial data, with the rest divided between internal operating data and external financial and operating data. That leaves companies with far too much historical information and not enough "leading indicators." The problem is not with the Balanced Scorecard itself, but rather with the ability of leaders to understand and focus on the right measures.

When companies have begun looking at their activities from a systems perspective (a result, sometimes, of Six Sigma efforts or related Business Process Management[4] methods), they have often made rapid and significant improvements to their Balanced Score-

2. Robert Kaplan and David Norton, *The Balanced Scorecard: Translating Strategy into Action*, Boston: Harvard University Press, 1996.
3. Janet Kersnar, "Swamped: Why Do Balanced Scorecards Fail?" *CFO Magazine*, November 16, 2004. www.cfo.com/article.cfm/3372320.
4. See Rowland Hayler and Michael Nichols, *What Is Six Sigma Process Management?* New York: McGraw-Hill, 2005.

cards. They are able to target more meaningful and varied critical indicators, even as the total list of items on the Scorecard is not increased to the point of overload. The key seems to be the ability to see linkages and essential aspects of the business that are not understood from the more familiar "organization chart" view.

This is not a pitch for you to use a Balanced Scorecard necessarily, though it can be a very useful method when done right. It *is* a pitch, though, for you to take a systems view of your operation or organization so you can better understand and define the measures and critical information you do rely on.

Let's take a little reality-based "demo" to see how it can help:

Stephanie (not her real name) is an aspiring Six Sigma Leader who is recognizing that too many of the decisions and actions in her organization are based on gut and not enough real facts. She asks three of her direct reports to come up with two critical measures for their respective areas of responsibility. Here's what they propose:

Sam (Sales):
   Average sales per account exec
   Total sales per quarter

Sully (Production):
   Capacity usage
   Units produced per month

Les (Distribution):
   Order fill rate
   Number of returns received

Stephanie can't complain that these aren't reasonable measures, but she isn't altogether comfortable with them either. Somehow they seem disconnected. So she calls together the three managers to take a look at the measures. She tells the team, "Let's take an end-to-end view of the business and see if we can improve on this list."

What they arrive at is shown in Figure 3.4. Not all the measures are different, and there is one more than the "first draft" list (seven versus six). However, there are some significant enhancements:

1. *Broader perspective* In the first list, Sam, Sully, and Les did what Stephanie asked: they came up with measures that focused on their areas of responsibility. But the success of the business *system* is determined much more by the aligned efforts *across* the various "subprocesses." Measures like "order to delivery cycle time" and "conversion rate" are real cross-functional measures that offer a better opportunity to gauge the real impact of each group's efforts on the business as a whole.

2. *Shared ownership.* If understood and applied correctly, the *team* of Stephanie and her direct reports will use these measures to identify areas where they need to work together to address issues or opportunities. "Return rate," for example, is not an issue that should only concern Distribution, it may have causes and implications across the business.

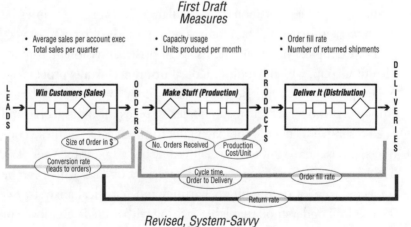

Figure 3.4 System-Focused versus Functional Measures

3. *A better Scorecard.* This may not yet constitute a complete Balanced Scorecard, but these seven system-savvy measures address costs, customers (returns, though we might want to add something a little more positive!), and internal processes. If we could track improvements in, say, order to delivery cycle time, it would indicate some "innovation." It may not yet be a perfect set of measures, but it provides a whole lot better view of the business than the first list.

Adopting a systems view of the business has other advantages to the Six Sigma Leader, which we'll explore a little later.

Guideline 4: Not All Facts Are Numbers

In a world of statistics and figures and signs saying "Billions served" it's possible sometimes for leaders and followers to become overly reliant on numbers. Not everything that happens can easily be quantified, and critical activities in your business may not happen often enough to put on a graph. But that does not mean you are stuck with guessing. You can still look for information about a situation, even if it's just a one-time event. Questions like, "Where?" "When?" or "Who?" don't give you numbers, they're just facts. Actually, specific facts about a particular situation may at times be much *more* informative than figures on hundreds of transactions.

For example, one of our clients is Uniprise, a division of United-Health Group, which handles medical insurance claims processing. A key portion of Uniprise's business is done on behalf of larger employers who have "self-insured" health plans for their people and need a service to handle the payments to physicians. In these contracts, thousands to millions of claims may be "adjudicated" per year. Tracking these transactions can generate a lot of data, which can be subjected to a lot of graphing, charting, and statistical analysis. *But* it's also well understood that issues arising with a single employee or dependent, say a misunderstanding or dispute over a claim, can jeopardize a client relationship even though the performance on the other thousands of claims might be *perfect*. If Uniprise leaders were to look only at the graphs, and not the facts, they could easily fail at one of the key success factors in their business.

Guideline 5: Take Responsibility to Get Good Facts and Data

One of the most common excuses leaders give for not using or for ignoring data is fear that it's not valid. While I'm somewhat sympathetic—getting *good* data is not easy—I also think that can be a cop out. To be an effective leader, you will need facts you can rely on. If you can't rely on them, you need to take responsibility to see how you can get better data!

The science of data collection can indeed be complex and technical, but the key questions you can ask to check your data and guide the organization toward better facts and data are not.

How Are We Defining This Measure/Data?

A great deal of the confusion about data arises from inconsistent definitions of the thing being discussed or measured. For example, we usually find simple concepts like "an order" are understood to mean very different things by different people/groups within a company. You need to ask questions to clarify and encourage clear and unambiguous measurement definitions—for example, what we mean by "an order"—both for specific instances as well as to improve your overall data-gathering systems.

An amusing example of misunderstanding data was told by a manager friend of mine whose boss received numerous financial reports in hard copy every day. One day, my friend asked the boss how useful the data was and his leader assured him the reports were a big help. He even pulled one out and pointed to a smiley face drawn on the cover page. "That tells me that our market share is up," the leader explained. "If it's there, I don't even have to look at the data."

My friend happened to see the person who generated that report the next day and asked about the smiley face. "Oh, that?"

she said. "When it's sunny out, I put a smiley face on every report I send out. It's just my way of saying 'Have a nice day.'"

Are We Counting Enough to Be Representative?

In data collection, sampling can be a huge advantage. We find a lot of leaders get uncomfortable with making decisions based on a sample of just 10 percent when, in fact, 10 percent can be a very reliable reflection of the larger world. The size of the sample is important, but a bigger question for leaders to consider is to what extent the sample is representative (see below). On the other hand, we find cases where far too few pieces of data are considered fully representative. I'd caution you that there are rarely perfect answers to these questions, but by asking them you can learn a lot and become more capable of knowing what to accept and/or reject.

Is Our Data Biased?

This is a little trickier—there are various types of bias—but an example would be a reasonable-looking sample that turns out to have come only from friends and relatives of employees. You need to look for hints that the results you're getting are somehow skewed because of the how, when, or who of the collection.

As you improve the questions you ask about your business, you will have an opportunity to focus your efforts to enhance the quality of your facts and data. As with any improvement, establish priorities and build on each step in creating more thorough, reliable information systems.

CHALLENGING ASSUMPTIONS

When businesses get into the deepest trouble, you can usually trace the source of their difficulties to an inability to see past a "truth" that is no longer valid. The willingness to challenge "received wisdom" is one of the hallmarks of Six Sigma Leadership. Without the readiness to question the status quo—to actually *introduce* doubt and deal with it proactively—you and your business become significantly more vulnerable to changes you can't control. Or you set off on ventures that leave you in serious trouble. In fact, the fundamental purpose of our 10-Second Rule is to give you a focused opportunity to examine your and others' assumptions before acting, or deciding not to act.

To some people, questioning assumptions or challenging accepted beliefs suggests being negative, cowardly, shaky. For a *leader* to do it threatens to undermine people's confidence. Clearly there is risk to pushing against the current view of the world or the expectations behind your current initiatives. But not to do so is usually worse.

Let's start with a nonbusiness analogy: I live in California, where, of course, the ground tends to move from time to time. You *might* assume that the best kind of building to withstand an earthquake would be a solid, more rigid structure: Just make it so tough that no jolt will knock it down! The reality, however, is that the best structures for an earthquake are able to give—they are built to move *with* the ground motion and absorb the shaking. In earthquake country you want your buildings to be both strong *and* flexible.

This is equivalent to the role of leadership "assumption busting"—the conscious act of testing commonly accepted beliefs about customers, markets, technology, etc. By being less rigid in your thought, you can prepare to be more flexible when the environment around your business starts shaking and you need to respond or adapt.

History and business lore are full of infamous assumptions and faulty "truths." You've likely heard of the comment by the then-head of Digital Equipment Corporation that "There is no reason for any individual to have a computer in their home." I'm fairly sure you knew that Internet commerce was going to put brick-and-mortar retail establishments out of business, right? More recently, U.S. automakers recognized the potential benefit of hybrid technology, but instead of using it to boost gas mileage, incorporated electric engines to improve *acceleration*.

One of my favorite corporate assumption stories involves the old, post-breakup AT&T and its grand strategic plan to win new customers and more lucrative business. With intense price competition in long-distance services, AT&T embarked on a costly effort to acquire an array of telecommunication services that it could sell bundled as an easy "one stop shopping" offering for consumers. The benefit: AT&T gets more of your business, and you only have to write one check. The problem was, customers not only didn't see that much benefit in the "one stop" approach, those who *did* sign on actually got upset when they saw services that they'd previously paid for separately all added up into *one bill*! One-stop shopping, the strategy that AT&T had invested billions in to achieve, just created sticker shock for the consumer!

In a business you *have* to operate every day based on "givens" and assumptions. These assumptions are not all bad; they help you move forward without having to question or debate every step or point of view *ad nauseum*. However, when critical assumptions are never challenged—especially if they are wrong—you're like a brick chimney in an earthquake.

So how should a Six Sigma Leader avoid being snared by faulty assumptions? Here's a suggested three-phase process that you can do in your head, or approach as a more deliberate assumption-testing exercise.

1. *Identify the assumptions.* It's easier, in my experience, to notice other people's assumptions than your own, so you may want to get help on this. Some clues to help you find the key ones:
   • Look for long-held "conventional wisdom," especially things held near and dear by veterans of your function or industry (remember, that veteran might be *you*).
   • Listen for assumption-based comments. Things like "That would never happen." Or "Customers really like/hate [blank.]." Or "We should have no trouble getting this done."
   • Examine your current operations (the status quo) and/or

your new initiatives (change efforts) and ask: "What are we assuming to be true, based on this plan or approach?"

2. *Test the assumptions!* Any assumption may prove wrong, so a smart leader will run at least a quick reality check:

   • First of all, assess the risks: "What's the impact if our assumption is wrong?" Only worry about the ones that will really get you into hot water if you're off base.

   • For assumptions with significant risks, examine the likelihood they might be wrong. For example, if your new product development effort is based on the assumption that a new technology will work, review the potential that the technology might not work. (By the way, in my observation the kinds of assumptions that tend to be most dangerous are those involving beliefs about people. Our expectations about how well others will accept new ideas, what their key requirements are, how ready they are to support our efforts—and even sometimes how "against us" they are—seem to yield the most surprises.)

3. *Adjust your actions/assumptions.* When you suspect some critical risks exist because of uncertain assumptions, you have then to decide what, if any, action to take. We'll look at some approaches in detail in the final two segments of this chapter, but your basic options are:

   • Do nothing for now. You may legitimately decide to let things ride to see if your worries are valid or not, or wait until you can get people to pay serious attention to your concerns.

   • Sound the alarm. This means "going public" with your suspicions that some key beliefs driving your projects or operations are faulty, and that some plan needs to be developed accordingly. This is the course to take when you can't respond independently and need others to help make adjustments.

   • Change your plans. Redefine your projects or processes, create contingency measures, or even try to influence reality to make your assumption true.

Adding a shade of doubt to the beliefs on which your organization operates takes courage. It need not be too dangerous, though, if you can combine your critical thinking with some fact-based analysis. Furthermore, as we'll see, borrowing from the scientific method can create an even more powerful balance between Certainty and Doubt.

ASK DOCTOR SCIENCE!

If you're really honest about it, a good portion of the "facts" that govern how our organizations operate are not really facts at all. Sure, there's plenty of data to be discovered, counted, and measured—things like number of orders, customers comments, weight of a shipment, length of a service call, performance of a product, etc. But these pieces of data tell us either what's happening now or what's already happened. They have great value, to be sure, but the things a leader has to "know" are actually predictions, not facts at all. Here's a short list of these kinds of pseudo-facts:

- The hot new technology or product in our industry
- The number of days or minutes it will take to get this order to the customer
- Our top three strategic priorities for the coming year
- The impact on our profitability from this acquisition
- The reason why return rates are up
- The real problem with the Sales team
- How many people we need to hire this quarter
- Who'd be the best person to run the new office
- The right pricing for the new product

A scientist and a Six Sigma Leader would realize that each of the pseudo-facts listed above and others like them would be most accurately called "hypotheses." They are not *guaranteed* to be true, but we *think* (or hope) they're true—in other words, they are educated guesses we make as we plan our actions and move the organization forward. Leadership, after all, is all about the future!

It's fairly easy to accept that what we "know" about the future is really a hypothesis. But it can also be the case with things happening today. For example, many Lean Six Sigma projects start with a "Problem Statement" that describes the pain they are trying to remedy. Some typical examples: "New customer mailers are going to the wrong addresses 12 percent of the time." "Detergent bottles are leaking." These descriptions are a great starting point to address important business issues.

However, very often the real problem turns out to be *different* from the one described in the initial statement. In other words, the Problem Statement is really a Problem *Hypothesis*—it describes what people *think* the problem is. (And that's why a typically large chunk of time in one of these projects is spent measuring and validating the problem; that is, refining the "problem hypothesis.")

"Solutions" or "initiatives" work the same way. Reorganizations, new marketing efforts, new compensation plans—leaders are launching programs like these around the world every single day. Their eventual benefit to the business is not a "fact" though; it's a hypothesis (or a bunch of them).

Here's a fairly simple example. Over the past few years a couple of our clients have launched the development of a "Corporate University" to consolidate and manage their disparate training activities. It's a reasonable idea; many companies have successfully created their own "U" that provides excellent programs for employees, leaders, suppliers, and customers. But having observed companies struggle to form a "university," it becomes clear that the concept of a centralized training organization is not *guaranteed* to be superior to what's already in place. In fact, there may be strong reasons why the decentralized existing approach works better. So, again, the Corporate U is not *factually* better, it's *hypothetically* better. The same can be said for that new ERP system, marketing campaign, office location, and so forth: none a sure thing, each a hypothesis.

To me, this is one of the most essential epiphanies of Six Sigma Leadership. If you can grasp and get comfortable with it, you can meaningfully improve your ability to drive success and avoid disaster. The notion of "management by hypothesis" really supplants "management by fact"—because we realize that there *is* no such thing as management by fact. What the Six Sigma Leader can aspire to is to operate by and based on *hypotheses that are more likely to be true.* How the heck do you do that? Well, let's ask Doctor Science!

As we see in Figure 3.5, hypotheses are a product of what we know, what we think, and what's driving us. Based on those hypotheses, we take action.

Unfortunately, too many "infallible" leaders follow the path much as it's shown here: they move from hypothesis to action on a direct path, with little conscious concern about the validity of their hypothesis. And as the actions roll out, relatively little attention is paid to learning and refining the hypothesis or plan. "Spare me the details, just get it done!" is what you're liable to hear under this mode of operation. A better, more proactive approach—when applied properly—is shown in Figure 3.6.

Before initiating action, the Six Sigma Leader does a "reality check" to see if the current hypothesis is reasonably valid: Are the facts on which it's based reliable? Are our assumptions solid or shaky? Are the goals and objectives that are prompting us to act the right ones? In this "Test Loop 1," the hypothesis either passes, is refined, or gets rejected/abandoned. Even a quick check can help avoid hasty or misguided action. In the process of testing, the "educated guess" becomes a "better educated guess."

What's labeled "Test Loop 2" in Figure 3.6 is much like on-the-job learning: After the organization has taken *action* based on the hypothesis, observations and information are compared to what was expected. Now the action can be refined and adjusted thanks to a *better* understanding of how well the initial hypothesis fit reality. In other words, the data is compared and evaluated much in the way a scientist compares experimental results to his or her hypothesis. If you want to be a smarter leader, perhaps some brushing up on the scientific method might be helpful!

Of course, the testing of management hypotheses is not quite the either/or scenario the diagrams suggest. All hypotheses get

Figure 3.5 Leadership Based on "Untested" Hypotheses

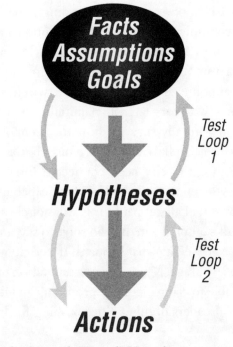

Figure 3.6 Leadership with "Tested" Hypotheses

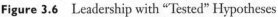

some unconscious testing or scrutiny: some undergo exhaustive review, some a minor check, some none. For a leader, having your hypothesis proven wrong (or "not quite correct") is not necessarily a bad thing. Any truly visionary change begins with a questionable hypothesis backed by conviction and commitment. But being balanced and savvy enough to recognize when there's uncertainty and to manage around it can be just as important to your credibility as pushing forth in spite of weaknesses in your facts and assumptions.

Here's a good illustration of the testing process and the role of the leader. In 2004, Philadelphia Mayor John Street announced that his city was embarking on an effort to make free wireless Internet access available to all residents. Mayor Street had a vision for interconnecting citizens and opening the Internet to people of all socioeconomic strata. Behind that vision was a hypothesis: "We can set up a wireless network throughout Philadelphia's city limits and offer it to people for free." Assuming there was conviction behind his plan (i.e., he was not just posturing), Street's initiative was based on some understanding about wireless technology and economics (his facts and assumptions) and a desire to offer broadband to all Philadelphians (goal). The concept proved appealing and a number of other cities, determined not to be left behind, have announced their *own* citywide wireless programs.

Now, about two years later, that initial hypothesis is still not proven. No one's totally sure yet how the technology will work. Limited pilot projects have shown promise, but as of this writing nowhere has an entire city been connected for wireless. Several companies have stepped up to offer their capabilities to *make* it work, but how it will all get paid for is still not clear.

How will this all play out? It's too soon to say, and I for one am looking forward to seeing what happens. If free citywide broadband turns out to be a mirage, Mayor Street's reputation may take a hit— or he may be able to claim credit for proposing an idea that "pushed the envelope." Leaders of other cities pushing for municipal wireless have, knowingly or not, staked some of their own political capital on Street's hypothesis.[5] For a Six Sigma Leader, there is no right or wrong answer to how much proof you should try to get up front before acting on your hypotheses. But we can provide some commonsense rules you can apply to your own planning:

1. The higher the risk of failure, the more you should consider additional testing of your hypotheses (Test Loop 1).
2. The less certain you are of your hypothesis when initiating action, the more you should be prepared to learn and adjust as you go (Test Loop 2).
3. If you're not ready to test your hypotheses or adjust your actions, you'd better be prepared for the consequences of failure.

I don't think business leaders are as aware as they should be that *their* jobs are often like that of an organizational scientist: forming, testing, refining, and rejecting and hopefully *proving* hypotheses about markets, products, customers, and people. Some leaders forge ahead with ambitious efforts that could have been better tested in advance, and fail. Others are paralyzed by uncertainty, missing the opportunity to evaluate their hypotheses, and never make progress. Both *action* and *inaction* can be helped by applying this "testing and refining" approach.

The Genius of the And in this equation is to strike the right balance at each level: Facts, Assumptions, Goals, Hypotheses, and Actions. Fortunately, there's one more aspect of Six Sigma Leadership that can help you manage the final outcome of your struggle with Certainty and Doubt.

5. "Wi-Pie in the Sky?" *The Economist*, March 11, 2006 (vol. 378, no. 8468) pp. 22–24. The article notes that: "All this means Philadelphia, San Francisco, Minneapolis, Portland, Chicago, and many other cities are participating in a great experiment."

PLANNING FOR FIRE

As noted at the outset of this chapter, supreme confidence on the part of a leader is admirable. But if it's not balanced by an understanding that even the best-tested hypothesis can prove wrong or that things can go awry, that leader is risking the health of the business. In the final section of this chapter, we'll look at some of the natural and needed thinking around accepting and managing doubt (aka "risk").

There's a fun workshop exercise I learned years ago that I'd like you to try. The scenario is this: You've been very successful in business and have made a substantial amount of money. You decide to invest a chunk of it to build a new luxury resort hotel. You have one concern: You're worried the resort might go up in flames, taking your investment with it. You're set to have a meeting with the architect and contractor who are designing and building the resort. As you head over to the meeting, you make a list of things you can build, buy, or install to reduce your exposure to the risk of fire.

What would your list look like? Go ahead, make your list . . . we'll wait. (Try to come up with at least 12 ideas.)

Okay, if you are much like the *dozens* of groups we've done this with, your list looks something like this:

- Fire extinguishers
- Alarms
- Smoke detectors
- No-smoking halls
- Proximity to the fire department
- Staff training in emergency response
- Water supply
- Fire hose access
- Helipad
- Insurance
- Chemical storage
- Emergency signage
- Evacuation routes

- Emergency lighting
- Sprinklers
- Wheelchair egress
- Building materials
- Kitchen maintenance

Now, before reviewing what you've come up with, here's a little background on "risk management." In my consulting work, I've often been asked, "How can we teach our people to take more risks?" Kind of an interesting question when you think about it, isn't it? Is that *really* what organizations want? Exposure to more risk? No. What organizations really want is to better *manage* risk. This means being better risk takers, being smarter about both incurring and avoiding risk. It also means better managing of the risk of being too timid or complacent in the face of shifting market conditions. Like so many aspects of being a Six Sigma Leader, the answer to "How do we manage risk?" is fairly common sense and can be boiled down to three steps:

1. *Identify what the risks are.* Most of us are pretty good at that if we try, though as noted in the discussion on Hypotheses above, those risks may be ignored or glossed over.
2. *Examine how to prevent the problems from happening.* That means looking for steps that will reduce the likelihood of a problem by investing some effort up front.
3. *Come up with contingencies that will limit the damage or consequences if things do "go wrong."*

Then, of course, you have to set some priorities and take action to put prevention and/or damage control measures in place.

Let's now examine our "fear of fire" list for the new resort hotel. The idea is to categorize each item according to whether it's a *preventive* measure (will keep a fire from ever occurring) or a *contingent* measure (will keep the fire small and/or limit damage and casualties). Let's go over my list of ideas. A "P" indicates a preventive action and a "C" means a contingent action.

- Fire extinguishers—C
- Alarms—C
- Smoke detectors—C
- No-smoking halls—P
- Proximity to the fire department—C
- Staff training in emergency response—C
- Water supply—C
- Fire hose access—C
- Helipad—C
- Insurance—C
- Chemical storage—P
- Emergency signage—C
- Evacuation routes—C
- Emergency lighting—C
- Sprinklers—C
- Wheelchair egress—C
- Building materials—P
- Kitchen maintenance—P[6]

The "score" on my list is typical of *many* groups with which we've done this exercise:

- 14 Contingent actions
- 14 Preventive actions

I'd imagine your totals are similar. (If your list has more Ps than Cs, congratulations! You get a gold star.) Hopefully you recognize that these totals are a bit out of balance. Instead of trying to keep from ever having to deal with fire, all our natural attention is focused on putting the fire *out* and rescuing potential victims. Now you know why the title for this section is "Planning for Fire."

---

6. Before you start arguing with my categories, remember "where there's smoke there's fire"—so anything that extinguishes fire, mitigates fire damage, protects people or property from fire, or responds *after* a fire has occurred is a contingent action.

The point is not that you should ignore contingency plans—they are very important and there are plenty of risks that may be beyond your capacity to prevent. And it's important to plan your contingencies in advance. The fire sprinklers, of course, are installed *during construction*, not rushed into place after the fire alarm goes off.

As a Six Sigma Leader, your focus should be to recognize risks, focus on the real show-stoppers, and prepare a balanced set of actions to either prevent and/or limit damage. To really prevent a problem, you have to attack and eliminate its cause. That's why "No-smoking halls," "Chemical storage," and "Kitchen maintenance" are good preventive actions because they address things that might ignite a fire. Most critical are the discipline and commitment to apply this "doubt management" approach to improve your chances of success and/or reduce the potential for nasty surprises.

In Figure 3.7, you can see this aspect of Six Sigma Leadership built into our action path. I call it the "Certainty and Doubt management" model and don't think it's really much of a stretch. There's certainly more we could add to it (for example, facts, data, and impressions on your Results feedback to the top circle), but in essence you find the primary "steps" and contributors both to applying facts to manage your business and confronting and coping with the uncertainties that impose doubt—and also derail results.

We've now explored some of the foundational aspects of Six Sigma Leadership. Leading is about change; leading is about balancing what's known and unknown to keep moving forward. In the next few chapters, we'll apply these core lessons to the aspects of leadership behavior that make Six Sigma Leadership truly effective.

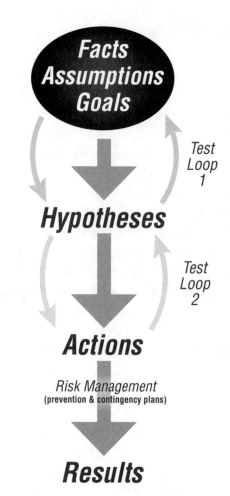

Figure 3.7 Integrated "Certainty and Doubt" Management

CHAPTER

Speed and Deliberateness

Time won't let me, whoo-woo
Time won't let me, whoo-woo
Wait that long
   —The Outsiders, "Time Won't Let Me" (1960s hit song)[1]

THE STANDOUT Number 1 on the hit parade of *Reasons Why I Can't Act Like a Six Sigma Leader* is "Time won't let me!" And it's been topping the charts for years. But that refrain makes a poor excuse not to take the time needed to build a more successful business. As I've heard countless leaders and managers comment through the years "We have time to fix it, but we seem never to have time to do it right the first time."

Speed is without doubt one of the most important factors in business success. The importance of staying one step ahead of the other guy is chronicled in hundreds of books and articles. A Six Sigma Leader must be adept at using speed as a competitive edge,

1. "Time Won't Let Me," Words and Music by Tom King and Chet Kelley. The Outsiders recording, released in January 1966, reached Number 5 on the U.S. charts. www.classicbands.com/outsiders.html.

looking for ways to keep the organization moving rapidly. These strategies include cycle time reduction, just-in-time processes, rapid iterative design, and time-to-market improvement. Even the ability to fail faster can be an attribute of business success.

But the need-for-speed has to be kept in perspective. Too many leaders and managers defend weak, hasty decisions based on shaky hypotheses by claiming they just don't have time to do otherwise. Checking facts or assumptions sounds good in theory, but not realistic when you're under a time crunch (and who isn't?). In other words, we are often in *too* much of a hurry. Being a Six Sigma Leader demands greater skills at getting things accomplished fast, but with the right time investment to get them done right. As we'll see, optimizing speed relies on discipline, understanding what you *mean* by "fast," and knowing when to just go all-out.

THE ILLUSION OF SPEED

The origins and persistence of the speed-above-all-else behavior go back quite a way. Figure 4.1 provides a simple overview of the evolution of management and speed.[2] We can look at it first as a lesson in history since the Industrial Revolution. In the earliest period (Production), capacity or supply was low relative to demand. As we know, that imbalance impacted price, but it also influenced business leaders' behavior. With demand so high, the smart manager knew that getting products to market should be the priority. Even if the goods being shipped were not "perfect," clamoring buyers would likely snap them up. The same held true when capacity and demand were relatively equal (the "Distribution" phase) since getting *your* goods on the shelves was still key to beating the competition.

In the Market phase, the third period, however, the equation dramatically changed: with supply exceeding demand, customers can be more discriminating. It was still important to get your prod-

2. I learned this point and borrowed this diagram from an old colleague, Greg Brower, who'd taught "Total Quality" extensively at GM in the 1980s.

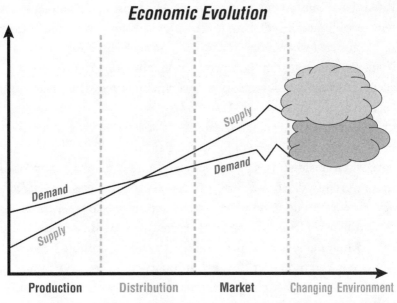

Figure 4.1   Evolution of Supply, Demand, and Competitive Conditions

uct or service to market, but it had to be good, meeting the needs of your target customers, or it would not sell. By the *final* phase—Changing Environment—competitors and potential customers are in a dynamic give-and-take where markets and product life cycles are increasingly narrow. In this case, there's no single prevailing dynamic for competition or theme to guide leaders on how best to drive their businesses' success. This is where the supply and demand lines disappear into clouds.

From a macro perspective, it's safe to say most economies are now into the cloudy world of the Changing Environment. However, I've noticed this same evolution at an individual *company* level as well—in fact, in many companies—and it heightens the need for the balance of Six Sigma Leadership.

Here's how it works. A company of any size and longevity is almost certain to have periods where things are *booming*. The firm's product or service is a winner, people are buying as much as they can produce, the firm may even be touted as the "next big thing."

Life is rosy, but of course, very hectic. With rising demand, a lot of new people are hired. Employees old and new are told, "Look, we've got customers breathing down our necks here so just do your best, get this done, and get product out the door." *Do it fast.* The accepted reality becomes: speed over deliberateness is the key to success.

It's little wonder that speed-at-all-costs becomes a hard-to-break habit. It's what people remember from those happy, crazy days when business was great—in fact, that's usually when most of them were hired. But while all-out speed probably was *the best business choice* when demand was high and supply was low, when things slow down that go-go approach turns into *excessive* speed. And that's when many companies, and their leaders, stumble.

As you might expect, this evolutionary phenomenon shows up most vividly in our high-tech clients. But the legacy of boom times is also a factor at companies in many other sectors that have been through high-growth phases or cycles: financial services, retail, construction, real estate, entertainment, and hospitality businesses are a few of those who've seen high-demand periods where the only way to survive is to move at a breakneck pace.

Lack of discipline, inefficiency, and higher error rates—a common side effect of moving fast—are tolerable when you have the revenues and profits to hide the costs. Speed is exciting, and after a while gets ingrained in the culture. But later on, speed becomes an illusion; the frenzy of activity hides the fact that very often the business's wheels are spinning, but getting little traction. Leaders then need to reset the *balance* between speed and deliberateness.

SPEED AS A DISCIPLINE

This phrase, "speed as a discipline," may sound like an oxymoron. To many, speed is assumed to come from abandoning discipline, charging ahead, worrying about the details later. But by now I hope you've picked up some hints as to why the discipline of a Six Sigma Leader can, perhaps paradoxically, actually boost your ability to drive speed—the right kind of speed—in your organization. In this section we'll examine the discipline of speed primarily in your "new initiatives" or change efforts; a little further along we'll explore optimizing speed in ongoing operations.

Discipline of Focus

In Chapter 2, "Change and Constancy," we emphasized how critical it is to focus your change investment on a manageable portfolio. If trying to do too many things at once will slow you down, then having focus can allow you to *speed up*. Let's compare two business approaches. Two of my firm's larger clients over the past decade have been GE and Sun Microsystems. Sun launched its "Sun Sigma" initiative in 1999, largely due to the influence and close relationship between Sun's long-time CEO Scott McNealy and then GE chief, Jack Welch. One of the remarks McNealy made as he compared the two firms was that, while Sun had *many* competing change priorities, GE had basically three. (Even today it still has three.[3]) GE, of course, was much larger and more diverse than Sun—though at the time Sun's market capitalization was quite high for its size.

Both companies have undergone major stresses since those days. Sun's—having been part of the dot-com "bubble"—obviously more severe. But GE has had to endure the shock of September 11, 2001, change in top leadership, energy cost pressures, and reorganization of some its major businesses. So even though they are two very different companies, it's reasonable to argue that GE's ability to move quickly, due in large part to its discipline of *focus*, has proven much more effective than Sun's.

3. The areas of focus have evolved over time. The three key strategic imperatives in General Electric's 2005 Letter to Stakeholders are: "1. Sustain a strong portfolio of leadership businesses that fit together to grow consistently through the cycles' 2. Drive common initiatives across the company that accelerate growth, satisfy customers and expand margins; and 3. Develop people to grow a common culture that is adaptive, ethical and drives execution." Not a bad list for a Six Sigma Leader! See: http://www.ge.com/ar2005/letter_sized.htm.

Discipline of Goals, Facts, Assumptions, and Risks

Thinking things over, checking your data, anticipating problems, and other seemingly sedentary activities are viewed by many to be the antithesis of speed. But they can increase your speed just as well—or at least allow you to go fast at the right time and get to real results much more effectively.

This point emerged dramatically in a study of the electronics industry conducted a few years ago by Andersen Consulting (now Accenture) and some major universities. This is a sector where the pace of change is so blinding and treacherous that, as one CEO is quoted: "We used to talk about product life cycles. Now we talk about *company* life cycles."

The researchers found, to their admitted surprise, what they termed the "Paradox of Deliberateness." It turns out that

> **. . . High-performing companies, despite their agility and flexibility for meeting changing market conditions, are actually more deliberate in their decisions to enter a new product market or adopt a new technology. In fact, decision-making speed in these strategic areas is inversely proportionate to success.**
>
> **On average, high performers take nearly *twice as much time* as their low-performing counterparts to make such decisions [emphasis added].**[4]

Agility and flexibility, combined with *deliberateness*?! This too is the Genius of the And at work, but unfortunately not the kind of thinking you run across every day in the business world. How does this work? Consider these examples of where deliberateness and speed work together:

- The student who studies and does his or her homework completes the test first (and gets a good grade).

4. A summary of the study, along with a list of academic partners, can be found at www.edacafe.com/technical/papers/Cadence/archive/vol2No4/prodDevTrends.php.

- The mechanic with an organized toolbox can get the repair done quicker.
- The new product development team that has a clear set of specifications, with pre-vetted technology, will get to market faster than the one dealing with many unknowns.
- The driver who gets directions and reads the map before leaving is more likely to arrive on time.
- The manager who carefully assesses the responsibilities and skills needed for a new position, and who evaluates candidates who fit the criteria, is more likely to pick the person who can "hit the ground running" and contribute right away.

It's natural, I suppose, to see deliberation as idleness. In the examples above, and whenever discipline is needed to allow for speed, some "prep time" has to be invested. That looks like downtime and people get very uncomfortable. A software industry consultant once told me she describes it as special form of liquor that's often imbibed by the leaders and sponsors of IT projects: WISCY (pronounced "whiskey"). Of course, it's really an acronym standing for: *Why Isn't Sam Coding Yet?!!*

I experienced the same impatience as I wrote this book! I frequently got the sense that if I wasn't chained to my desk pounding the keyboard, I wasn't making progress. So I planted myself and ground away, pushing to get the chapters done. Then, finally, I took a break—feeling guilty—and lo and behold, while pouring coffee, catching up on the news, or taking a shower, a helpful idea occurred to me. That "idle" deliberation time actually helped me get more accomplished in 5 or 10 minutes than I often can in an hour or more of focused writing.

To overcome the danger of excessive impatience—to build the habit of deliberateness so you can unleash greater speed—a smart leader has to get comfortable with "downtime" or "prep time." And you have to learn to use that invested time in the right way. Here's a list of some suggested ways to use your time (most of which should ring a bell if you read the last couple chapters).

- *Check your goals.* Are we working on the right things, going in the right direction? (Going fast the wrong way is just accelerated reverse.)
- *Assess your facts.* Do we have the information necessary so we don't have to stop, back up, change plans, etc.? What additional data or verification will help us move forward effectively?
- *Review your assumptions.* Are there implied "facts" or expectations that may actually slow us down?
- *Test your hypotheses.* Can we validate our plans against reality? (More on this in a few moments.)
- *Manage your risks.* What potential problems can we prepare for so they don't bring things to a halt later?

You need not review all these items all the time, nor do they need to be followed in this order. In fact, if you were to cut your "deliberation plan" down to two items, the most important would almost always be *Goals* and *Risks*.

Discipline of Scope

Another very important influence on the speed of change efforts is the size or scale of the task. This is an area where the lack of discipline can be especially frustrating, to me at least. At practically every company we've consulted with over the years, I've heard people—leaders included—acknowledge having frequently gotten bogged down in "boil the ocean" initiatives. Peruse the mainstream business media and you'll see a pattern: Failed huge-scope initiatives are costing shareholders (and taxpayers) millions if not billions each year, while creating problems for employees and customers. Yet the tendency to launch big, hugely scoped projects persists.

Often it seems that the reason for a "boil the ocean" effort is that leaders are not sure which part of the ocean they ought to boil, so they just overfill the pot. Equally challenging is the perception that a smaller scope means "settling for less." For leaders with passion and big appetites, it's hard to accept that carving off a *piece* of the pie is better than trying to swallow it whole. Having vision and setting ambitious goals, however, is not incompatible with scaling down so you can achieve results sooner and build on that progress.

In his excellent book *Leadership*, former New York Mayor Rudolph Giuliani shares a great example of the use of scope, even in light of a huge challenge. Faced with a growing crime rate that was creating fear and hurting the great city's image, Giuliani launched a large, ambitious effort to tackle the problem. But instead of trying to knock out crime in a single blow, Giuliani started with a small jab: clear New York streets of the "squeegee people." These were the people who'd stand on the approaches to bridges and tunnels surrounding the city and "voluntarily" spray water on car windshields, wipe them off, and then demand payment for "cleaning the windows."

It was not a major crime—in fact, for a while it was not even seen as illegal—but it did make a bad impression on people coming to New York and Giuliani thought it was a good place to start. The mayor directed the police to cite the squeegee people for jaywalking. The police soon found that the squeegee people usually were wanted for more serious violations and could be put into custody. In no time, the entrances to New York City were much more inviting.

Fortunately, scoping a project to be something manageable is *not* as hard as leaders tend to think, although it does require an investment of time, thought, and even some research. The better you understand the issue or opportunity, the more likely you'll know where to focus and where the "sweet spot" is likely to be. I doubt most of us would intuitively know that squeegee people would be a worthwhile starting point in the battle against crime. Even the former prosecutor Rudy Giuliani only learned it by taking advantage of crime statistics that had previously been ignored.[5]

5. This example adds a reminder to our discussion around using facts and data from Chapter 2. While usually "less is more" will help you get better focus on relevant facts, it's also possible that you should pay closer attention to the data you're already getting. That's what officials in NYC did as they started to find effective ways to use their resources against crime.

No matter how much data you have, though, scoping always requires some leadership judgment. With that in mind, here's a checklist of possible ways to slice "world hunger" down to something where progress can be made with reasonable speed.

- *Explicitly narrow the problem/opportunity.* The goal here is to say both what is "in" and "out" of scope, line small bumps on the side of a highway that alert you when you're getting off track. There are two steps:
  - Describe the problem or objective in terms of what it *is*. For example: "An estimated 30 percent of Customer IDs in the database are duplicates. Our goal is to eliminate all duplicate IDs."
  - Describe explicitly what the problem or objective *is not*. Continuing the example: "We will not be concerned with updating any client information or other aspects of the database organization."
- *Limit the breadth.* Here, the point is to clarify what activities or tasks are "in bounds" for investigation or solutions. This is where the big picture systems view of the business can provide valuable insight. Figure 4.2 illustrates scope as the span

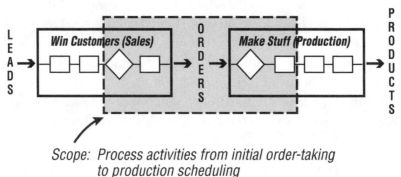

Figure 4.2 illustrates:

Goal: Streamline order management process to improve cycle time & reduce rework

Scope: Process activities from initial order-taking to production scheduling

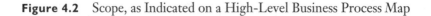

Figure 4.2 Scope, as Indicated on a High-Level Business Process Map

of activities in business processes that will be examined/ affected in a change initiative. The example here indicates discipline in keeping the scope narrow so the project can move faster.

- *Target a segment or location.* This is a simple scoping approach, in which a new initiative is focused on a limited geographical area or number of locations, and/or a certain customer of product/service types. For example, one of our clients was trying to cut cycle times to deliver spare parts in its Asia region. Based on data showing the worst cycle time perfor- mance was in India versus other Asian parts depots, the proj- ect sponsor asked the team to narrow their efforts to India. That tighter scope enabled solutions to be implemented much more quickly—not to mention achieving significantly reduced delivery times.

- *Use a "multigenerational" approach.* Any change effort may benefit from a multigenerational plan, though this is most often relevant for larger-scale, more ambitious initiatives. As the name suggests, the Six Sigma Leader defines a vision or goal for success, but then plots a path to achieve that goal through a sequence of projects or major phases. The multi- generational concept not only helps manage resources, but can also provide stronger overall results by building new capabilities in a more appropriate sequence.

It's likely you've used or observed some or all of these scoping approaches at one point or another. (You can even mix and match them, by the way. For example, apply a multigenerational plan to a project in a limited set of locations.)

Are there times when a huge-scope effort is warranted? Defi- nitely! When major threats or opportunities confront your or- ganization, you may have no choice but to commit to a large, dramatic initiative. Many industries at various times encounter periods of upheaval or a shake-out where make-or-break change is required. Today's telecommunications industry is one example (and it seems to go through these cycles fairly regularly) of where a high stakes struggle has various players vying to be the "pipeline of choice" for consumers and businesses. Cable companies, "traditional" phone companies, Internet services, and wireless providers are all investing billions to try to win the technology and preference battle.

But even when you're launching a "bet the farm" initiative, there's value in checking facts and assumptions, being more focused, and scoping. Speed and deliberateness *still* need to be balanced, even when speed is of the essence.

DEFINING AND INTERPRETING SPEED

A colleague back in my days as a PR account executive had a card on her desk with one of my favorite all-time sayings: "Everything takes longer than you expect. Even when you expect it to take longer than you expect."

I've repeatedly observed that the expectations and perceptions around how long things take, or should take, are big factors influencing how effectively a leader, and an organization, will balance speed and discipline. There are really two elements to this challenge. They tend to interact and are therefore not always easy to differentiate, but let's try to look at them separately. The first is easiest: How time is counted. The second is trickier: How time is perceived.

Issue One: Measuring Time

In Chapter 2 we talked about the importance of clear definitions in gathering and interpreting data. Poorly defined and communicated time frames lead to misunderstandings that can create unnecessary pain. Here are a couple of examples.

Operational (Cycle) Time

"It'll be there tomorrow." "It'll take three days." "We'll be back soon." "The promise date is June 30." Each of these is a real quote from a real business making a commitment to a colleague or customer on an issue of time/speed. The question that so often arises is "What does that mean?" I would say a lot of our clients have gotten a lot smarter about being specific when communicating time commitments, but there's still a lot of vagueness. These examples tie closely to issues around understanding customer needs, which we'll examine in Chapter 7. The main lesson is that you need to define and measure speed in terms that are clear and meaningful to everyone. If we tell someone, "It'll be there tomorrow" it may be perfectly acceptable. But if they have a 10 a.m. meeting and need "it" for the meeting, you've now created more fear and concern than may be necessary.

Project (Completion) Time

It's common for projects to feature a Goal Statement describing the intended objective. For example, "Reduce invoice discrepancies to Tier 1 customers by 40 percent by March 2." This looks good at first glance, but not if the business leader and project manager have differing interpretations of what "by March 2" means. There are at least two ways to understand the statement:

1. The project's solution will be implemented by March 2; or
2. The 40 percent reduction in invoice discrepancies will be documented by March 2.

These mean two very different things. Typically a project leader will focus on *implementation*; a business leader will be more interested in *results*. Neither leader in this case is right or wrong, they just have different views of "completion," and thus the time span of the project. With clearer communication, misunderstanding and frustration might be avoided. For example, the smart project leader could include two dates in his or her Goal Statement: "Reduce invoice discrepancies to Tier 1 customers by 40 percent. Solution to be implemented by March 2 and results to be confirmed and documented by April 15."

Some smart habits to consider when dealing with the time measurement challenge:

1. Insist on clarity around setting "target dates." The dates, or hours, themselves may shift (though of course you want to avoid that if possible), but what's to be accomplished at a particular day or time should be as unambiguous as possible.

2. Try to be careful about pushing unrealistic time frames. It's tempting and sometimes a good tactic to set an aggressive schedule to push for speed. But there are some potential downsides as well:
   a. As noted, excessive speed leads to mistakes and missed opportunities.
   b. You can eventually undermine your ability to set target dates. Many times I've heard people confess that "The dates set by the boss are totally unrealistic, so nobody believes them, and we just assume we'll miss the deadline."
   c. People can get discouraged if they think they can't meet a date (and that their input is not taken seriously).

3. Use experience and data to set target dates. To be *more* realistic about your dates, the best time estimates are based on looking at expected durations of different tasks or phases and using those discrete (and usually more accurate) estimates to arrive at a total time.

Issue Two: Perceiving Time

Your impatience level, opinions about how long something *should* take, and what you identify as "time well spent" will almost unconsciously affect your ability to balance speed and discipline. A Six Sigma Leader is not immune to those influences, of course, but is more aware of the real impact of speed: when it's better to accelerate, when it's better to slow down, and how to manage the risks on either side.

Earlier, we discussed the "Paradox of Deliberateness" where researchers found electronics companies that took *more time* before deciding what products to launch had a consistently higher success rate. In a field as dynamic as electronics, you'd think that deliberation time would be hard for leaders to accept. After all, if the goal is to "Beat the other guys to the market" who can stand to spend time thinking?

But obviously that extra deliberation time is not really idle. These leaders—exhibiting habits of Six Sigma Leadership—are making a different choice of how to *invest* time than their more impatient competitors. They perceive the discipline of making careful decisions as a valuable part of the overall cycle time of bringing things to market!

Balancing speed and discipline ties together these two issues of how time is measured and valued. In Figure 4.3 you can see two different approaches to managing project speed and success.

Company A on the left represents the "speed at all costs" bad habit (used by the poor performers in the Accenture study). A few important factors are at work:

- The preproject "deliberation" time is considered part of the overall project duration. In essence, leaders tend to account for that period in determining whether the project is "progressing" or not.
- That up-front time investment is viewed as necessary, but not critical, to the success of the effort. So it gets cut short pretty rapidly.
- By failing to carry out the necessary "due diligence," the project moves into high gear prematurely. It may be completed "on time"—though it's also a candidate for major delays—but the final result is disappointing.

Company B is guided by folks with Six Sigma Leader "best practices" ingrained in their DNA! (It may have come naturally; perhaps they picked it up from a book—or it may have been learned in the school of hard knocks.) In any case, here we see some very different perspectives in play:

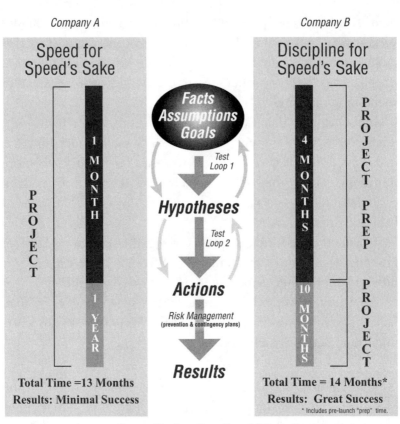

Figure 4.3 Approaches to Project Speed and Discipline

- The preproject time is a separate investment, managed with its own special set of outputs. It's not "counted against" the total project, so there's more patience for those "test loops" to be done right.
- By investing the time to deliberate, the overall time span for the project is not dramatically lengthened because once the "Start" button is pushed a lot of the uncertainties about how to execute the change have been dealt with. This practice I've called "front-loading the trauma."
- The overall results are better.

It's impossible to guarantee that spending additional up-front time will always speed up execution. Each case is different and the right balance needs to be assessed for the particular situation. And that's the key point: The Six Sigma Leader pays more attention to the overall effect of balancing speed and deliberateness. "Front-loading" work—testing assumptions, clarifying goals, etc.—is *valued* instead of shortchanged. Time is measured carefully, but also put in the context of the whole cycle instead of expecting that each activity can be speeded up without impacting the final result.

FAILING TO SUCCESS

An underlying premise behind most of the concepts of Six Sigma Leadership covered so far is that success is best achieved by moving as close to the limits of risk as you can afford, while avoiding any actual pain. A good analogy—especially in a chapter about speed—is a sailboat. To maximize speed, the sailor has to optimize the pressure on the sail *almost*, but not quite, to the point of flipping the boat. When risks are higher (say, there are sharks in the water) the person at the helm will rightly back off a little more from the edge because the potential costs of capsizing are more significant.[6]

But what about when a *new* boat is being designed? Or when the costs of not being at the limit are higher than going past it? In other words, is there a case when *making the boat flip* might actually be smarter than not flipping? The answer in a business context is "Yes!"

One of my colleagues earlier in my career inspired me by enthusiastically talking about how we were going to "make mistakes at a high rate of speed." Later, I saw this attitude exhibited in some companies that *deliberately* put products on the market knowing they are not yet nearly perfect. Even later I heard this strategy described as the "fail fast" approach.

There's a lot of value in understanding, and using, a fail fast strategy in an environment where speed is critical and excessive deliber-

6. The point at which the sailboat tips over is technically known as the "vanishing point."

ateness has its own risks. Often, the risk management paradigm of leaders and businesses as a whole (best reflected in the phrase "don't screw up") promotes behavior where ideas are not tested under the harsh conditions they'll have to endure in the real world. A lot of the time (probably most) this is the right call. Keeping the sailboat from tipping over is usually smarter than getting into a cycle of capsizing and righting the boat. But as a leader, you need to be aware of when it *is* worthwhile—and safe—to capsize the boat.

Life in the (Fail) Fast Lane

The conditions for a true "fail fast" approach—where your mistakes are in plain view of your customers and even competitors—include the following:

- Getting something on the market—either alongside and/or ahead of your competitors—is key to your success.
- Your customers are resilient, mature, or savvy enough to handle any problems caused by your product or service's "failure."
- Your customers will not "blacklist" you for failure—and may even see you as a partner in helping them by taking the fail fast risk.
- You're able to invest the time to support your customers in the event of a failure.
- You have the focus and resources to observe, learn from, and respond to the failure with solutions and/or a "newer-and-better" product or service.

One of the standout technology stars of the 1990s—Silicon Graphics—became a leader in 3D computer imaging by providing products that did what no one else's could do. But, as I learned working with them on some consulting projects before their star began to fizzle, those early products were anything but "plug and play." The technology was new, however, and their customers— movie special effects firms, petroleum exploration companies, and others where 3D graphics were a huge advantage—were prepared to take what they could get and invest the time to make it work. Silicon Graphics was there, and it gained huge market share. Theirs was a classic fail fast strategy.

Fail fast has even worked in financial services. In terms of the number of cards issued, the most successful new credit card product introduction in history was the American Express "Blue" card in 1999. It was the first broadly marketed credit card with a computer chip embedded and was something like the Macintosh of the credit card business: a really "cool" product targeted at a new generation of emerging young, discerning Internet users. Blue stood out amongst a herd of decidedly dull competitors.

The technology capabilities of the Blue card as pitched were a bit beyond what American Express could flawlessly deliver at the time. The initial graphic design actually called for a translucent card—which was shown on the original TV ads—but that proved technically unfeasible and was scrapped before Blue was introduced. And the chip itself didn't really offer any value-adding functionality beyond the existing "magnetic stripe" already on every credit card on the market.

At the time, people at AmEx with whom we worked had differing opinions about whether it was a good strategy or not, but Blue was a clear example of a fail fast approach. More time could have been taken to perfect it, but the Blue rolled out and the results were a big success, despite the bugs. It was, and continues to be, a highly fashionable and popular product that many of American Express's competitors have since tried to emulate.

More recently, one of the most high-profile users of the fail fast approach has been Google. Over the past five years, the search engine champion has launched more than 100 new products. Not all have succeeded by any means. Froogle, the comparison shopping engine, for example, was a flop when first introduced and as of this writing has yet to distinguish itself. But Google's approach is to try out ideas, see if they fly, keep refining those that resonate, and drop the losers quickly.

Note that a fail fast strategy is *not* the same as enticing "early adopters." Any new product or service can be initially targeted to that segment of the market eager to try new things. But in many cases, if the early adopter is unhappy with the product, he or she *will* put you on a black list. That makes fail fast a losing proposition. In the case of the original Macintosh computer, for example, early adopters were those *least* likely to tolerate a machine that caused them headaches. They were sold as an easy-to-use computer that was different from the more technically inclined PCs already on the market. In the consumer products industry, as another example, fail fast is usually a strategy to be avoided.

Fail Sooner, Fail Safer

If your circumstances don't seem to warrant a true fail fast strategy—and most *do not*—there are other, less risky, ways to "make mistakes at a high rate of speed" that can both accelerate and improve your progress. As a leader, you don't necessarily want all your riskiest ideas or projects to appear (falsely) perfect by keeping them under ideal "laboratory conditions." You want to expose the bugs, find the weaknesses, push the envelope. And you want to do it when you can best learn from and respond to the failures.

Figure 4.4 shows a simple "project cycle" for any change effort (from a new benefits program, to a reorganization, to a new product) and suggested "fail sooner" strategies. Your goal should be to push your sailboat to the edge at the most appropriate point in the development process based on the project, customers, and risks.

Playing things safe can be helpful, and small wins can create momentum, but in most cases, the sooner you find the breaking point in your ideas or products, the less it costs and the more opportunity you have to recover. A test market of a new TV service delivered via fiber optic phone lines is a good example of what may be a too-timid approach. The offering from Verizon is being tested at this writing in Keller, Texas, a new suburb that's sprouted north of Fort Worth. The conditions for the pilot (which would fit in the "Build/Test" phase in Figure 4.4) are almost optimal. Rather than

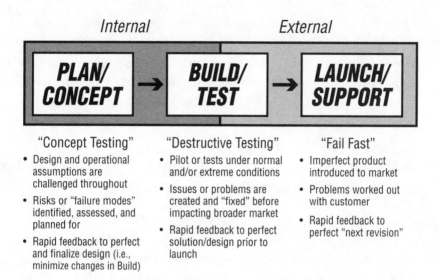

Internal   **External**

PLAN/ CONCEPT →	BUILD/ TEST →	LAUNCH/ SUPPORT

"Concept Testing"
- Design and operational assumptions are challenged throughout
- Risks or "failure modes" identified, assessed, and planned for
- Rapid feedback to perfect and finalize design (i.e., minimize changes in Build)

"Destructive Testing"
- Pilot or tests under normal and/or extreme conditions
- Issues or problems are created and "fixed" before impacting broader market
- Rapid feedback to perfect solution/design prior to launch

"Fail Fast"
- Imperfect product introduced to market
- Problems worked out with customer
- Rapid feedback to perfect "next revision"

Figure 4.4 Approaches to Pushing "Failure" and Driving Speed

going head-to-head with one of the big powerhouse cable firms, Keller is served by a regional franchise. Local approval came easily (Verizon is already the local phone company) and the new suburb's infrastructure allows easy upgrade to broadband "pipes." The town is affluent and more tech-savvy than the typical U.S. community. Texas, where further tests are planned, has passed laws making Verizon's efforts much easier than in other states.

To promote the service, moreover, Verizon has gone to some significant lengths: door-to-door salespeople, pizza box advertising, public events, and demonstration kiosks are among the activities that have led to a fairly strong initial adoption of the service.

It would be unfair to call the Keller test a waste of time. Verizon is getting some positive customer response to the service. Customers like the signal and see some clear advantages. But many of the hurdles that will have to be overcome to make the service successful elsewhere are not present. So there's still a long way to go before finding out how really viable the service is.[7]

7. "Battling for the Eyes of Texas," *BusinessWeek*, March 20, 2006, pp. 34–36. As the article comments: "certainly this small laboratory isn't emblematic of markets ahead."

Including "fast failure" as a legitimate option is another example of the balance and flexibility that defines Six Sigma Leadership. Most often, you'll likely want to keep your boat upright, but tipping it over at times may be the right call. Being a risk-*provoker* is as much a part of smart leadership as knowing how to manage risks.

EVERYDAY SPEED (LEAN LEADERSHIP)

The principles of the "Lean Enterprise"—which focus on speed and efficiency in ongoing operations—are becoming an integral part of the processes of many leading organizations. By focusing on waste, planning, inventory management, and scrutinizing tasks based on their value to the customer, many firms have been able to take huge chunks of time and cost out of their processes. For the Six Sigma Leader, an understanding of Lean principles is essential to optimizing speed while maintaining discipline.

Principles of Lean Speed

Lean emerged from the "Toyota Production System" developed in Japan in the 1970s. In developing these principles Toyota had some advantages: First, the imperative for change was a matter of survival; it led the company to challenge some long-held assumptions about how to run a successful business. Secondly, unlike U.S. and European auto companies, Toyota did not have decades of success that made it hard to shake off those old beliefs. As it turns out, Lean principles are applicable to many types of business, not just manufacturers. Here's a quick summary of some of the core concepts behind Lean speed.

Value

Every activity in a business should be scrutinized for how it adds value to the final product or service provided to the customer. Tasks that do not add value can be considered "waste" and need to be reduced or eliminated. A lot of activities previously thought to be "essential" in a business turn out to be non-value-adding when evaluated from the perspective of the customer. (More on this in a moment when we look at Lean Leadership.)

Flow

In an optimal operation, a service or product should be continually flowing from inception to the customer. Breaks in the flow—for example, waiting for review by the boss, sitting in a warehouse, rework to correct mistakes—add cycle time and create a poorly flowing process. Speed of the flow should be aligned to the customers' needs.

Pull

Creation of a product or delivery of a service should be initiated by customer demand or requests. Everything should be "built to order" and in the exact quantities demanded (also known as "single-piece flow").

Perfection

Everything in the business should be organized and managed to prevent mistakes and defects that add to waste and slow responsiveness.

These concepts may sound innocuous, until you understand what sacred cows are threatened. For example: the traditional *sales forecast*. Lean thinking reasons that a forecast is a guess and will never be perfect. Managing based on a guess always leads to waste (unused inventory) and risks shortages (if we underestimate demand). To replace the forecast, though, you have to rethink the entire "value stream."

A client of ours that manufactures sporting equipment had a common practice of ordering raw materials in volume to get a lower price, then building to forecast. But because their market was volatile and products were redesigned constantly, they would end up with a huge volume of obsolete finished product. Looking only at the cost of raw materials, it looked like a good choice. But calculating the *total* cost—including the melted down obsolete product—it would have been better to order and build "just in time" and pay a premium for the raw materials. It took a while for this reality to sink in, however. The first time I met with the client I heard the company president badger other executives repeatedly for "better forecasts!"

Lest you think Lean may not apply to you, we have clients applying Lean to streamline operations in hotels, financial services, retail, and many other nontechnical or product-related businesses. Product and process design are also huge areas where Lean concepts can be applied. So is what *you* do!

Lean and Leadership

Some of the least Lean aspects of many organizations are the *management* activities. My colleagues and I consistently find a high proportion of "non-value-adding" tasks in arenas such as sales, marketing, order management, human resources, finance- etc. involved decisions, sign-offs, reviews, and other activities involving leaders. Ask yourself if you've ever heard this comment: "We're ready to go, but we're waiting for the boss to decide."

Any Leader who's demanding speed also needs to ensure his or her *own* intrusions on the work process—well-intentioned though they may be—don't slow things down unnecessarily. Creating Lean leadership processes requires some fairly straightforward steps:

1. *Recognize leadership as a non-value-adding role.* I can sense the egos getting a bit riled at that one . . . Of course, leadership is critical to a successful business. But as viewed by your paying customers, on an everyday basis you are probably not really adding anything all that essential to the process. Think of what you do as being akin to the conductor of an orchestra: While the leader wields the baton, the music produced by the musicians is the final product the audience pays for.

2. *Identify and evaluate your value-adding activities.* Once you've become at least open to the idea that a leader's role in daily activities is to guide but not hinder (i.e., can be non-value-adding), you can begin to examine and optimize your contributions. Some of the work you do may actually be value adding from a customer point of view, especially if you get involved in actually designing products, delivering services, or winning customers (leaders do that too), but it may well be less than you think. A great value-adding leader example: One of the most successful advertising agencies of the past couple of decades is Hal Riney and Partners of San Francisco (now a unit of global ad giant Publicis). The agency produced some of the most recognized and effective ads of the 1980s and 1990s, including the Bartles & Jaymes wine cooler campaign for Gallo, and Ronald Reagan's famous "Morning in America" TV spot created for the 1984 presidential election. Agency founder and president Hal Riney was more than a "conductor." He not only wrote much of the copy for his clients' commercials, he was the familiar, soft-spoken, avuncular voice of many of the agency's famous spots. His was a truly value-adding presence for his customers.

In looking at *your* value-adding efforts, it's a good idea to test your assumptions about whether you are really the right person for those tasks. Like Hal Riney, your talent may be irreplaceable, the economics of the business may require you to take on some of those tasks, or you may just be a "hands-on" leader.

On the other hand, you could be doing what I call "raking the lawn." This term was inspired by my Dad, who after assigning my brother and me to spruce up the yard when we were kids would invariably walk by, look at what we were doing, and say, "Here, let me show you how!" Several minutes later, the lawn was all raked. (Thanks, Dad!) A lot of impatient leaders fall into this habit; it feels good but it can send the wrong message to your people, slow things down, and detract time from *leading* the yard work.

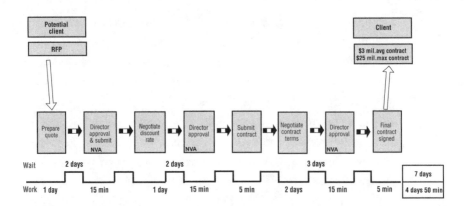

Figure 4.5 Impact of "Non-Value-Adding" Leadership Activities on a Project

3. *Take steps to "lean out" your leadership and management.* The goal is to identify and differentiate the useful leadership interventions from those liable to unnecessarily slow down the work, and stop getting in the way when it's not really critical.

Figure 4.5 diagrams a typical sales process with time data included along the bottom (this is a modified "Value Stream Map" format). As noted, the wait time in the process is all tied to the Director's reviews, which from the end customer's perspective are non-value-adding steps. Out of a total 11-plus days to complete a sale, 7 are spent waiting for the Director to review the documents. If that sounds exaggerated, guess again: We find *many* such processes where as much as 80 percent of the elapsed time is just "on hold" or non-value-adding time.

As noted at the outset of this chapter, the ability to drive speed, but balance it with the deliberateness needed to stay in control and achieve your goals, is one of the toughest "balancing acts" of Six Sigma Leadership. We've looked at some of the more important factors that create imbalance and ways you can approach your work—both projects and "ongoing operations"—to ensure you are setting the right pace. We'll look at other dimensions of speed and deliberateness in Chapter 6, where the focus will be on balancing short-term and long-term goals.

Next, however, let's take a look at another critical element of smart leadership: the tug-of-war between Teamwork and Independence.

Teamwork and Independence

We don't accomplish anything in this world alone . . . and whatever happens is the result of the whole tapestry of one's life and all the weavings of individual threads from one to another that creates something.

—Sandra Day O'Connor

ONE OF THE marvelous paradoxes of any successful organization is that every achievement demands a blend of collective spirit along with individual effort and talent. In this chapter, we'll explore some of the specific dimensions of teamwork and independence that a Six Sigma Leader must both control and unleash (another paradox) in order to create a more durable and appealing tapestry of success.

WHAT IS LEADERSHIP SUCCESS?

One of the principles I sincerely hope you'll take to heart from these pages is that *real* leadership success is best defined by the positive impact you make, and *leave*, on your organization.

That's not the only goal, of course. I also hope you are among the many individuals who apply Six Sigma Leadership to boost your *personal* success, satisfaction, income, career goals, etc. The "Genius" is to achieve both objectives, to create a legacy that both you and the organization benefit from, with the greater good taking the lead in driving your individual success. Scanning the bookshelves, however, and seeing so many management books that focus primarily on *personal* success suggests that the higher ideal of "organization-first" is not as prevalent as it should be. There are other warning signs.

Executive pay has been a hot and controversial topic for the past few years. Unfortunately, it reinforces the view that many business leaders put their self-interest above the interest of their employees and other stakeholders. Among many similar news stories, I recall a recent example about two senior executives from different companies who have potential pension plan payouts of over $80 million each. Is $80 million too much? I don't know. We can hope the directors of these companies are basing their compensation judgments on sound criteria. (It may be $80 million is *less* than what these leaders deserve.) Making a lot of money is one of the expected rewards of being a top executive; it's not new and it's by no means wrong. But it's hard to avoid getting a sense that in general the personal gain too often takes priority in leaders' minds over driving lasting business performance. Simply from the commonsense perspective of fostering teamwork in an organization, a smart leader will know that balancing a significant income *and* a sense of proportion are essential. Here is what the great leader Atilla had to say on this subject: "Care more for the rewarding of your Huns than for rewarding yourself. Your own rewards will then far exceed even your greatest hopes and dreams."[1]

The personal versus organizational focus of many leaders is also evident in what I'll call the "Make your Mark" syndrome. This is the almost compulsive behavior of many new leaders to initiate change as soon as they take over, regardless of the potential nega-

1. Wess Roberts, Ph.D., *Leadership Secrets of Attila the Hun*, New York: Time Warner Books, 1990, p. 79. This is actually a comment written by Roberts in a fictional but very worthwhile review of leadership principles that often echo ideas in this book.

tive impacts. Of course, there may be valid reasons to shake things up: A new leader may be arriving to correct a bad situation or replace a leader who's lost control or gotten into a rut. And eventually every leader needs to take action to establish his or her own credibility and to continue moving the organization forward.

But I've observed many, many cases where immediate changes have more to do with the new leader's personal preferences or desire to just to *do something* than with real organizational needs. And in quite a few of those instances, the net effect of the change is negative: Worthwhile projects get squelched, culture change gets frustrated, talented people get discouraged. That's where leader ego or ambition trumps the value to the business.

The common phenomenon of leaders protecting their own turf is another example of confusion between organizational and individual agendas. Barriers or silos—and the mistrust that goes with them—have plagued organizations since the first specialization of labor. (I can imagine the scene around the pyramids in ancient Egypt: workers moving huge stones complaining about the tomb designers, "These guys just don't *get* it!")

What's wrong with a leader pushing for his or her group to get more resources, authority, or recognition? Nothing—so long as it's balanced with the broader needs of the organization. But that advocacy often appears self-serving or ignorant of the entire business environment or the perspective of other groups. And so the organizational barriers get higher and thicker.

I got an early taste of this misplaced advocacy in my first job out of college at a radio station in Southern California. It came in a staff meeting when our Ad Sales Manager—an industry veteran— proclaimed to the entire station that "Nothing happens until there's a sale, baby!" Most of us were young and fairly open minded, so we thought about that comment. We had to agree that without ad revenues, our paychecks would bounce, so he had a point. On the other hand, advertisers need an audience for their commercials, and listeners would only tune in if the on-air personalities were appealing. Once the spot was aired, we needed the accounting people to collect money from the advertisers and get it to the bank. And you had to have a studio, microphones, and a transmitter, all maintained by the engineering staff. In other words, no single department in the radio station, once you started to think about it, could claim to be the key. All were essential.

So the Sales Manager's boasting—or organizational advocacy—turned out to seem narrow-minded and disrespectful of the other, non-sales folks in the room. Everyone needed to pull together to make the organization a success. It was a lesson I've always kept in mind.

When leadership success is measured by ego, head count, or budget it can lead to some very imbalanced choices. When leadership success is measured by the value of the contribution to the greater good, then the organization prospers. For a leader, it can be like good career karma—what goes around for the business as a whole comes around to the individual's personal fulfillment and growth.

This may sound a little naïve. If you don't "look out for number one," you'll never get ahead, right? Well, as always, our theme is *balance*: putting success of the larger organization first does *not* mean forgetting your own interests. Fighting for what you believe in, or seeking recognition for your achievements, is not incompatible with putting the organization's success first. Applied properly, that emphasis should give you a stronger case for your value because of your commitment and because a leader who's also a *team player* is much more likely to *deliver* value to the organization.

A VISION OF LEADERSHIP TEAMWORK

One of the key points made in Chapter 3 is that the too-common image of the isolated, infallible leader is fraught with danger—especially in the complex world of 21st-century business. The more leaders are cut off from information, or assume they have all the answers, the greater the risks of misjudgment and failure. In a complex organization (even with as few as 100 people), the potential for serious disconnects between various elements of the business becomes high—in fact, almost guaranteed, thanks to some of the barrier-inducing factors I've just described.

But these dangers can be dramatically reduced if and when leaders can work collaboratively to better align and coordinate their efforts. In fact, the organizational and personal benefit you can achieve as a Six Sigma Leader will always be much greater if you can enhance the teamwork with other leaders, including peers, those at other levels of the business, and even in partner organizations.

Many companies and departments do have a "Leadership Council" or "Executive Committee" or other body that brings together the senior group. But the caliber of the teamwork among those groups is often poor, and rarely is much attention paid to how that collaboration can be *improved*. More often, as suggested by the problems of individual focus described above, they become a forum for each leader to talk about "my group" but not to facilitate real understanding of how the different groups—starting with their leaders—might work together more effectively.

Clearly we need to look at *how* leaders can play nicer together, but since it's often not natural—and certainly not easy—you need to be *committed* to the goal of better leader collaboration. So let's first review some of the rationale for building leadership teamwork and then how to overcome the obstacles to building that teamwork.

Teamwork and Its Benefits to Leaders

There can be many ways of defining a *team*, but I prefer the simplest and most essential definition:

A group of people working together for a common goal.

Looked at that way, it's clear that the key ingredient to building any team is that *common goal*. Without it, all you have is a bunch of people working! For leaders, of course, there often are *numerous* goals to which they and the organization aspire. So really, the vision for leaders is to create an atmosphere of committed and effective *teamwork*—the ability to define and strive collaboratively to achieve various and evolving common goals for the benefit of the larger organization as well as all its constituents.

Teamwork is not just idealistic; it has practical value. But because it requires commitment and effort, you need to remind yourself and others why it's worth the trouble. (You'll note these reasons align with goals of Six Sigma Leadership.)

Broader Knowledge and Perspective

Greater complexity and specialization tend to create ever-narrower views of the organization and the world around it. The multiplication of "Chief" titles mentioned earlier is evidence for this thinning span of authority. By listening to and learning from other leaders, understanding their needs, challenges, and especially how the different pieces of the organization impact one another, leaders can much more clearly see the "big picture."

Improved Return on Change Investment

In Chapter 2, I presented the case for a balanced "portfolio" where change initiatives focus on critical needs and balance risk and reward. A related ingredient in the Six Sigma Leader's change management skill set is a more effective alignment of resources to cross-functional opportunities. These are the "sweet spot" projects where results tend to be significant while being much easier to coordinate than larger-scale, company-wide campaigns (see Figure 5.1).

This enhanced change portfolio management across an organization is almost impossible without strong leader teamwork. Recognizing opportunities, defining shared goals, setting priorities, and allocating talent and other resources are all activities destined to fall short if leaders can't cooperate and collaborate effectively.

Better Use of Facts and Data

Here again, the goals outlined in Chapter 3 turn out to be significantly enhanced by the ability of leaders to share information and—as a structural solution—to develop aligned measures based

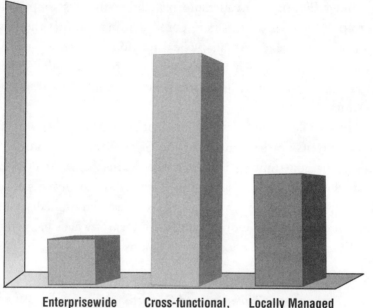

Figure 5.1 Change Portfolio with Improved Leadership Teamwork

on an integrated "system view" of the business. (See Figure 3.4.) Better *use* of facts and data, by the way, includes paying attention to the data, seeking to *understand* what the facts mean, and then responding proactively—not reactively—while *sharing* responsibility when appropriate.

A brief example: Executives at XYZ Company are meeting and see a report indicating a downturn in sales for the third quarter. The old-school response would be for heads to turn toward the head of Sales and for someone to ask, "What the heck is going on?" That's when the Sales leader might feel like a character on those airline commercials that ask, "Want to get away . . . ?" The assumption—or perhaps hope—in grilling the Sales leader is that sales volume is exclusively a result of the Sales department's efforts rather than, realistically, an outcome of many variables—plenty of which are usually *not* controlled by Sales.

Under Six Sigma Leadership principles, the first step would be to try to put the numbers in context (it may be that the lower figures in Q3 are a normal, cyclical phenomenon or are missing some regions). Next—if the problem is a real one—the smarter leaders would begin a discussion of what might be causing the downturn.

This would include exploring various issues *elsewhere* in the business (outside the control of the Sales group) that might be causing or contributing to lower sales. This behavior does not mean the XYZ Sales leader gets a free pass whenever sales go down. It simply means that leaders look past the immediate data and work together to more effectively interpret what's happening. And, if needed, plan a coordinated response.

Faster Response to Challenges and Opportunities

Speed of action is often squandered when consensus is hard to come by and/or when resources and support are not provided from the top. Conversely, if leaders are agreed on the direction and goal—or are at least prepared to get behind it—efforts tend to pick up momentum.

A testament to the positive impact of leadership teamwork is the resurgence of Motorola. After being blindsided by rivals such as Nokia and Ericsson in the mobile phone market, the company's board brought in veteran high-tech executive Ed Zander as CEO. Zander challenged the engineering-oriented company to shift its perspective from inward (warring tribes, technology) to outward (customers, value). That meant working together for a common goal: a new compensation scheme tied 25 percent of salary to customer satisfaction. "If you understand only one thing about our evolving culture, let it be this one," Zander wrote in an e-mail to employees. "You work for this company . . . not just your sector or your country office. To offer seamless mobility, we must tear down artificial barriers between our technologies, products, and customers. We, too, must be seamless."

This teamwork has been a key to Motorola's successful new products and to a new spirit in the organization. The company's performance tells the bottom-line story: record sales and expanding market share, growing strength in international markets, and a new flair for design drawing attention and building customer enthusiasm.[2]

By now, the trend should be clear: all the benefits of Six Sigma Leadership we've examined so far, and those we've yet to examine, can be augmented when managers and/or executives apply more effective collaboration. But teamwork among leaders is still no more of a slam dunk or panacea than any other single dimension of Six Sigma Leadership. Complex problems and uncertain situations can still defy easy answers, no matter how open to teamwork a leadership group may be. And leaders working as a team have to be careful not to assume they have *all* the answers: an insular leadership group, which fails to draw on information and input from people close to customers and real work processes, can turn out to be as big a disaster as a single closed-minded leader.

Nature of Leadership Teamwork

Teamwork among leaders is almost certain to be different from that in other types of groups. After all, you and your leader colleagues are the people who want to be, and who are used to being, *in charge*. We know that leaders will tend to advocate from the viewpoint of their own role and function, as well as (like all of us) experience and biases. Whenever personal egos take over, the going gets rough. But success is possible. The new standard of Six Sigma Leadership is to place higher value on and continually strive for better leader teamwork, but not to expect *perfect* behavior or perpetual harmony.

2. Elizabeth Corcoran,. "Making Over Motorola," *Forbes*, December 13, 2004. www.forbes.com/forbes/2004/1213/102_print.html; Motorola Q1 2006 Earnings Release.

In fact, perfect harmony should probably be a warning sign. *Good to Great* describes the type of interaction among executive teams that helped create a dramatic upswing in their companies' fortunes. One of the companies profiled is Nucor, the steel company that has managed to survive and succeed while most U.S.-based steel companies have undergone successive years of difficulty and decline. The leadership team at Nucor is described by Collins as a contentious group of very bright people who reshaped the company through an ongoing series of debates—often extremely heated—wherein consensus and commitment were formed. Notes Collins, "Like Nucor, all the good-to-great companies had a penchant for intense dialogue. Phrases like 'loud debate,' 'heated discussions,' and 'healthy conflict' emerge repeatedly. They didn't use discussion as a sham process to let people 'have their say' so they could 'buy in' to a predetermined decision."[3]

What about the role of "internal competition" between groups within your business? In many businesses, this friendly rivalry is seen as a strength and part of a culture that gives them an edge. This is true—when the impact of internal competition *adds* to the success of the organization as a whole. Leaders who challenge their teams to be Number 1 in safety, or sales, or customer satisfaction can effectively tap into people's innate desire to succeed. On the other hand, when the result of the competition prompts purely *self-serving* behavior—winning at the *expense* of the larger organization—then it's gone too far. The trick for leaders is to watch out for and avoid the potential downside of internal competition.

There's an activity my colleagues and I conduct in process and product design workshops that illustrates how the negative side of competition can creep in. Small teams are asked to design, build, and fly paper airplanes. They're judged on two customer requirements: distance flown and straightness of flight. Participants are

3. Jim Collins, *Good to Great, Why Some Companies Make the Leap . . . and Others Don't*, New York: Harper Business, 2001, pp.76–77.

clearly told that they are *all* employees of the same hypothetical company—Huge Aircraft—and that the goal is to have the most total successful flights possible.

As you'd expect, the teams automatically want to "win" by creating the best designs. That challenge can spark some terrific outside-the-box thinking. One team came up with what will always be, in my mind, the most remarkably innovative design: a crumpled-up ball of paper! (Remember, I said there were no rules as long as your "plane" flew far and straight.) Most "regular" paper airplanes curve and/or crash and are of inconsistent quality; the "ball of paper" planes flew consistently and straight as an arrow every time. Clearly that team "won" with the best design.

But remember, the assignment is to design *and fly* the plane to make customers happy—to win more business for Huge Aircraft. That's where competition can prompt some not-so-good behavior. In this case, the "paper ball" team wanted to conceal their idea from other parts of the "company." They actually conducted a "fake" test flight of a *regular* folded paper airplane just to fool other groups and not expose their innovative aircraft. Instead of sharing their design, they kept it secret. So when all the teams flew their planes the total company performance was fairly average—because only one team was using this breakthrough design.

Encouraging competition can energize people and add fun and inspiration to the job, but if it is not balanced by some level of teamwork and a *shared* benefit, there may be subversive behavior arising beyond your knowledge or control. It's another example of why the new standard of leadership needs to promote the *right* kind of competition but eliminate the traditional forms that undermine business performance.

The vision of leadership teamwork is not about being in perfect synch, and as we'll see, it depends on initiative and individual commitment. But it can create an environment where synergy and talent can multiply achievements and build a more durable, and rewarding, organizational culture.

BUILDING LEADERSHIP TEAMWORK

By adopting the smart habits described throughout this book, you pave the way for enhanced teamwork among organizational leaders. Similarly, by reaching out and engaging fellow leaders in collaborative efforts, you create a climate where the balance and flexibility of Six Sigma Leadership can grow.

What can you do to facilitate better collaboration in your own "leadership team"? Here are some suggestions that include both attitudes and actions.

Define and Accept Shared Goals

The term *shared* is important; it's deliberately different from *common*, used earlier in my simple definition of a *team* (a group working toward a *common* goal). It's a subtle difference, so let me illustrate with an example.

The leadership group of LeanTech, a global manufacturer, has just completed its annual goal-setting offsite meeting and come up with a list of nine critical objectives for the coming year. Each is assigned an executive sponsor. Here's a sample of the goals (three of the nine) and each one's assigned sponsor:

- Improve workplace safety and reduce days lost due to on-the-job accidents. Sponsor: *Chief Safety Officer*
- Expand sales in emerging markets. Sponsor: *President of International Division*
- Introduce three new high-margin products. Sponsor: *Chief Development Officer*

Everyone on the LeanTech leadership committee has signed on to the goals and accepted his or her area of sponsorship. Looks great, right? Unfortunately, in typical practice, those goals are viewed by each leader as someone else's responsibility: "I've got my goals, they've got theirs." If the Chief Safety Officer and his team begin to suspect some product design issues are increasing accident risks in manufacturing, it becomes very difficult to get the attention or help of the R&D group. The Chief Development Officer is pushing everyone to get the three new products to market. "Safety is someone else's concern," becomes the perceived message. When pressed, the CDO will likely cite lack of time and resources as reasons for leaving the safety effort to others.

To change this scenario: to begin working toward the vision of collaborative leadership, you need to start with the goal-setting process itself. When the organizational goals are set, the explicit understanding and agreement should be that these are *shared* goals. The LeanTech executive group not only signs on to the list and the sponsorship, but also to mutual responsibility for all the goals and to cooperation in achieving them. It's a subtle but meaningful difference in the type of commitment from each leader that ideally will lead to greater teamwork in pursuing the various goals.

It may well be that, recognizing the need for shared commitment to *all* nine goals, LeanTech's executives decide to pare down the priorities. If *six* goals, focused on the most critical business needs, is more realistic than nine and permits the kind of teamwork needed to *get them done*, that is, I would say, a great thing.

How do you encourage leaders to *share* goals? That may take persuasion, clout, or both. The role of the senior-most leader—department head, CEO, etc.—can be key to defining the vision of shared goals as well as establishing systems for shared accountability. Often, however, that's not enough—especially when each leader has a fair amount of autonomy and/or the systems for accountability are not very effective. To begin influencing thinking toward sharing goals among a group of leaders, one suggestion is to openly ask questions like these:

- Can this be achieved if the "owner" can only work within his or her own organization?
- What will each of us do if [the sponsor] comes to us, or our people, for help?
- If these goals are really critical, can we all share in accountability if they are not achieved?

At least if you can start to demonstrate a willingness to share goals with your colleagues you may serve as a role model—and very possibly make a meaningful contribution to achieving some worthwhile results.

Use Scorecards and Dashboards

Shared goals and a spirit of leadership teamwork are supported by common measures. As described in Chapter 2, the "systems view" of the organization—where key business processes are seen as interdependent and their links are understood—provides a context for using measures that more accurately reflect the performance of the business. These more integrated metrics allow leaders to look at key indicators together and ask "How are *we* doing?" rather than just "How is Department A doing?" or "How is Department B doing"?

Remember that at first the measures are likely to be unfamiliar, and often they will need to be refined over time. But they can end up providing a much more meaningful view of the organization and create a unified perspective that can facilitate leadership teamwork.

Apply Joint Oversight and Responsibility

Goals and measures are ingredients required to engage fellow leaders in reviewing performance and progress toward key objectives. Joint oversight does not mean all leaders participate in every project review or get every report. However, the broader leadership group should be kept up to date, especially on important strategic efforts, on a regular basis. Particularly important is to report on areas where multiple groups within the organization need to get involved, provide resources, etc.

The communication and discussion that can emerge from joint oversight can be a big help in promoting better balance and flexibility toward your multiple priorities. More commonly in the companies I observe, each individual leader or group grumbles about being asked for help from so many other parts of the organization—meanwhile complaining that those same groups won't help them on their own initiatives. What you end up with is "lip service" support that doesn't come through when it's really needed.

When you and other organizational leaders get involved in more meaningful performance and progress reports, you can also look more closely at successes and shortcomings to improve in the next quarter, project, or major initiative.

Adapt Your Mindset

The biggest step in becoming a more consistent and effective team player with other leaders is to recognize the reality of interdependence and the limits of independence. As we'll see, independent initiative is still essential, but the traditional scenario where a leadership group is much like a bunch of chiefs getting together to share stories about their respective tribes—but never to talk about how the tribes are cooperating—needs to be replaced by a more cooperative and collegial approach. All the things I'm suggesting here won't change much without that change in attitude in favor of leaders working as a team.

POINTS OF INITIATION

Size is a great advantage to a business, but it brings many challenges. Most of my professional life has been about assisting large companies. I've done this from a platform of a consulting company that now numbers about 60 people. I've come to think this experience—viewing the contrast between bigger and smaller organizations—has allowed me to see things that might not be so obvious had I been in only a corporate role my whole career. As scale increases, so does the challenge of balancing teamwork and independent action, which is critical to sustain momentum, innovation, and success while avoiding chaos.

Let's start with a look at my own company, back 15 years ago when it was only a one-person business. When I was running the show alone, the entire company was 100 percent informed of everything that was going on (except perhaps when my memory failed). If we ran a marketing campaign, called a client, sent an invoice, made coffee, no one was in the dark. After we added our first employee, she and I worked about 12 feet apart from one another, so it was still easy to keep everyone in the loop.

Jumping ahead: Now we have a team of people spread around the world. As we've built the Pivotal Resources organization, of course we've sought smart, ambitious, creative, skilled, energetic individuals. But after a while it dawned on me that those bright people could start doing things that neither I, nor anybody else, might know about. They could accomplish big things or they could cause problems! Of course, I could micromanage the place, but that would just create other problems. For any leader, it really comes down to a question of trust and letting go.

All this led me to the concept of *Points of Initiation*. Each smart person we bring on board adds a new opportunity to strengthen the company. He or she has a great idea and goes after it; sees a problem and tries to fix it; etc. That's exactly what you want them to do. Except . . . more Points of Initiation create the risk of duplicate or conflicting efforts, communication gaps and inconsistencies. There are organizational Points of Initiation, too: we call them departments, locations, business units, levels of management. There, groups (or their leaders) can take action, launch projects, do deals that may be great news or *bad* news if they aren't aligned with the rest of the business. The challenge for any organization, big or small, is to channel those Points of Initiation and coordinate the flow of energy so it benefits the business and does not, in effect, blow the place up.

Why *don't* companies just flame out from too much random, uncoordinated effort? You might expect chaos to reign if you have, for example, a 3,000-person company and each is a potential Point of Initiation. There are two answers:

1. There actually *is* a lot of chaos, but it's factored into the way things work. It's kind of like the "background radiation" astronomers and physicists have detected as a residual of the Big Bang: so much a part of the natural environment we almost don't notice it. When people spend time around the water cooler or in e-mails talking about routine problems and frustrations, for example, they're displaying evidence of this constant, residual wasted energy.[4]

2. Businesses also have ways, some obvious and some subtle, to limit and control the Points of Initiation. Not every person or group is an initiator, nor should they be. Take for instance the staff in a Customer Service Center: the service representatives have pretty clear job descriptions, support tools to respond to customer inquiries, and a predefined escalation path when a customer's issue can't be easily resolved. These procedures are in place to ensure the work is done correctly, but also to control unnecessary "improvisation" for individual service reps.

    That does not necessarily mean that the Service Center leaders would be angry with a representative who proposed a change or identified a problem and brought it to their attention. But if a *lot* of people started speaking up often, that would start to be viewed as too much (i.e., more initiative than we can handle). Job descriptions, supervision, functions, and specialization are all, in essence, methods that help reduce or channel initiative.

You can probably see the potential downside of these control mechanisms already. By managing initiative-taking or limiting its boundaries, you also tend to discourage innovation and confine

4. This can be quantified by measuring "Cost of Poor Quality." Some of these costs are obvious: returned products, customer complaints, system crashes, etc. But others are hidden, or take a little work to find: crossed signals on a project, duplicate lists of customers, continual rewrites of ad copy, long lead time to ramp up a new product or service, expensive software that rarely gets used. Attacking these problems is often a focus of Lean Six Sigma projects.

people to addressing problems only within their organizational unit (i.e., department, location, or silo). After a while, it becomes part of the organizational culture to lay low and mind your work. People may tackle the smaller, local issues, but bigger, cross-functional ones are left alone. And even the local problems can often fester until they get to be really serious or urgent and require emergency attention.

So to summarize, organizations face a two-sided problem that is very hard to balance:

1. Eager people taking uncoordinated and misguided initiative that (even when well-intentioned) wastes resources and adds to chaos
2. A lack of initiative or attention to problems, created in part by efforts to quell uncoordinated activity

What can a Six Sigma Leader do to find the right balance: reduce existing chaos, encourage initiative, and yet keep it focused in the right direction? The first step is to recognize the challenge. As I said, my role as an "outside observer" helps me see the effects of both the chaos *and* the chaos-reduction efforts. When I describe the symptoms to leaders they invariably identify with the problem: "Yeah, that's us all right!"

Next, you need to get a little upset about it! A Six Sigma Leader always wants things to be better, and while you don't want to drive yourself or your people nuts with dissatisfaction, you should also be prepared to push beyond the status quo. George Bernard Shaw observed that "Reasonable people adapt themselves to the world. Unreasonable people attempt to adapt the world to themselves. All progress, therefore, depends on unreasonable people." To build your business, some unreasonableness is a valuable ingredient. Or as Jack Welch once told a group of GE leaders: You were all the "good kids" in school, but what we really need around here are some "bad kids."

Third, you need to look for small ways to influence change. Asking better, more focused questions can help you drive or guide people's efforts in a more appropriate direction. And then listen. Encourage a culture that tolerates a certain amount of silence and reflection. Apply the 10-Second Rule here—don't just blurt out a bunch of potentially annoying questions without thinking them through. But there are some fairly straightforward questions you can ask on a routine basis. Table 5.1 shows some to consider, depending on whether you want to expose an ignored problem, slow someone down, or encourage/guide someone's initiative.

Keep in mind the following "tips" about the questions and approach suggested in Table 5.1:

- By asking questions, you're prompting other people to begin thinking the way you do. You're getting them to examine issues more closely, look for more information, think about whom to talk to, etc.
- It's still okay to be directive if necessary, but it's better to probe first and get other people to come to the right conclusion (with your help) on their own. Then you may not have to *tell* them what to do.
- Note that these questions seek a balance between teamwork and independent action. Taking initiative is essential—too many of the chronic issues that plague organizations persist though lack of anyone's taking them on. But failure to reach out to others can lead to narrow and ineffective or redundant solutions.
- Note also that these questions focus on *defining the problem or issue* rather than leaping to a solution. This is a core of Six Sigma Leadership. If the solution is apparent, the next step may be to take action—but the first priority is problem definition!

When appropriate, you or your people should consider escalating bigger, more critical or persistent issues for consideration as part of the broader "change portfolio." Also, beware of letting initiatives you launch informally add up to too many simultaneous priorities within your own area of the business.

Focus on a Suspected Problem	Stop or Slow an Initiative	Prompt or Redirect Action
Ask when you see an issue you think may need attention or further investigation.	Ask when you think someone is taking action unnecessarily or without sufficient information.	Ask when someone is being too reticent to act or is heading in the wrong direction.
What exactly is wrong here?	Are there other issues that might be more important?	Do you think you might be in a good position to get something done about this?
How often does this happen?	Is it possible this is just a one-time event?	If you/we don't take the lead on this, who else might?
What is this costing us?	Have you checked to see if anyone has looked into this before?	Doesn't this issue seem to fit pretty well with your role and skills?
How is this affecting customers?	How does this compare to other problems we need to work on?	Can we really solve this on our own, or should we get other people involved?

Table 5.1 Sample Questions to Promote, Guide, or Limit Initiative

A Six Sigma Leader gets more accomplished by paying constant attention to the need for people to step up and take action, while also guiding initiative to the best benefit of the organization and customer. Over time, these smart habits can create a culture that more effectively values and drives the *right* kind of action. To make

Focus on a Suspected Problem	Stop or Slow an Initiative	Prompt or Redirect Action
Ask when you see an issue you think may need attention or further investigation.	Ask when you think someone is taking action unnecessarily or without sufficient information.	Ask when someone is being too reticent to act or is heading in the wrong direction.
Have we tried to solve this before?	Can we get a little data before going any further?	What kind of benefits can we achieve if we can make some progress here?
Do we have any data on this issue?	What other groups might be better able to deal with this than we are?	
Has anyone investigated the problem?		

Table 5.1 (continued)   Sample Questions to Promote, Guide, or Limit Initiative

this work, however, you may need to adjust the way you address problems yourself.

LOOKING UP AND OUT

A few years ago we were consulting with a large, well-known financial services firm to help build capability in redesigning critical processes. Part of the assignment was to identify areas where current processes presented a significant opportunity to be re-engineered. We had impressive success in some areas of the business. For example, a new customer "on-boarding" process was revamped at an immediate savings of over $2 million per year, with several times that in increased revenues. But, despite these results, my memory of the engagement is one of frustration.

We saw opportunities where the potential benefit far surpassed the other successes we'd helped achieve. But on these other areas, I could never figure out how to get any traction. We saw chronic disconnects between the firm's product development/marketing groups and its operations/service group that created constant problems in launching and supporting new products. Most disappointing was the reaction from the head of the group responsible for managing the handoff from Marketing to Operations. Despite having the best vantage point and authority to try to tackle these big opportunities, he simply would not step up to the responsibility.

I wish this were an isolated example. However, all too often there's an obvious reluctance among even senior leaders to take initiative outside their own "boxes." It might be okay to stay quiet and not make waves if you're content to be a run-of-the-mill leader, but it won't cut it if you're aspiring to be a Six Sigma Leader! A bit more on the evidence/impact of leaders failing to step up:

- Some of the big scandals and corporate implosions of recent years—Enron, WorldCom, Tyco—were aided by leaders who saw the writing on the wall, but ignored it or failed to speak out until too late. Of course, we can't say whether earlier action might have prevented scandal and collapse, but aside from a few "whistleblowers" the action of the majority of the leadership was not inspiring.
- Investigations into wrenching national catastrophes such as the September 11, 2001 attacks and Hurricane Katrina have uncovered appalling insularity and lack of initiative across large groups of leaders.

- In dozens of business change efforts I and my colleagues have supported through the years, one of the biggest hurdles is getting teams and their leaders to seriously "reach out"—as more than just a token message or meeting—to other parts of their organization to gain real collaboration. One recent example involved an effort to increase revenue for service contracts where the operations group stalled for months before finally engaging in meaningful discussions with their sales account execs.

What's missing is what I call the "Up and Out" perspective. The common response, when managers or leaders see a problem or opportunity, is to turn their attention "In and Down"—to look at how they can address it in their own area, to manage the challenge as far as they can independently (if they elect to do anything at all).

There's nothing bad about the "In and Down" perspective; taking responsibility for cleaning up your own act is part of smart leadership, too. However, by not *also* looking Up and Out, you miss the opportunity to leverage your efforts and/or to address them at a more effective level. You may be failing to call attention to an issue that many other managers are coping with, where you might pool your resources to come up with a more effective solution. You may only be able to provide a small impact on a bigger challenge that would best benefit from a systems-focused, end-to-end view. You may be spending time fixing something that some other person or group in the company has already solved. Those are the shortcomings of not taking the Up and Out view *as well as* the In and Down view.

Looking Up and Out takes at least a small bit of courage and some knowledge of the organization beyond your own comfort zone. A smart leader will take the time and initiative to become familiar with other parts of the business, so you can be a better team player and more effectively look and communicate beyond your official boundaries.

Try some of these questions to help you orient yourself in the Up and Out direction:

- Is it possible other parts of the business have this same problem? Might they have some solutions we can "borrow"?
- Who else might be, or should be, aware of this opportunity? How can I reach out to them to compare perspectives?
- If I tackle this myself, will it really address the problem or just a piece of it? Would a more holistic approach be worth exploring?
- Should this be on the agenda for our next project portfolio discussion? What facts or data would be useful to explain/verify the situation, costs/benefits, etc.?

You may legitimately decide, after reflection on these questions, to handle the situation on your own, but at least you will have done the kind of "reality check" that is too often skipped, and yet is a prerequisite to organizational teamwork in facing challenges and opportunities. The goal is proactive effort and outward diplomacy, not suicide missions.

BRING ME SOLUTIONS!

As a conclusion to this chapter on balancing teamwork and independent initiative, I'll offer a comment on one of the more commonly heard requests of leaders: "I don't want you to bring me problems, I want you to bring me solutions!"

Like me, you've probably heard this comment many times—and perhaps occasionally even uttered the sentiment yourself. It's a natural, reasonable expectation that your team members should make decisions on their own initiative instead of running to you with every difficulty. After all, isn't that what you're paying them for?

But this rule can also create much bigger problems if taken too literally or applied too strenuously. Think about it: Do you *really* want people fixing things—or taking the time to develop solutions—without ever talking to you first? I see this "solutions only" admonishment having the unintended effect of stifling open discussion of common issues. It emphasizes the "In and Down" behavior, when many of the more challenging issues facing companies today require "Up and Out" teamwork.

Like every aspect of smart leadership, the key is balance: In some situations, you want only solutions. But in others, you should hope people are talking about problems so they can be handled in the most effective, comprehensive way—or at least so you can help determine the best approach.

One of the criteria for determining whether an opportunity should fall into the "locally owned" category or the "let's take a team approach" column involves whether you need a short-term or long-term solution. It's that aspect of Six Sigma Leadership that we'll explore in the next chapter.

CHAPTER

Now, Tomorrow, and Next Year

Sensus, non aetas, invenit sapientem.
[Good sense, not age, brings wisdom.]

—Syrus, first century B.C.[1]

BALANCING YOUR TIME HORIZON

In this chapter, we take a closer look at how a Six Sigma Leader can address the dual challenges of managing time and balancing priorities. We'll consider some methods you can use to optimize your change investment. And the chapter explores how time does not always have to be an enemy of change.

The concept of portfolio management can help us again. One of the common practices of bond investors is to purchase notes with different maturity dates. Diversifying the maturity dates balances your risk and lets you decide how to reinvest your money on a regular basis, rather than reallocating your entire bond nest egg all at once. When planning efforts to build for the future of your organization, a Six Sigma Leader applies much the same philosophy: some efforts need to mature in the short term and others in

---

1. From Rose Williams, *Latin Quips at Your Fingertips*, New York: Barnes & Noble Books, 2001, p. xxiv.

the long term. The challenge is in knowing *which* are the appropriate activities to focus on for the near-term payback, which are the most appropriate longer horizon efforts, and how to manage each for success.

Time is a relative concept, so let's agree on some terms. For the purposes of selecting and strategizing initiatives based on their time horizon, I'm using the following guidelines:

> *Short-term:* Implemented in less than 3 months; results measurable in less than 4 months
>
> *Mid-term:* Implemented in 3 to 12 months; results measurable in less than 15 months
>
> *Long-term:* Implemented in more than 12 months; results measurable in more than 15 months

Long term, of course, can go well beyond one year, while some short-term efforts may take just a couple of days or weeks.

The appropriate mix of short-, mid-, and long-term efforts will vary depending on the needs and opportunities in your business. Because cycle times are shorter, you will usually have quite a few more short-term projects getting completed. However, as we noted in Chapter 2, risk increases when the number of short-term efforts gets too high. These are often prompted by "Points of Initiation" that don't coordinate very effectively. Short-term overload diverts resources from the mid- and long-term efforts. Longer-term efforts have different challenges: waning enthusiasm and momentum, for example, are a common plague on extended initiatives.

With these challenges in mind, the main leadership question can be stated as:

How do I identify the right kind of opportunities and approaches for these different time horizons to ensure outstanding results?

Too many leaders tend to shrug off this question as either easy (it's not) or something for subordinates to worry about. If you are a CEO or consider yourself an "idea person," you may think of this challenge as too tactical for your role. But be very careful: struggling with this question is important to any level of leadership and a skill every leader should want to master. Here are three reasons why.

1. *Your subordinates look to you as a model in this area.* The care you take in checking and validating efforts can have a huge influence on your people and your business. If you're prone to rush headlong into every problem, you're likely to find people following your lead, and soon there will be a lot of ill-advised activities under way with all their consequent confusion and collateral damage. Conversely, if you demand exhaustive research and validation before getting *anything* started, people may become hesitant to respond even to immediate issues. (The former is more common than the latter; both outcomes, of course, are unfortunate.) The bottom line? When Six Sigma Leaders maintain a balance between observation and action, facts and gut, they model key behaviors that will significantly influence their potential for success.

2. *Determining whether you should take a short-, mid-, or long-term approach to a critical business opportunity is the central dilemma.* I hear stories all the time about leaders who direct their teams to build a big solution in response to problems that would yield to one or two quick fixes. In reality, the most effective change leadership involves a tight integration of the various time scales: short-term projects pave the way for implementation of long-term transformations. The better you can apply a "triage" approach to your challenges— knowing which are life-threatening emergencies, which can get by with first aid, and which require long-term treatment plans—the better you can allocate and coordinate your efforts.

3. *The keys to success are usually quite different depending on the time horizon of the opportunity.* The critical questions for a possible short-term effort, for example, should focus more on managing risk. For a long-term initiative, your initial priority will usually be on defining a change vision. If you can get clearer on how these different types of effort have to be managed differently, you can

spare yourself and your people a lot of frustration—not to mention getting efforts moving faster and with greater focus.

Let me reiterate: While the topics in this chapter tend to get very close to aspects of project *execution*, they are really about *leadership* that drives effective execution. I'd urge and warn you to check yourself when tempted to think "Hey, I've got people who do this, it doesn't concern me."

THE USUAL SUSPECTS

One of the more common examples of "unconscious incompetence" in leader-driven improvements is what I call "usual suspect" solutions. The phrase is inspired by the classic movie *Casablanca*, where Police Captain Louis Renault (Claude Rains), knowing full well the identity of the man who pulled the trigger, tells his men, "Major Strasser has been shot. . . . Round up the usual suspects!" Usual suspect solutions can be applied to short-, mid-, or long-term efforts, but they're all drawn from a standard list of things that are just assumed to be a good idea.[2]

Here are some of the most prevalent usual suspects—and a summary of their rationale and potential downside:

> *Training.* Assumption: If people aren't doing what we need or how we need it, they must lack some key skills of knowledge. Training will turn things around!
>
> Challenge: Training is unlikely to have any impact on, for example, poor processes or equipment, unclear goals, or counterproductive incentive plans, just to name a few.
>
> *Automation.* Assumption: If we can just get people out of the process, or quit putting everything on paper, things will be cheaper, faster, and better.

2. Usual suspect solutions also remind me of words my French teacher warned about in high school. These were terms that look the same in both English and French, but which actually mean different things. For example: "assist" in French doesn't mean "help," it means "attend," as in attending a concert or play. There were called *faux amis*: false friends!

Challenge: Equipment can be every bit as temperamental as people, and computerizing a convoluted process can just make it harder to change. And if you check the price tag, most automation is not cheap!

Inspection. Assumption: We can't trust people to do things right every time, and these machines aren't reliable, so we'd better have someone take a look to make sure we catch any mistakes. The micro-managing leader version sounds like this: "I want to see and approve every [*insert item name*] before anything goes out of here!"

Challenge: The risks of relying on inspection have been pointed out hundreds of times. For one, you can't catch everything. Moreover, you're sending a message that if you make a mistake someone will weed it out. But it's so tempting . . .

Add people. Assumption: We have so much to do and not enough resources. The only way we can handle it is with more bodies.

Challenge: More people can add complexity, communication challenges, and require time to get up to speed. There might be ways to reduce the burden on existing people—for example, by eliminating unnecessary tasks or tightening priorities.

Eliminate people. Assumption: Costs are high and we can get by with fewer hands.

Challenge: It may be that the work just takes a lot of people to get done. Reducing staff could end up cutting productivity, slowing service, and/or losing key talent.

Reorganize. Assumption: Our reporting structures are getting in the way of effective operations. If we shift around who reports to whom, it will make us more efficient, effective, and focused.

Challenge: Changing the "silos" will likely do nothing to streamline how work gets done and may actually make people more internally focused—i.e., concerned about their boss rather than about the customer.

Outsource. Assumption: We spend a lot of time doing this and it's not really our area of expertise. We should let someone *else* do it for us so we can optimize our own core competencies. Challenge: Your outsource providers are going to want to make a profit on the services you may now be doing at a "break even." And they may have many other customers, so your clout in getting what you need may be much less than with your current/former "in house" group.

There is nothing wrong, necessarily, with *any* of these usual suspect solutions. In the right circumstances any one of them may be an excellent answer to the opportunities or ills facing your organization. Unfortunately, though, each is often applied with the untested assumption that it's the *best* solution when there may be alternatives that are better, less costly, less risky, etc.

Faced with the temptation to push ahead with an attractive usual suspect solution, take a deep breath and ask yourself: "Will this action really move the organization forward?" If someone else suggests one or another of these usual suspects as the obvious path forward, gently remind him or her that their pet solution is really a *hypothesis* and ask how its validity might be tested. For example, if the proposal is to hire more people, reframe the solution as follows: "If we hire X more people in the call center, we will reduce customer hold times and abandoned calls by Y percent." Now you can assess whether the *solution hypothesis* is likely to be true!

SHORT-TERM EFFORTS

Short-term or quick hit initiatives often appear deceptively easy. A fast solution tends to be associated with "low risk"—when in fact *any* change has risks, and moving too quickly boosts the chance you or your people will miss potential problems until it's too late. So even short-term opportunities need to be chosen carefully and managed properly, or unanticipated risks may be exposed. When it comes to leading change, what you don't know *can* hurt you!

Despite these caveats, rapid response and simpler solutions are an essential and valuable aspect of change leadership.[3] Some of the special benefits of short-term projects include:

- People thrive on success and progress. Being able to spot an opportunity and achieve results soon is rewarding and encourages more improvement.
- Short-term wins can help you learn about the business, customers, process, etc., and pave the way for even greater growth and improvement (more on this later).
- Time and resources for analysis should be reserved for the opportunities that need it. If the situation is right, as the slogan goes: *Just do it.*

Ensuring your short-term efforts are *successes* and not disappointments starts with selecting opportunities that are a good fit for rapid action.

Basic Criteria for Short-Term Projects

Depending on your role as a leader (for example, how much you delegate, how many people you have working for you, etc.) your direct involvement in identifying short-term opportunities will vary. But even if you aren't involved in actually selecting or okaying quick improvements, you *should* know how to help your people make the best choices (including avoiding risky ventures) and review the "portfolio" to make sure efforts are well invested.

The need for a proposed short-term initiative can arise from various sources. For example:

---

3. There's a common, mistaken impression that a "quick fix" falls outside the bounds of Six Sigma improvement. In fact, a fully mature Six Sigma system actually helps identify and execute appropriate short-term solutions (along with other types of projects). It's true Six Sigma programs *start* on bigger problems, and many efforts get "stuck" there—which is why the false assumption that a quick win is "not Six Sigma" gets formed.

- *An emergency or unexpected problem.* Machine failure, cost increase, legal action, rule change, customer demand, key employee departure, etc.
- *A simple problem that's finally getting attention.* Customer data not being updated promptly, an important scheduled maintenance test not being done correctly, etc.
- *A discovery from or subset of a larger project.* For example, a group looking at automating sales lead processing discovers some leads are being sent to the wrong office and initiates a "quick fix."
- *A formal improvement or process analysis activity.* Work-out session, *Kaizen* event, balanced scorecard project, etc.

Of these scenarios, the emergency response understandably gets the least scrutiny before being given a green light. Still, an ill-advised quick response can just exacerbate the problem,[4] so having *some* validity check should be considered a best practice (see Table 6.1).

The common term used for a problem with an obvious solution—a "no brainer"—should be at least a hint of a warning about the risks of attractive quick fixes. As a leader, you certainly don't want people taking that term too literally! To streamline screening, the main focus should be on assessing risks.

Leveraging Small Victories

If a quick win is chosen correctly and works well, it can have an impact far beyond its immediate results. When it's part of a larger initiative or in concert with other efforts, the right short-term fix

---

4. Experts who investigate catastrophic failures or accidents, such as nuclear plant incidents, refinery explosions, and even plane crashes, often find well-intentioned "corrective actions" actually contributed to the eventual disaster. While the emergencies I'm talking about here are usually not quite so sensitive or time critical, the same phenomenon can occur where a chain of failed "fixes" leads to a much bigger problem. (See the comment later in this chapter on GE's experience with the Work-Out method.)

Short-Term Opportunity Validation Questions

Scale and scope	• Situation is contained within a single department, location.
	• Effort won't duplicate or clash with other groups' projects.
	• Costs can be absorbed within current budget.
Ease of execution	• Expertise is available to put potential/planned solution in place.
	• Few or no technical obstacles.
	• Short-term window (less than 3 months) looks feasible.
Risks	• Potential impacts on other parts of the business are understood.
	• Planned action can be taken without significant support from other groups.
	• Resources are available to address any unforeseen problems.
	• If a solution is already identified, we're sure it will work.
Results	• Benefits/results and potential problems can be monitored during implementation.
	• Solution/action is sustainable.
	• Someone will take responsibility for tracking impact and documenting results.

Table 6.1   Criteria for Screening a Proposed Short-Term Change

may serve as a catalyst for much more important achievements. That's why a Six Sigma Leader tries to avoid having too many *isolated* short term efforts and instead engages in smaller changes that can add up to bigger ones.

In Chapter 4, I used the example of former Mayor Rudy Giuliani's targeting "squeegee people" in the much larger effort to reduce *all* crime in New York City. In fact, Giuliani's interest in getting a quick win was inspired by a principle called the "broken windows theory." Developed by researchers James Q. Wilson and George Kelling, the theory suggests that visible disorder in a community—litter, graffiti, broken windows, and other signs of neglect—are both a sign of crime and a factor leading to more crime. It's like the old line about the camel's nose in the tent: once the beast's nose is in, pretty soon you're going to have to host the entire camel.

So the focus on unsolicited windshield washing helped eliminate an intrusive sign of disorder, and in doing so helped to reverse the spiraling crime rate in New York City. The results were even better than expected. By taking the squeegee population off the street—many of them with outstanding warrants for other crimes—untold numbers of criminal acts were avoided.[5]

Not every short-term change will be part of a longer-term effort, and not all initial successes can be done quickly. But seeing change as part of a connected process *over time* is an important feature of Six Sigma Leadership that we'll explore again later in this chapter.

SELECTING THE RIGHT CHANGE STRATEGY

Before moving on to look at mid-range projects, let's first review some of the key issues around *strategies* for change. The symptoms of Unconscious *In*competence often befall leaders in this critical area.[6] There are three core change strategies, as profiled in Figure 6.1.

5. Giuliani, pp. 42–43.
6. My firm Pivotal Resources probably supports well over 200 business change projects each year. The challenge of either *not* having a chosen strategy (i.e., the question is never asked) or clearly having the wrong strategy arises on at least a third of those initiatives.

1. *Improve:* This is commonly equated with "incremental" change or "continuous improvement," though terms such as *fix, enhance,* or *tweak* also are apt descriptions. The Improve strategy means you've directed your people to find a way to achieve results *within the current structure, design, or architecture* of whatever you're changing.

2. *Design:* Now we're looking at "exponential" change to a product, process, or service; in other words an "overhaul," "startup" or "major upgrade." A completely new object or process—imagine the first MP3 player or your organization's first overseas operation—we call a "greenfield" design. Most efforts, though, are a "redesign" of some existing activity or offering.

3. *Manage:* How can "manage" be a change strategy?! It *is* different from Improve or Design. The Manage strategy is about setting up the leader/manager practices and supporting tools to enable better decisions on when, where, and how to promote effective change. A good baseball analogy would be (*a*) keeping your eyes better focused on the ball and (*b*) knowing when to swing the bat. On a day-to-day basis, you just *do* the Manage work, but sometimes you need to create or improve your *ability* to Manage—that's when it becomes an option for your mid-term initiatives.

I can use the example of one of our clients, Sun Microsystems, to illustrate these three change strategies and how *leadership choices* can be so important. Sun's tremendous success in the 1990s was based on its dominance in the "enterprise Web server" market. As companies began to take advantage of the Internet to sell products and serve customers, they needed enormous computing power to run their Web sites and process transactions. As their slogan said, Sun "put the dot in dot com" by providing the processing infrastructure that all Web-based operations needed. Sun became a Wall Street darling, but there were some challenges behind Sun's market dominance.

Before scoring big with Web servers, Sun's core business was high-end workstations: powerful desktop computers used by engineers and others who needed extra computing power. Sun's pro-

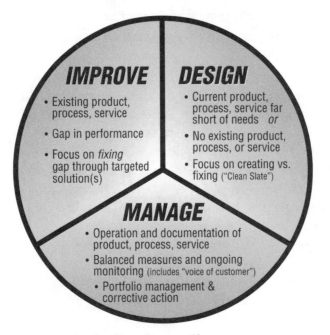

Figure 6.1   Strategies for Organization Change

prietary operating system, Solaris, was the platform of choice for many companies that needed both networking and processing capabilities.

Even today, those of us using personal computers know that every once in a while our machines will crash, freeze, or start running slow and we'll need to restart them. Sun's workstations likewise were good, reliable pieces of hardware and software, but they were designed for power and throughput rather than bullet-proof stability. However, when Sun began to sell Web servers, it was a whole different story; a higher level of reliability was critical. If a Sun customer's Web server crashed or had to be rebooted, it didn't just mean an engineer was idle for a while, it meant customers *could not access the Web site*. Web downtime led to lost revenue, unhappy end users, and bad publicity. The trouble was that this higher standard crept up on an unsuspecting Sun—plus the systems themselves were more complex and sensitive. Sun's leaders recognized the scale and importance of the challenge and launched a series of initiatives to address the need for better availability. These touched on all three change strategies. For example:

Improve:
- Find and eliminate causes of server crashes.
- Improve the effectiveness of "failover" mechanisms (technologies that would keep a system from going down if a crash were imminent).
- Speed up response time to restore a system that went down.

Design:
- Overhaul components where "fixes" would not sufficiently improve availability.
- Build criteria and practices into the design and testing process of new products to "build in" availability.

Manage:
- Build better measures and reporting on performance of installed Sun servers.
- Create more cross-functional oversight of product availability performance.

"Manage" is about running the current operation and being better able to target improvement and/or design opportunities.

Leaders need to be aware of the importance of articulating the right strategy. For example, in the Sun Microsystems effort, a senior manager asked a team to create and implement a measurement system for a key area of the business. Unfortunately, while he looked at this initiative as a "fix," it was actually much more complicated than this leader realized. And sure enough, the team could never get enough traction to make progress on the new measures.

Another fairly common strategy challenge is to launch a Design effort when the time, resources, and/or commitment are just not there. For example, I worked with a group at American Express that was challenged to redesign the process for production and fulfillment of "smart cards" like those used in the Blue card mentioned in Chapter 4. The potential for a redesign was indeed compelling: demand for smart cards was far above forecast and more new products were planned around the embedded chip technology; cycle time to produce the cards was seven days versus two for the old magnetic stripe technology; cost per unit was about 10 times higher for smart cards than the magnetic stripe. Over time, however, the focus of the design team and its sponsor were clearly overwhelmed by day-to-day priorities and there was not enough commitment to a ground-up redesign. Instead the project evolved into a series of improvements, but not a full-scale redesign.

As this example illustrates, the choice of strategies is not always black and white and you have to apply some intuition to make the *best* choice. Even if you start in one direction and decide to change strategies, that's okay too . . . as long as you make a conscious choice and reevaluate it as you go. The biggest mistake is to let resources continue to be wasted trying to apply the *wrong* strategy.

Table 6.2 (pages 156–157) gives some examples of business challenges confronting leaders and approaches that might apply under each of these three core strategies.

It's very possible to address a single, larger opportunity with projects under all three strategies, as Sun did in its efforts to improve system availability.

Being conscious of the choice and management of the right (or best) change strategy is an important and valuable skill for leaders who want to optimize the value of their change efforts. Strategy can also provide a guideline on what the likely time horizon for your investment will be. Improve initiatives almost always fall in the short- to mid-term range, while Design falls in the mid- to long-term. Manage efforts—where you're boosting your effectiveness in overseeing the operation—fall in all three horizons.

MID-TERM PROJECTS

Now we can look with a more focused perspective on opportunities that fit the middle time range—roughly between three months to a year. For ease of discussion, I'll assume these are primarily *Improve* efforts; in the following section on long-term initiatives I will address those mainly as Design initiatives.

Driven by time pressures, leaders are often compelled to question why *everything* can't just be a quick fix! Of course, you know better. But just in case, we can summarize the need for mid- and long-term initiatives in five main reasons (and all may apply to a single situation):

1. The nature of the problem or opportunity is unclear. (For example: we may not even be sure it's something to be concerned about.)
2. An appropriate solution is not identified and needs to be determined.
3. The solution is complex enough that it can't be implemented rapidly.
4. The money for the solution is not available and has to be budgeted.
5. It requires time to gather organizational support to ensure success.

Hurrying has its costs. Mid-term projects are like a track meet's 1,500-meter race. Compared to the 100-meter sprint (short-term efforts) you must set a more deliberate pace to achieve victory.

Basic Criteria for Mid-Term Projects

Table 6.3 (pages 158–159) is a guide to screening potential mid-term change efforts. Note that any option that passes this assessment still may not be the *best* project—you also need to evaluate and prioritize *across* the various potential investments to ensure you have a well balanced portfolio.

Not all these items will be known up front, but you should be able to apply the reasonableness test to most of them before putting a prospective opportunity on the list of viable initiatives.

	Manage	Improve	Design
Appropriate when	• New or better measures are needed. • Documentation is poor. • Requirements/specs are not clear. • Performance monitoring is weak or ineffective. • Oversight responsibility is poorly handled or not well defined.	• Problem or opportunity suggests gap in existing product or process. • Key factors creating gap can be narrowed to a few root causes. • Basic design of the process or product is adequate for current needs. • No immediate need or capacity for major overhaul/redesign.	• No current product or process. *or* • Current product or process not adequate for business needs, market, strategy. • Multiple factors must be changed to close gap (no main root cause). • Risks are manageable.
Scenario: **Concern over new product development cycle time**	• Establish measures of current process cycle time to improve management and identify issues.	• Identify one or two key factors slowing down time-to-market and apply focused changes to get products ready faster.	• Conduct an end-to-end review and realignment of new product development practices to reduce cycle time, cut

156

		development costs, and improve product success on the market.
		• Form joint Sales & Accounting design team to review and revamp contracting and invoicing to reduce payment cycle time, save money, and improve customer satisfaction with billing process.
Scenario: **Past Due Accounts** **Receivable** **increasing**	• Initiate bi-weekly review involving Accounting and Sales Management.	• Short-Term: Hire Collections firm to bring in payments. • Mid-Term: Gather data to confirm severity of the problem and look for patterns that suggest a cause. Implement solution to reduce past due accounts.

Table 6.2 Criteria and Examples for Each Core Change Strategy

Mid-Term Opportunity Validation Questions

Nature of the opportunity	• Situation requires time to validate the problem, verify the benefit, and/or determine the best solution.
	• Potential opportunity, based on financial, customer, or strategic benefit warrants an extended effort.
	• A short-term fix won't be sufficient (or, we've already tried those and failed!).
	• There is an appropriate leader to serve as sponsor over the course of the effort.
Scale and scope	• Focus can be narrowed to a reasonable segment of the organization or process without overly diminishing benefits.
	• Effort can be aligned with and won't duplicate other groups' projects.
	• Costs for the initial investigation phase can be absorbed within current budget; additional budget for solutions is accessible if the ROI is clear.
	• We can launch the project without *knowing* the full cost of a solution.
Feasibility	• Expertise is available over an extended period to investigate, plan, and implement the change
	• We can get approval to start even without a known solution.
	• Anticipated technical capability is available or can be developed.

Table 6.3   Criteria for Screening a Proposed Mid-Term Project

Feasibility (continued)	• Mid-term window (3–12 months) looks achievable. [*Note:* your window may be less than 12 months.]
Risks	• We can avoid being pushed to a "usual suspect" solution. • Resources will be available consistently, or can be obtained. • Unintended consequences can be anticipated and managed. • Buy-in among key stakeholders is achievable.
Results	• There is a clear measure we can use to track results/impact. • An "owner" is available or can be selected to sustain the change. • Likely results are compelling to drive commitment even if/when issues arise. • Success will have a meaningful benefit to the business.

There's usually another advantage to mid-term initiatives: They can be stopped if and when they turn out not to be viable or when priorities change—and often without significant negative ramifications. Short-term projects tend to have a momentum that can be hard to stop, and long-term efforts a size and level of investment that makes their cancellation difficult. But these "in between" initiatives can be redirected or terminated based on what you learn as they progress. But you have to be prepared to actually kill an initiative if it's not working out—something leaders are often unable or unwilling to do.

Validating Opportunities, Urgency, Causes, and Solutions

Mid-term projects, as suggested by their time frame and the screening criteria above, are usually somewhat exploratory. You can't *just do it* because it's not really clear what you *should* do—or even if you *should* do something. To lead or sponsor these exploratory efforts you have to know and be good at posing the critical questions that lead to results. I'm going to walk you through these key questions here, and touch on some of most useful ways to answer them. In the interest of full disclosure, this is the part of this book that comes closest to the techniques that, for example, a Six Sigma Green Belt might apply. Remember (before you skip ahead) that as a *Leader* you don't necessarily have to be able to answer the questions, but you can be much more effective just by knowing when to ask them, and what the right answers should sound like.

Question 1: How Thoroughly Do We Really Understand the Opportunity or Gap?

Chapter 3 introduced the notion of the "problem hypothesis." That's the essence of this first critical question. Here's an example: One of our clients, a service industry leader, recognized an issue with customer wait times at its locations worldwide. The problem was initially defined as "customers are unhappy about waiting for service." However, in checking further, they discovered that waiting itself was really a minor issue—customers did not mind standing in line. The refined problem was described as: "Customers are upset about waiting for service if they see a staff member performing other tasks, but not attending to customers." A subtle, but important difference in the real problem!

Leaders—especially those with a lot of experience—can be particularly prone to flying past this first question, assuming they already *know* the problems and gaps. Here are some follow-up questions to check how thoroughly the opportunity is understood:

- What exactly is the pain we're trying to remedy, or the gap we're trying to close?
- What facts (measures, observations) do we have to verify that this is a real problem or opportunity?
- What assumptions are we relying on?
- What steps can we take to validate/refine our knowledge of the opportunity?
- How might we focus on segments of the opportunity so we can narrow our scope?

The goal here is to ensure the situation prompting the project is real, well defined, and not somehow being misread. The last question can help manage the size of the opportunity so that it's achievable.

Warning: As a leader, you need to be on guard for opinions being presented as facts. A couple of ways to avoid that trap are:

1. Be sure to phrase these as "open ended" questions—just as I've presented them here. If you turn them into Yes/No (closed-ended) questions, it's too easy for people to give you simple, one-word answers and not even test their *own* thinking.
2. Have this discussion with people from different parts of the organization or process. That way you can surface differences of opinion (or interpretations of the facts) more quickly.
3. When in doubt, ask to see the data yourself. Make sure people are using common definitions for what's being measured, and ask them to verify and validate the data.

Question 2: How Well Have We Verified the Causes of the Opportunity or Gap?

Much as you and I know problems should be addressed at the root cause, the temptation to move directly to solutions is strong. Even when you *are* committed to getting a good explanation for a problem or opportunity, several factors can make it difficult:

- *Experience:* Knowledge of the business, product, or process is an advantage and a disadvantage. Relying purely on past experience (what you might call the "been there, done that" approach) can lead you to miss new or unknown factors.
- *Lack of facts:* Data to help tease out causes is often not easily accessible, even with solid information systems.
- *Weak analytical ability:* Good analysis relies on a combination of skills, starting with asking good questions, testing assumptions, developing hunches, and following clues.

By no means does every problem demand intensive cause analysis. In the customer wait-time example mentioned above, once our client learned that the real problem for customers was seeing people doing other work and not *helping them*, the mystery behind the situation was pretty much eliminated.

The basic steps in a fact-driven root cause approach, where you rely on observation and testing versus experience and consensus, are as follows:

1. *Clarify the nature of the problem.* This is the "problem statement" that's been checked by the data.
2. *Look for patterns in facts about the problem.* Patterns help us isolate the problem and provide clues about what's behind it. For example, if a decline in sales is found to be particularly high in one location, or one product area, it gives a hint that something special about that place or product will reveal the main cause.
3. *Develop hypotheses—or suspected causes.* One or more proposed ideas of what's behind the problem.
4. *Test the hypotheses against other facts.* In the most objective approach, you look for situations or data that will *disprove* your hypothesis. For example, if you suspect a new incentive

scheme is leading to a sales decline in Region A, you need to check if the same incentive scheme is used anywhere else. If it is, say in Region D, but the sales there are doing fine, you've just raised big questions about your suspected cause.

5. *Continue until you've verified your hypothesis.* When the facts fail to disprove the suspected cause, you're probably right!

Figure 6.2 shows the steps in this fact-based approach with another example, tied to where in the business system your investigation leads.

The alternative to this "check the facts" approach is what we call "experiential" cause analysis—which basically means you develop hypotheses based on a guess or past experience and try to gain agreement on that cause. The weakness is that your experience may not fit current realities and may miss some key facts.

A few years ago, I was working with managers of a plant making telephone equipment, where yield levels had been going down. Since the business was in the throes of being sold, its leaders assumed poor morale must have been causing employees to lose focus, make mistakes, etc. Hypothesis: *Poor morale is causing defects leading to rejected phones and declining yields.* But when we examined

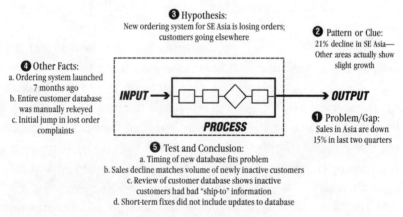

Figure 6.2   Steps and Example of Fact-Based, Root-Caused Analysis

the issues causing the defective products, a clear pattern emerged: The rising problems all involved primarily *automated* steps in the plant. The activities where people's poor *morale* would logically be expected to lead to higher defect levels were not affected. It took about a 15-minute discussion to fairly simply refute the suspected cause hypothesis which the managers' *experience* had led them to accept without much question. (Turns out there had been a series of job reassignments in the plant, unrelated to the sale, leading to poor equipment maintenance.)

Not every situation leads to an "ah-ha" like this one, of course. But this same logical, objective approach works in any environment and does not have to be tied to a major project or initiative to work.

Question 3: Have We Evaluated and Chosen the Best Solution?

Knowing the causes behind a situation can still leave you with plenty of options on how to resolve it. It can take strong leadership discipline to warn people to avoid usual suspect solutions, which can always sneak in.

One of our technology clients had been suffering high costs for handling returned parts and materials for several years. It was discovered that the group dealing with the issues—the Materials Review Board—would take weeks trying to get various groups to agree on how to deal with returned items. So millions of dollars in inventory was sitting unused.

The solution: *outsource it.* Unfortunately, that just moved the issue to an organization that knew even less about the issues than the internal Review Board. So after the outsource effort tanked, the process was brought back in house and the process was streamlined to eliminate all the previously required sign-offs. It turned out that empowering the group responsible for managing products returned by customers worked great—but outsourcing looked easier at the time.

Creativity—or at least avoiding the same group of ineffective solutions—is key in any situation where you're looking to make positive change. Getting people to "think outside the box" is *not* easy; a smart leader must realize that not everyone is good at thinking of new ways to get work done. At the same time, some practical and challenging questions can help jolt people outside their comfort zone, which can be a spark for more effective, if not startlingly innovative, solutions:

- What are some different ways we might approach achieving our goal?
- How will this address the opportunity at the source or root cause?
- Are we sure this is not just an easy or comfortable fix as opposed to the *best* one?
- What are some ways we can enhance the likelihood the solution will work?
- How can we test the change quickly and safely to prove that it's viable?
- If we conduct a test (or pilot), how will we evaluate the results—and then use what we've learned?

You may note that these are not the standard "cost versus benefit" related questions. A leader who serves simply to approve or reject a team's proposal will typically ask those questions—and you should too. We'll look at bit more at approaches to drive creative solutions in connection with long-term initiatives.

To summarize, here are the high-level questions to drive a mid-horizon effort:

1. How thoroughly do we really understand the opportunity or gap?
2. How well have we verified the causes of the opportunity or gap?
3. Have we evaluated and chosen the best solution?

As a follow-up to question three, you also should probe to ensure effective and thorough execution of the change. Because those issues most often fall on the people side of change, I'll address those issues in Chapter 8.

COMPRESSING OR EXTENDING THE TIME WINDOW

Before moving to long-term change efforts, a few words about the options to consider when planning to tackle a critical opportunity. Generally, you have two tactical approaches to choose from, which might be described as the "frontal assault," or the "stealth attack." As these descriptors suggest, the frontal assault is more aggressive, and therefore has the potential of achieving results faster—but it can also be riskier.

Table 6.4 profiles the two tactics, highlighting their differences and some of the well-known methods that fit under each.

One way of distinguishing between these two tactics is that the rapid, frontal assault approach accelerates, and in some cases skips, the "Test Loops" described in Chapter 3 (see Figure 3.6). The stealth approach applies more care to testing and validating hypotheses about the problem, cause, and solution/design.

Which tactic is better? By now, I hope you can answer that question yourself.

The answer is, "Whichever is most likely to achieve, or maximize, success." It's not strictly an either/or proposition; you may apply a rapid-attack mode to achieve one set of goals and take a more careful, stealth approach to address another part of the same opportunity. Making smart choices on how and when to target results is one of the defining skills of a Six Sigma Leader.

LONG-TERM VISION AND INITIATIVES

The balance and flexibility of Six Sigma Leadership applies to how you deal with immediate challenges while also maintaining the long-term perspective. Like walking along a wall, to stay balanced you need to pay attention to where you're placing your feet, but you move *much* more smoothly if you keep your eyes focused out ahead.

Table 6.4 Overview of Accelerated and Deliberative Change Tactics

	"Frontal Assault"	"Stealth Attack"
When to use	Accelerated Approach: Issue or opportunity is attacked using a "target team" (or network of teams) with the assignment to build a solution. Objective is to hammer out a solution rapidly with faster and less in-depth analysis. Rapid response is critical. Risk of failure is tolerable or is overwhelmed by need for speed.[7]	Deliberative or Investigative Approach: Team is assigned to delve into the issue and develop thorough understanding of the opportunity, requirements, causes, etc., based on facts. Speed is important, but effectiveness of the solution or design is critical. Time can and should be invested to allow more clarity and creative thinking.
Challenges	Can be very intense process, with forced consensus and high demands on leader to "accept or reject" recommendations.	Maintaining momentum, avoiding over-analysis.
Improve methods	Kaizen "blitz," Lean Event, Town Hall Meeting, DISC (Define, Investigate, Streamline, Control).	Plan-Do-Check-Act; DMAIC (Define, Measure, Analyze, Improve, Control).
Design methods	Work-out, reengineering, acquisition integration	DMADV (Define, Measure, Analyze, Design, Verify); IDOV (Identify, Design, Optimize, Verify); Lean Enterprise

7. While risk management may still be a high priority in the Frontal Assault method, there also may be a "fail fast" approach underlying this tactic. (See Chapter 4, "Failing to Success.")

The difficulty of maintaining both views is often noted as a shortcoming of modern businesses. The importance of "meeting expectations" on a quarter-to-quarter basis drives dramatic fluctuations in a firm's market valuation, even when the *actual* value of most companies changes much less rapidly. (What's changing is the market's *perceived* value of the company.) Clearly, that type of scrutiny can have a big impact on leaders' behavior. I've been in meetings with executives who've fallen into the habit of checking their company stock price a couple of times *an hour*.

It's little wonder, then, that many companies find themselves falling off the wall—their leaders are looking at their feet and fail to notice a turn. Well-known examples include Motorola's failure to see the switch to digital cell phones; IBM, Digital Equipment, and others failing to adapt to the move away from mainframes; old-line retail companies' failure to adapt to the competition posed by Wal-Mart and Costco.

By ensuring you make longer-term efforts an integral part of your leadership plan, you help counter the shortsightedness that makes organizations vulnerable. Investing in the farther-out future keeps your eyes looking ahead and encourages you to think about the opportunities and threats that you'd miss by just focusing on your feet.

Compelling Reasons to Launch Long-Term Projects

The portion of your portfolio allocated to longer-term efforts may well have its own mix. Some are more operationally oriented—such as adding plant capacity or putting in new order management software—while others will likely be more strategic—for example, introducing an entirely new product line or entering a new market. Engaging in an investment that will take a year or even multiple years to bear fruit should be entered into *only* under the right conditions. Those long-term initiatives that require a significant up-front investment or that will be difficult to stop once launched need to be more carefully examined before you make a "Go" decision.

Table 6.5 provides a guide to some of the more critical questions in identifying and assessing worthy potential long-term change efforts.

The *most* important factor prior to launching any long-horizon initiative is committed and engaged leadership. Next would be the caliber of the people who'll work on the effort. Over an extended time frame, the passion, commitment, and creativity of the initiative leaders will be key to overcoming any obstacles, maintaining energy, and achieving the goal and vision.

Defining the Vision

Some people are cynical about the idea of a "vision." They can take a lot of time and effort for what can, in the end, seem like a very few short sentences. To a leader who *already* has a personal vision of where he or she wants to take the organization, they can seem unnecessary. But in spite of those misgivings, having and effectively communicating vision is one of the most critical skills and priorities of a great leader—and a foundational aspect of Six Sigma Leadership.

Here are some key realities about a vision that I hope will encourage you to develop and use them more effectively:

> *They work.* The compelling value conveyed in a vision often sustains people through the most difficult times working toward significant achievements. For example, consulting on a process design project, we can observe the energizing impact of a vision. Over the course of an extended initiative you can see a design team's spirit start to flag as they confront issues and challenges that need to be overcome, or when their most creative ideas seem impossible to implement. However, teams can often be re-engaged and their spirits boosted after only a brief pause to review and discuss their project vision. With the right people and the right message, it's like a mental energy drink.

Long-Term Opportunity Validation Questions

Nature of the opportunity	• A compelling organizational, operational, or competitive opportunity. For example, avoiding a dangerous threat or creating an entirely new/updated capability (product, process, service, technology, etc.).
	• Requires a sustained effort based on size of the challenge and/or complexity of the change.
	• Fixing current issues may be helpful, but will not address the bigger challenge.
	• There is consensus among a group of leaders that the initiative is critical (leadership alignment is key to supporting and sustaining over the long haul).
	• A single leader with appropriate authority will serve as an engaged sponsor over the course of the effort, taking accountability for success.
Scale and scope	• Scope is large enough to require an extended effort, but still specific enough to be defined and actionable.
	• Other important initiatives can still proceed without being totally stalled by this effort; unnecessary or conflicting initiatives can be cancelled.

Table 6.5 Factors for Validating and Assessing a Potential Long-Term Initiative

Scale and scope (continued)	• Budget can be handled through long-term investment process (e.g., capital expenditures, R&D, long-range planning).
	• We can control the direction of the project so it doesn't expand to become too unwieldy.
Feasibility	• We have the commitment and talent needed to create the new capabilities required.
	• Resources are available; additional resources may be obtained if the business case is sold.
	• Project management and cross-functional cooperation are strong enough to keep things coordinated and minimize overlaps or gaps in discovery and execution.
	• We can manage the scope and risks to prevent large time and cost overruns.
Risks	• We can stay committed to the vision and maintain momentum in spite of obstacles (predicted and/or unforeseen).
	• Conflicting short-term priorities won't badly disrupt this effort.
	• People can be comfortable with uncertainty and ambiguity as the project rolls out.

Long-Term Opportunity Validation Questions

Risks (continued)	• The project can be flexed, or even cancelled, if the situation demands.
Results	• A relevant baseline of the current state can be used to assess impact over the long term. • Management and support systems to help sustain the change are available or will be developed. • Resistors can be brought into line, or worked around, to allow the transformation to be sustained. • Success will have a meaningful benefit to the business or the effectiveness/capability of a key part of our operation.

Table 6.5 (continued) Factors for Validating and Assessing a Potential Long-Term Initiative

Not everyone needs to get it. The *primary* audience for your vision is the group of "thought leaders" and key initiators in your organization. It's not realistic to expect everyone to understand or feel the thrill. So you need to focus on that core group in composing and communicating your message.

Brevity and detail are both important. A brief, well-worded synopsis or slogan can describe the core message, but a more detailed explanation of what the vision really means to the business is essential as well. (In creating a vision, it's often easier to enumerate and agree on the detail first and compose the "slogan" afterwards.)

They need to be used. As we'll discuss in Chapter 8, the vision becomes both a guide and a critical tool for marketing the initiative and maintaining momentum.

Testing a vision with key constituents can be a good "reality check" before deciding to "green light" an effort. Ideally you should sense other key people with that "fire in the gut" unless you *personally* are ready to actively lead the initiative.

Laying out the Roadmap

Achieving an ambitious vision through a long-term initiative is almost always broken into phases. As noted in Chapter 2, the most effective path is usually what many of our clients call a "multigenerational" approach. It's not a new idea, really, but more conscious planning for how to segment a longer effort into achievable sub-projects boosts your likelihood of sustaining progress over time.

Creativity and Contradictions

Some of the more valuable insights into achieving real innovation in recent years have come from the discoveries of the late Genrich Altshuller, a Russian scientist and researcher who developed his initial ideas studying thousands of patented inventions over a period of decade. The technical aspects of Altshuller's methodology are beyond the scope of this book, but every Six Sigma Leader will benefit from some of his discoveries:

- Inventions fall into patterns and types, which have been developed over the course of human history. Rather than trying to "create" from scratch we can learn by investigating those past innovations and applying them to our situation.
- Opportunities for breakthroughs arise from *contradictions*. In other words, it's at those points where the challenges tend to

seem the most bleak—or where the goals seem most at odds
with one another (for example: *To be the highest quality, lowest
cost provider*) that the greatest potential for substantial
progress arises.

This second point seems most inspiring and resonant with the
principles of Six Sigma Leadership. It means that your vision to
embrace the habits of balance and flexibility as a leader are an
opportunity for *you* to make a breakthrough in how you lead. Each
point where we need to apply the Genius of the And is a contradiction, and a chance to innovate.

Throughout this chapter I've touched on a variety of concepts
that are essential to a varied and robust system of business change
efforts—which is one of the foundations of Six Sigma Leadership.
It's tempting to delve deeper into execution—and at times indeed
we've examined hints and approaches you as a leader can encourage, based on the time frame you've defined for an initiative.

But even when it looks a bit "tactical," I'd strongly urge you to
think of these all as *leader* questions and skills. A manager or executive who only assigns tasks and takes no responsibility or interest
in *getting things done* will never be a Six Sigma Leader. And I'd pre-
dict that over the long term those leaders will not meet the needs
of the 21st-century organization.

We'll return to issues related to execution in Chapter 8—at that
point looking at an element of leadership we're skirted around thus
far: the people you lead. First, though, in the next chapter we'll
look at another constituency you might consider even more
important than your fellow leaders or employees: your *customers*.

Customer First . . . and Last

If you work just for money, you'll never make it, but if you love what you're doing and you always put the customer first, success will be yours.

—Ray Kroc

Every company I've worked with over the past 20 years has had a policy or vision statement of some kind claiming, in essence: "We are committed to meeting or exceeding customer expectations 100 percent of the time." That's good business, and my guess is they all mean it sincerely. However, there's a big gap between *claiming* to be customer focused and *actually* putting the customer first. Like the difference between wanting to lose weight and actually losing weight, intention is good, but by itself is not enough.

If you're already slim, of course, losing weight is not a good idea—and this same contradiction is true with customers. There's a point at which commitment to customers must be balanced with the interests of the business. That tension is expressed succinctly in the following vision statement: *To completely satisfy customer needs profitably.*[1] You can aspire to achieve total customer satisfaction, but that goal has to be balanced with your own business and financial self-interest.

As if "satisfaction" and "profitability" weren't hard enough to balance, there's the added difficulty of staying abreast of *changing* customers, markets, and opportunities. This is where "focus on the customer" can—and does—get companies into trouble. By concentrating on satisfying *today's* customers, selling them the products and services they want *now*, you can fail to pay enough attention to finding opportunities to serve *tomorrow's* customers (who may be an entirely different group from the customers you have now).

All the skills that are key to Six Sigma Leadership are put to their ultimate test in this challenge of balancing customer needs and your organization's self-interest *today* while being always ready to change with the customer, or to begin serving new customers.

On the one hand, it would be wrong to paint too bleak a picture of the landscape we're about to enter. There are, of course, millions of reasonably satisfied customers served by profitable companies every day. On the other hand, there are plenty of reasons to be dissatisfied with the general performance of companies in serving their customers. For example, in a 2003 white paper, customer satisfaction research firm J.D. Power & Associates noted:

> **. . . research covering a variety of different industries shows that most service-based companies reach optimal levels of customer satisfaction less than 50 percent of the time.**[2]

Even with *100 percent* satisfaction, your customers may still go elsewhere. But it's hard to see that when times are good. As one

---

1. This was the "vision statement" for Six Sigma developed by our client GE Capital back in 1996.
2. "Enhancing Retail Level Customer Satisfaction: Common organizational issues that impact performance; Using customer satisfaction data to optimize performance," J.D. Power & Associates white paper, May 2003.

CEO put it: "When the fish are jumping in the boat, you're focused on building the biggest boat you can."[3] In other words: Happy customers may be your worst enemies!

In this chapter, I'll begin with the "bad news," looking at a variety of reasons why being customer focused might seem nearly impossible. But I promise that feeling won't last long. The balance of the chapter will review ideas and approaches to building a more solid and practical approach to increasing customer focus balanced by the need for flexibility and long-term success. These approaches will increase your odds of staying connected to a group of satisfied—and profitable—customers.

By the way, while much of what's here will relate to leaders serving "external" customers or stakeholders, these concepts can be translated and applied quite easily by leaders who serve *internal* groups.

THE LOST CUSTOMER

Back in the very early days of what's now called Six Sigma, managers at Motorola put together a simple way to measure process performance based on counting "defects." Counting defects is by no means the *only* good way to evaluate your business; however, Motorola's choice led to a subtle but important awakening for a lot of companies.

Trying to count defects in a business led to some key questions: What *is* a defect? Who decides? Where do you *look* for them? There could be a lot of arguments over what a defect really was. An engineer, trained to build electronic components a certain way, might have one definition; a manager might have a different interpretation; and so on. Multiply that by every *individual* engineer, manager, or employee and soon you have hundreds or thousands of so-called defects—or at least that many dueling opinions on what is or is not a defect.

3. "Sun Down," *Forbes*, vol. 17, no. 11, May 22, 2006, p. 47.

As a result, Motorola decided to consult a "higher authority": Rather than trying to argue over it, they defined a "defect" as any failure to meet the requirement of an *external customer*.[4] How is this a breakthrough? Because trying to understand and quantify "defect" this way exposed a weakness shared by many, if not all, businesses:

> **Much of the understanding about what's important to external customers did not come from those customers themselves, but from internal groups defining or deciding what customers want.**

As the measure was applied and as more scrutiny was placed on identifying "defects," a lot of circumstances arose where it became clear that the "customer focus" companies were claiming to practice was not quite as effective as they'd believed. It turned out there were a lot more defects, as defined by customers, than there should have been. This gap, by the way, was found to be just—if not more—serious when service companies and groups like sales and finance departments began counting *their* defects.[5]

Where Did We Put That Customer?

Figuring out what customers want is *not* an easy thing to do, but Six Sigma Leaders first have to understand and address the factors that undermine customer focus. In other words: How do you keep from losing your connection with the companies and people who pay your mortgage? The reasons behind the Lost Customer tie into many of the challenges of 21st-century business:

---

4. There are still some complications to deal with, but in general this would mean that if a cracked resistor or other "internal" defect did not affect the performance of a piece of electronics according to the customer's requirements, it was not a defect.

5. Contrary to what some people assume, measuring "defects" works just as well in sales, customer service, finance, or other less-tangible processes as it does with physical products like a cell phone or a shoe.

Size and Silos

The nature of the modern corporation is like an extremely dense object. As the business grows, there's more and more "mass" on the inside while the surface area—the part that has contact with the "outside world"—grows more slowly. Customer information that does filter through doesn't lead to any action because an employee fails to understand its significance or, worse, it gets ignored because of the most damaging excuse in business—"That's not my job."

When people *do* engage with customers, the nature of that contact is usually limited by their function or role. This is true even in small organizations; roles like accounting, logistics, sales, and so forth get specialized even when you have only 5 or 10 people in a firm. The challenge for a larger business, however, is that those role-focused people are less likely to understand the "big picture" of that customer's experience or relationship.

Lack of Empathy

Empathy may be a strong word, but I think it's appropriate—especially when you think of the kinds of pain companies sometimes inflict on their customers. These pains tend to be associated with "Customer Service," and poorly trained or insensitive service staff can certainly aggravate the issue. But what shows up in a service environment is often a sign of insensitivity permeating through the whole organization and just manifesting itself when a client calls or a customer walks into the store.

There's a Monty Python sketch about a woman attempting to get a new Gas Cooker (stove) that touches on many of the factors that indicate what I mean by lack of empathy. In the first place, the name on the order form is misspelled, so the delivery people nearly refuse to deliver the cooker. Then, they can't install it. She waits for weeks and finally two men from the "Gas Board" show up. When they explain she has to call the Maintenance department, empathy falls to new lows:

MRS PINNET: Oh, will they come and fix it?

FIRST GAS MAN: No no, they don't come out.

MRS PINNET: Ooh, can you fix it?

THIRD GAS MAN: No, we can't go around doing maintenance.

FIRST GAS MAN: We haven't got the staff.

FOURTH GAS MAN: (walking in): Not unless it's a special.

MRS PINNET: What's a "special"?

SECOND GAS MAN: It's a 2-7-6 or a 3-9-B.

MRS PINNET: Well, can't you phone somebody?

SECOND GAS MAN: Not on a Friday.

(A fifth gas man walks in.)

MRS PINNET: Well what can you do?

FIRST GAS MAN: We could try head office.

FIFTH GAS MAN: No, that's emergency only.

FIRST GAS MAN: Yeah, yeah . . .

MRS PINNET (getting agitated): Look, look—I waited three months for you to come round! I haven't been able to cook a meal since Christmas! This is an emergency!

FIRST GAS MAN: No it's not.

SECOND GAS MAN: Nope, nope, an emergency is contingent upon there being immediate danger to life.

MRS PINNET: Oh dear.

FIRST GAS MAN: Mind you, we can, er, endanger your life for you.

MRS PINNET: Can you?

FIRST GAS MAN: Yeah.

THIRD GAS MAN: Just lie down on the floor.

SECOND GAS MAN: Yeah.

MRS PINNET: Ooh, that's marvelous.

SECOND GAS MAN: Right. Harry, get the pipes!

SIXTH GAS MAN (entering): Right-o, mate.

FIRST GAS MAN: We'll soon have you asphyxiated, love.

MRS PINNET: Ooh, really?

(She lies down. The gas men crowd around her. The sixth gas man leads a rubber pipe to her mouth.)

SECOND GAS MAN (Calling outside): Send out for form P-3BE!

MRS PINNET: Ooh, that's lovely, thank you.

FIRST GAS MAN: Oh, don't mention it, love—all part of the service. Get us a P-B-E, Charlie?

SEVENTH GAS MAN: Oh, righto. Get a PBE, Frank?

As absurd as it is to think of asphyxiating a customer so she can get fast service, I'd bet most people have one or more horror stories where it felt like it came close! The Gas Men are insensitive, but if you pay attention you should recognize that their behavior is a function of the business systems around them.

What's Important

In another part of the Cooker sketch, the crowd of Gas Men gets into a long discussion/gossip session about which depot handles what deliveries and which facility does what repairs and on and on. Each is eager to show what he knows about the company and spout a lot of details that have no relevance whatsoever to the customer standing right there. Here, you can observe probably the biggest factor that makes customer focus so challenging: Most of what people care about, and in fact are *asked* to care about by their management, are things *internal to their business*. This is really the "bridge" between the Size and Silos challenge and the Lack of Empathy. The silos create the internal focus, and internal focus leads to cluelessness about what customers really consider important.

Think of how senior executives usually describe their company's goals. Here are a few common phrases:

- Grow revenue by 15 percent per year over the next three years.
- Capture 30 percent market share.
- Enter five hot global emerging markets.
- Launch two new products per quarter.
- Boost gross margins by 3 percent in the coming year.
- Make one major and one minor acquisition each year.

Rarely in these pronouncements is the emphasis on the customer's experience. Leaders get into the habit of defining success in terms of the company's goals, when those are really outcomes of what is done for customers. Driving financial performance, lowering costs, and other worthy objectives, without explicitly tying them to the critical importance of the customer, can have the unintended consequence of causing people to turn even *more* internally.

The good news is that the overall situation is better today than in the recent past. Driven by tougher competition, the need to connect with tighter and tighter market niches, and a savvier customer base, companies are trying to nurture their customer relationships. Positive signs include:

- Solution- and consultative-selling replacing old fashioned "push" methods
- Loyalty programs seeking to delight customers by adding benefits and recognizing their role in the business's success
- Customer Relationship Management applications that can quickly deliver detailed information about customers
- Web access giving customers 24/7 accessibility to information, services, and purchases and providing greater transparency

It's important to remember that improvement in customer focus does not mean the problem of disconnectedness is solved. The tendency to turn inward is a natural effect that can easily reappear. Mergers or reorganizations, for example, can prompt people to turn inward as they worry about where they stand in the new structure. It takes active, consistent leadership to sustain an outward-looking organization.

Supply Chain Inefficiencies

Who *is* the paying customer? The answer may not be easy when you have a group of suppliers and/or a distribution channel to contend with. If your business depends on carving out "shelf space" to get your products to consumers, sells goods through an on-line retailer or a bricks-and-mortar reseller, or provides materials or components for a final product, you have the obvious need to keep that "next step" customer happy.

Unfortunately, it's often a struggle for power in a supply chain, where one player—for example, a major retailer, or the provider of a key part or material—will try to leverage its position. When that happens, it can hurt the end consumer—especially when the fight over pushing costs down or taking a big share of the profits removes the incentive to improve service or create innovative new offerings.

So the Lost Customer stands outside many businesses waiting to be found. And companies display behaviors that show they aren't all that sure how to find the customer. Here are a couple of other examples:

- Ford itself created a big decline in sales of the Lincoln Continental—one of its more profitable models with a highly loyal customer base—when it removed the keyless door lock feature in a cost-cutting move.
- Motor oil manufacturer Quaker State realized that the labels on its synthetic oil products confused some customers. The CEO invited its top engineers to observe customer focus groups being held to clarify the problem. Viewing the customer discussions from behind one-way mirrors, the engineers were very surprised that no one in the focus groups could even define synthetic oil. One of the engineers announced that, in the future, they would have to find smarter customers for their focus groups.

These and countless other small and large examples of customer "disconnects" stem from failure to ask simple questions: What will this mean to, or how will it affect, the customer? Getting to the answer, as we'll see, can be tough—especially when you consider the obstacles to determining what customers want.

THE LAW OF THE IGNORANT CUSTOMER

In *The Six Sigma Way*, I related a story from a workshop with a group of commercial insurance salespeople at GE. In the session, when we got to talking about customer focus and knowing customer requirements, this group immediately started grumbling. The problem: Most of their customers bought insurance based on one factor alone, price. When I suggested that the salespeople would do well to talk about adding value and winning through service, all I got was a lot of glazed expressions. Finally, one member of the group blurted out, "There's a lot of *ignorant* customers out there!"

Over the last couple of years, I've come to see that comment as one of the more insightful observations I've ever run across about the challenges—and opportunities—of business. Because the truth is, most businesses have different versions of the same problem these folks had. Almost all of us have ignorant customers; and almost all of us *are* ignorant customers.

Hey, Who Ya Callin' Ignorant?!

Imagine that we turn the challenge of customer focus around and see the world from the eyes of your customers. Like the people you lead, they are part of a larger organization; or, if they're consumers, they have hectic lives, homes, kids, jobs, and many other distractions. With some rare exceptions, no matter what kind of business you're in, the percentage of attention your customers or their companies devote to what you do for them, or what they buy from you, is very small.

If you're a leader in a business-to-business company, you could claim that your buyers are well informed and see their purchases as important (i.e., not routine). But I'd suggest that if you look at the situation a little more closely, you'll find those cases are less common than you might expect. Usually one or more of the following comes into play:

- The prospective customer has never bought this particular product or service before and is trying to determine what's important so he or she can make a good choice.
- A procurement group has been told to coordinate the purchase, but they are not sure what the real requirements are and are struggling to get good input from their internal client.
- A technical buyer is making the decision independently, but her understanding of her own organization is not that strong and her contact or influence with users is limited.
- A committee is involved, with varying perspectives and no clear alignment around or understanding of the purchase.
- It actually *is* a routine purchase and your customer is buying from you based on a long-term contract, relationship, or other factor.[6]

We tend to overestimate—sometimes dramatically—the amount of attention and/or expertise customers bring to their purchase decisions and their vendor relationships. For most current or potential customers, what you sell them is just a small slice of their busy lives, whether at home, work, or play. The tendency, nevertheless, is to treat them as all-knowing beings who have thoroughly thought through their needs and are making very considered judgments on our products and services.

Surveys, focus groups, phone interviews, and other techniques that ask customers "What do you think?" are helpful, but have to be taken with caution. In fact, any method to learn customer preferences, requirements, expectations, or needs should be taken with a grain of salt. So here's how I've come to summarize it:

---

6. Situations like strategic alliances or close ties between two companies ("Our CEOs are very good friends and have forged our two companies' relationship.") are not necessarily exceptions to this issue. It still does not guarantee that specific offerings or needs are not subject to customer ignorance.

The Law of the Ignorant Customer

Customers rarely, if ever, understand or can communicate their own requirements as well as we'd like, or expect.

Reasons for the Law

- Customers have *other* important priorities.
- Rarely are they experts in our products/services.
- Customer organizations have silos, too!
- Priorities change to match the latest crisis.
- They may not really understand their *own* customers' requirements.
- What they *think* they know could well be wrong.

As a leader striving to create a customer-focused organization—or more importantly to be *more successful in meeting current and future needs* (which is the real goal!)—you must accept the Law of the Ignorant Customer. Once you do, you can be free to close the gap of ignorance between your organization and your customers—or if there is no gap today, to prevent one from growing in the future.

The Customer Is Always . . .

Bob Neuman, veteran consultant, coauthor, and my colleague at Pivotal Resources, often challenges executives and managers to complete this phrase: "The customer is always . . ."

"The customer is always . . ."

Quick! What's your first thought? Before you read further, try making a note of your response.

The customer is always _____.

Most people favor: "The customer is always *right*," perhaps the most traditional formula about customers on the planet. But hearing it so often does not make it true—and I think there's compelling evidence that the customer is not always right![7] You may want your

---

7. Actually, the phrase is attributed to H. Gordon Selfridge, the founder of Selfridges, one of the best-known department stores in the United Kingdom. Note: Selfridge died penniless and insane.

people to *pretend* customers are right to keep them happy, but even that spirit of accommodation needs to have some boundaries.

You may ask: So, Pete, how do you complete the phrase? That's a fair question. So here goes.

"The customer is always . . . ?"

Important.

Any customer offering to buy your wares or services is worthy of attention or care. One of the more challenging issues for a business is to determine how to say "no" to a customer, in an appropriate way and at the right time. Here are some cases that illustrate the challenge:

- A large client of ours decided to discontinue a "perfect service" guarantee program because it found customers were abusing the offer (issuing complaints just to get freebies) and it was not positively impacting overall customer satisfaction levels. Employees were spending so much time dealing with the increased levels of complaints that other service was suffering.

- Companies with warranties or service contracts on their products—which range from fairly inexpensive home appliances to autos to multi-million dollar computer systems and heavy equipment—are often confronted with the uncomfortable situation of a customer expecting repairs or support that is expired or was never paid for to begin with. While some are good at saying "No," I've heard stories of significant accommodations made to customers for unpaid support costing tens of thousands of dollars and up. As leaders explain, "It's not easy to tell customers you can't help them."[8]

- In the constant pressure for greater efficiencies, customers in many industries are constantly pushing for lower prices. And they are rewarded because their vendors often agree to reductions, though it means increasingly tight margins and

---

8. The temptation to say "yes" in this arena can even become a smokescreen to hide your own shortcomings. When Lee Iacocca use to pitch Chrysler's great warranty program, on the one hand it showed a sign of confidence—but it could also have been viewed as a message that: "You *might* have some issues with our cars, but please buy them anyway.

the commoditization of goods and services. Turning away business, or risking loss by being underpriced by competitors, is a frightening prospect.

Suddenly changing a "Yes" to a "No" with customers is usually not a good idea. Any change in policy or approach has to be carefully managed and deployed. Employees also—especially those who work directly with customers—need to be prepared to follow new rules and deal with any concerns/complaints.

Here's a recap of the challenges of connecting your organization and its customers, as well as those *potential* customers whose money and loyalty mean growth for your business:

1. *Keeping an organization really focused on customers is a major challenge.* Organizational structures, local politics, and other forces tend to create an inward focus and unconscious misunderstanding of real customer needs/requirements. Most businesses are producing "defects" they aren't even aware of.
2. *Customers are often unable to communicate—and may not even understand—their own needs and requirements.* Businesses tend to inflate their own role in customers' lives and yet put high reliance on customers *telling* them their needs fully and in detail—failing to take the Law of the Ignorant Customer into account.
3. *Customers are important, but agreeing to their every request is a dangerous habit.* Patting yourself on the back or bragging about saying yes whenever something goes wrong for a customer can be called "responsive," but it can also be an unintended way of hiding deeper issues.

Back to the weight loss analogy from earlier in the chapter. To build a more customer-responsive organization you can't just go on a crash diet. The suggestions and new habits below are things you have to build into your routine, so if you're tempted to launch a "campaign" to get close to the customer, just be sure to position it as a new set of permanent skills you're seeking to develop/

upgrade. And leadership (your) efforts need to be consistent. In the book *Satisfaction*, Chris Denove and James D. Power IV note that the unraveling of customer focus starts at the top:

> **Employees say to one another, "Just go about your job in the same old way and in a few months management will forget all about customer satisfaction and move on to something else." The unfortunate fact is that at many companies this is exactly what happens.[9]**

THE CUSTOMER'S CUSTOMER'S CUSTOMER

Begin by taking a bigger picture view of the environment in which you and your customers exist. According to the Law of the Ignorant Customer, the services and/or products you provide are just a piece—a small one—of their overall world. By taking a "systems view," you can better understand how your offerings and the value of your relationship fit in that bigger customer environment.

The systems view we first looked at in Chapter 3 was more concerned with defining the internal workings of your operation, to better understand dependencies, develop measures, etc. Now the focus shifts downstream (to the right) to where your products and services are bought, used, and evaluated by customers, and by *their* customers.

Figure 7.1 gives a generic view of the downstream system. The grey-shaded area—what you might call the "mystery zone" for many businesses—is presented very generically here. You may already have a very good idea of what happens with or to your offerings after the customer receives them, but in our work we find that in many organizations a lot of it really *is* a mystery.

A sampling of questions that you can examine when looking at the "mystery zone" include:

- How exactly are our products/services used by customers?
- What is the value they hope to get out of what we provide?

9. Chris Denove and James D. Power IV, *Satisfaction: How Every Great Company Listens to the Voice of the Customer*, New York, Portfolio: 2006, p. 121.

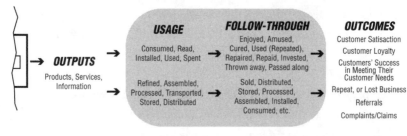

Figure 7.1 Downstream Look at the Business System

- Are there different needs among different customer "subsets" (members of the family, groups within the organization, etc.)?
- Is there value they *could* derive that they don't recognize?
- Are there aspects of our product/service that we think are valuable that customers really don't care about?
- Where would competitors' products/services be used and/or compared with ours?
- What do we know, or could we learn about *their* customers that would help their businesses be more successful?

Adding detail to this downstream view, you and your people can get better insights into the chain of events that lead to customers' impressions of your business. Table 7.1 compares a typical, internally oriented view of what happens downstream with a more realistic view.

An example of how a company learned some critical lessons from a downstream view is the Merry Maids housecleaning service. When a Merry Maids team enters a client's home, they scatter. Some workers go for the bathrooms; others the kitchen; still others the bedrooms and living areas. When the company started, it put heavy emphasis on ensuring customer satisfaction. Before leaving, the team leader would check hundreds of items to ensure the home was cleaned properly. Trouble was, Merry Maids had assumed it knew what customers valued in creating the exhaustive

Common View of "Customer Experience"	More Realistic View of "Customer Experience"
a. Customers receive the product or service;	a. Customers receive the product or service;
b. They decide if they're happy with it or not;	b. They get ready to use or consume it;
c. [*Optional*] They tell us in a survey how they liked it.	c. They put it to use or consume it;
	d. They respond to how it works, tastes, feels;
	e. [If not a consumable] They maintain it for continued use or sell it to their customer
	f. They get further feedback on how it works in their own environment or from *their* own customers
	g. Based on this succession of steps, they form a total opinion about the product, service, purchase experience, etc.
	h. [*Optional*] They tell us in a survey how they liked it.
	Notes: f) may continue if the supply chain has more than one step prior to reaching the end user. h) is a joke—don't just do a survey!

Table 7.1   Simplified and Realistic Views of a Customer's Experience

checklist. Looking deeper (this did require some research), they discovered that each customer actually has one or two essentials that he or she wants perfect—Merry Maids called these "hot buttons." Customers would be forgiving if the cleaners occasionally missed some other details, but failure on a hot button item was unacceptable. Merry Maids adjusted its approach; now they identify each individual customer's hot button items and work to ensure that, if nothing else, those customer-defined criteria are done right every time.

So, to summarize the tasks in building a more thorough understanding of your customers and the broader environment and use of your products and services:

1. Start looking at the customer experience—and how their view of your organization is formed—as an ongoing *process* rather than an event.
2. Accept that to really gain insights into customers and their needs, you'll have to be ready to test and even abandon your assumptions about customers and the world around them (meaning your world, too).
3. Be ready to look at the customer "experience" much as a satellite photo-map Web site (such as Google Earth) does: from miles high, or from right at ground level.
4. Engage your people in this expanded view, and communicate what you learn to others in the organization. Giving everyone that broader, more intimate understanding of your customers helps reverse the inevitable tendency toward being internally focused and promotes more customer-focused thinking on a daily basis.

This last point is important. As a leader, *you* may have the advantage or privilege of understanding the big picture, while the people who work for you might not. On the other hand, they may see details of which you're oblivious. The goal of completely satisfying customer needs profitably can't be assigned to one department or level of the business; it needs to involve a broad cross-section of the organization.

ASKING, INTERPRETING, TESTING

I usually fly with American Airlines or one of its global partners and am generally a pretty satisfied customer. A few years ago, they put on an extra effort to try to find out *how* happy I was. I learned quickly: When I saw a flight attendant coming down the aisle with a sheaf of pink paper, I would try to look very busy. I knew from previous flights that those pink pages represented a customer survey on steroids. It was *full* of detailed questions about me, my flight, my view of every aspect of the service I'd received, my seat comfort, the food, etc. Altogether, the survey took nearly an hour to complete. They were very friendly and even provided me with a pencil.

I can't fault the airline for being interested in passenger feedback. But I've seen what happens when companies collect these types of comprehensive surveys. Not much. That's because, without knowing what specific information would be most relevant, they instead ask for everything, hoping they could answer whatever question might come up, or that each function or department would sift the data and find something relevant to its own work. Even with good intentions, the work required to sort through and analyze all those questions would be daunting. Just the executive summary would likely take hours to review.

This example is pretty typical, I'm afraid, of a lot of well-intentioned "voice of the customer" efforts. One huge survey, or even a lot of small ones, won't unlock the mystery of your customers. Realistically, you can never *fully* understand them (for one thing, their needs are usually changing), but through persistent and effective effort you *can* reduce the mystery.

The best mystery-reducing approach is an iterative, investigative process akin to the validation cycle introduced in Chapter 3. As presented in Figure 7.2, you begin with goals and form questions (defining what you want to learn), draw initial conclusions or hypotheses (noting what you *believe* customers want), and then further evaluate and refine the hypotheses based on additional facts. The amount of evaluation is based, of course, on how reliable your conclusions are and how critical it is to be absolutely certain.

For example, let's say the issue is to understand the required delivery date for a product. If that's already specified in a contract, you might not do any hypothesis testing (though some reconfirmation still might be a good idea). On the other hand, if you're working to improve delivery time performance across a range of customers (and their needs are not spelled out in a contract), you'd probably want to check your hypotheses fairly carefully.

One of our clients actually began a "delivery time improvement" effort thinking that all customers would prefer that their

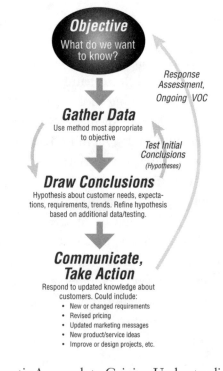

Figure 7.2 Systematic Approach to Gaining Understanding of Customers

orders arrive "as soon as possible." When they tested that view, it turned out that accuracy according to a promised or scheduled delivery time ("Bring it when you said you would") was the more accurate requirement definition.

Beware of assuming the only way to "gather data" is by talking to customers. As we've noted, they may not even know their own requirements. Often more informative is to observe/measure response to various situations in the "real world." That's the principle of test marketing, but it may be possible to conduct your own tests or experiments without turning it into a costly pilot program. I think companies often miss out on opportunities to use "everyday" observation of customers that could offer insights.

Figure 7.3 illustrates this approach. In this scenario, a mortgage origination company has two offices that each handle the loan application process differently: one sends out a generic application; the other tailors the application based on information from the prospective borrower. It's like an experiment already in progress. To take advantage of it you need to:

- Make sure other variables are controlled so you can draw meaningful information; and
- Create a sound plan for measuring the results.

In this example, by the way, it appears the tailored application is much better from a cycle time perspective and actually helps boost customer satisfaction.[10]

Here are some additional reminders and encouragements to help you apply this more scientific, yet realistic approach to unlocking the mystery of the customer:

- Objectives and hypotheses can and should be targeted to *specific* aspects of how you serve your customers. You can probe,

---

10. Any data of this type should be checked for statistical validity to avoid false reading of the results.

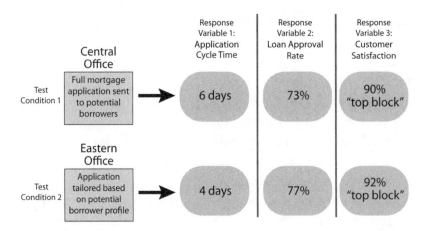

Figure 7.3 Using Real-Life Conditions to Test Customer's Needs/Wants

for example, on invoicing, product/service delivery, service calls . . . any area that's important to your business and your customer.

- Setting priorities is critical so you aren't swamped with data, as well as to avoid overloading customers with questions (like the airplane survey did). Set your targets based on
  - The areas or issues most likely to impact your current and future success in meeting customer needs; and
  - Areas where you feel your current understanding of customers is most weak or vulnerable (i.e., where the mystery is deepest).
- Reach out and across the organization, teaming with other leaders or support areas of the business, to further narrow your focus, avoid redundancy, and define responsibilities.

Your drive and guidance is essential to apply this discovery-based approach. It takes persistence, curiosity, and a willingness to challenge your own assumptions—that is, the usual paradoxical mix that defines Six Sigma Leadership.

FINDING THE MIDDLE GROUND

What you learn as you take a closer, more discerning look at your customers may not be comforting. You may find customer needs that you are not meeting (e.g., defects or lacking features), including some that, as of now, you *can't* meet (technically or profitably). You may find customer demands or expectations that in reality are irrelevant or obsolete (a function of the "ignorant" customer's not understanding his or her own process or your product). Discovering that you're missing the mark with a customer can be deflating: it's like you work so hard and they *still* aren't happy.

But it's just too dangerous to live in blissful ignorance, or to pay lip service to customer focus while failing to really listen to their input. The good news is that there are a variety of ways to close the gaps between what customers demand and what you deliver. Table 7.2 provides some simple guidelines on how to respond in different situations when there's a gap between what customers are *asking for* and what you are currently *delivering*. The first column indicates whether the customer's perceived need is realistic, or inflated. As noted, the actions you take should be screened based on the importance of the gap, costs, etc. (In other words, apply portfolio management methods.)

A critical dimension we could add to Table 7.2 is your *competitors'* current profile: Can they deliver on the need? Are they? If the competition is meeting a customer's perceived need (even one you are certain is unnecessary), you may be forced to match them *unless* you can reeducate the customer to see why they are demanding more than is needed.

As noted, saying *"No"* is a viable option, especially when a customer is asking for things they don't really need. But before you get to "No," it's smarter to try to help customers see why their demand will not add value—to educate them on their real needs or negotiate a satisfactory middle ground where you *and* your customers are happy.

Real Customer Need?*	Technically and/or Financially Feasible?	Action
No	Yes	1. Try to educate consumer. 2. Just do it anyway. 3. Just say "No."
No	No	1. Negotiate, reset customer expectations. 2. Just say "No."
Yes	Yes	Launch effort to close gap (based on priority of need).
Yes	No	1. Negotiate with customer for alternative ways to meet needs. 2. Launch innovation-focused effort to develop capability (based on priority of need, potential profit, etc.).

*Customers believe they have a need, but is their view right or wrong?

Table 7.2 Options to Close Gaps between Real/Perceived Customer Needs and Delivery Capability

Not all gaps arise because of the *customer's* perceived needs. It's also common for a company, or even an entire industry, to serve up services, features, and/or benefits that are of little to no interest to the customer—or that cater to a very small group who are a poor reflection of the market at large. Where I observe this most these days is in software applications, where there are modules and menus and options far beyond what most mortal users could ever fathom. That leads to the frustrating chore of having to search through drop-downs and help pages to find fairly routine instructions among all the other "power user" features. You may get stuck in what one of my clients once described as an "arms race" with competitors and market perception where—despite your better judgment, or even without realizing it—you are escalating the sophistication of your offering or adding "weapons" that provide marginal value.

However, it's also possible, should you find your business in that kind of race, that something akin to unilateral disarmament may be a smart strategy. That's one of the distinctions of Apple's hugely successful iPod. It's been boiled down to the basics so no customers have to feel like they're ignorant or not getting their money's worth because they don't use or understand all the other buttons and menus that come on the product. It takes some Six Sigma Leader-like guts, however, to take the risk of jumping off the arms race treadmill.

PAY (NO) ATTENTION TO THE CUSTOMER

As hard as it can be to develop and maintain customer focus, understand and eliminate defects, and break through the challenge of the Ignorant Customer and the internally focused business, often a more fundamental challenge is staying ahead of *bigger* shifts in market and customer behavior.

Smack in the middle of Los Angeles is a remarkable natural wonder, the La Brea Tar Pits. This is a site where, even today, large pools of oil form at the surface of the earth in what looks like a marsh (technically it's an "oil seep"). Through thousands of years, animals—many now extinct—wandered into the pits, were trapped, died, and left their bones to be preserved by the tar. Many species have been excavated from the site, including mammoths, mastodons, sloths, camels, and ancient horses. At the nearby museum there's an entire wall with skulls of saber tooth cats— dozens of them—that met their demise in the tar.

If I were a saber tooth cat, I'd probably feel pretty confident that I could take care of myself. I've got powerful muscles, huge teeth, good eyesight—not likely to run into a lot of trouble. But somehow a lot of my tough cat buddies got stuck in a tar pit and today there aren't *any* of us left around. Likewise, when you're a well-paid leader of a successful enterprise you can feel pretty powerful. Sure you're always hunting for your quarterly numbers, and that's a challenge, and you've heard about other companies stumbling into the business equivalent of the tar pits. But it's hard to imagine that could happen to you; in fact, it's just easier not to think about those tar pits.

How do you keep from becoming a saber tooth cat? There are three key Six Sigma Leadership habits that can help you reduce your odds of extinction:

Accept the Reality of the Tar Pits

There are oily swamps out there, waiting to trap any business that fails to watch out. Of course, it's not comforting to dwell constantly on your own potential demise. Calling attention to the bigger dangers that may threaten you with extinction can seem like negativism. Plus, it is possible to over-react to threats and create undue panic.

But the numbers of company and industry failures and downturns where leaders failed to respond in spite of clear danger signs, or missed out on great opportunities, suggest that it's smarter to see every clue as worthy of attention than to dismiss it as trivial.

Threats or opportunities that fall outside the normal frame of reference of a successful company can seem unimportant or can be easily misread. For example, when Xerox was first developing the technology that became the first commercial photocopier, the world was making copies with carbon paper or mimeograph technology. IBM, to whom Xerox offered its patents, paid for a market research study. But the research firm made a huge mistake: it considered only the market the new invention would *replace*, not the

market it would *create*. The study concluded that even if the revolu-
tionary machine captured 100 percent of the market for carbon
paper, it would still not repay the investment required to develop
the copier. The research failed to recognize that the copier would
not really solve an existing problem or replace a current technology,
but actually provide a whole new capability: rapid, multiple repro-
duction of documents. IBM declined to acquire the Xerox patents.

The nature of the business tar pits is that they often start forming *right where you are*. To stay out of them is to keep moving to
new areas of solid ground where you can be a saber tooth cat
again—for a while, perhaps. From a customer perspective, this
means accepting the reality that your customers are a moving target and your long-term success means adapting to their changing
needs and preferences.

Listen Ever More Carefully to the Customer, and the Customer's Customers

The biggest tar pit of recent years was the demise of the dot-com
boom in early 2001. Could anyone have seen it coming? Well, as
related in the book, *The Eye of the Storm*, at least one, Cisco Systems, *might* have predicted a crash but did not pick up on the signals. In late 2000 and early 2001, Cisco's sales were still strong and
their customers sounded as optimistic as ever. Meanwhile, however,
there was also a noticeable jump in customer requests for extended
credit terms. In other words, companies buying Cisco products for
their new e-commerce ventures were starting to run low on funds
as profits did not materialize. Cisco leaders were hearing the *positive*
signals, but not paying sufficient attention to other indicators and
eventually had to write off $2 billion in inventory.[11]

The dot-com boom was a big tar pit that caught a lot of companies and investors.

---

11. Robert Slater, *The Eye of the Storm: How John Chambers Steered Cisco Through
the Technology Collapse*, New York: Harper Business, 2003, p. 243.

Individual companies get trapped as well. McDonald's is a good example of a company whose hugely successful business approach—based on streamlined processes and high consistency—began to grow tar-like. First, consumers had become more health conscious. Second, McDonald's customers' expectations in areas of quality, service, and cleanliness had grown more stringent, and McDonald's was not meeting them consistently. Same-store sales and the stock declined while the restaurant chain was losing 1 to 2 percent of its customers each year.

The good news is, leadership and a new focus on the customer experience have brought McDonald's back. James Cantalupo, who became CEO in 2002, criticized the company for inside-out thinking. He initiated changes from new menu items, to posting nutritional information, to measuring and communicating customer data. Within six months of Cantalupo's changes, same-store sales began rising. Corporate profits and the stock price rose.

The lesson of these and other stories from the tar pits is that leaders need to be highly attuned to a *variety* of signals from customers and markets. It may be too late when you start seeing the symptoms of a change in your current sales numbers, read about a new product that could undermine your entire business, or start smelling oil seeping from the ground.

Ignore the Customer

Since customers are not always in tune with their own needs or preferences, smart companies and leaders know that sometimes gut is more important than research. The classic story of the New Coke (pun intended) back in the 1980s was a case where what consumers *said* ("Love it") and what happened ("How dare you take away my Coke?") turned into a near catastrophe.[12]

---

12. As Malcolm Gladwell points out in his book *Blink!* the research methodologies that led to the Coke fiasco did not take a "big picture" view and concentrated on a blind taste test.

A positive example—and one of a company that got itself into, and then out of, its own tar pit—is Motorola and the RAZR cell phone, mentioned in the last chapter. The stylish flair of the hugely popular thin, black mobile phone was developed despite going counter to the research. As *Fortune* recounted: "Motorola's 'human factors' unit dictated that phones more than 49 millimeters wide would be deemed uncomfortable by consumers. The RAZR team concluded otherwise. Their only data points: their own instincts."[13]

Balance Change and Constancy

Many of us in business today—leaders, managers, academics, consultants—note how rapid change is making things increasingly difficult and dangerous. I agree; in fact it's a big reason why the new standard of Six Sigma Leadership is so critical. But Six Sigma Leadership is about balance and flexibility, which means also paying attention to other signals. And the fact is, some of our faith in the breakneck pace of change is probably exaggerated.[14]

This reality was brought to light in an article by author, intellectual, and former Oxford lecturer, David Bodanis, who pointed out how much of our modern "technology" is fundamentally old school stuff. He mentions jet airplanes, credit cards, four-wheeled vehicles powered by an internal combustion engine, even the graphical user interface on the latest computers as decades-old technology.[15]

13. See "RAZR'S edge: How a team of engineers and designers defied Motorola's own rules to create the cellphone that revived their company." money.cnn.com/2006/05/31/magazines/fortune/razr_greatteams_fortune/.

14. We probably also underestimate the pace of change in the past, either because it's a distant memory or simply because we weren't around to notice it. It was a mere decade from the first flight at Kitty Hawk to the first scheduled commercial air travel. Radar was conceived, perfected, and put into widespread use within the time frame of World War II.

15. David Bodanis, "Slow Forward: Is the Speed of Technological Change an Illusion?" *Discover* magazine, June 2006, pp. 46–49.

One of Bodanis's hypotheses is that success with current technology is actually squelching innovation today. Too much is invested in our current infrastructure—and the owners of that technology have too much to lose—to make rapid roll-out of new ideas or technologies acceptable or affordable. The rapid growth of the Internet, cellular/mobile phones, and other new offerings undermines that argument somewhat, though the fact that some of these technologies—especially wireless phones—were much faster to take off in less developed countries shows there's an advantage to not having an existing capability to get in the way of the new. And it certainly fits with the history of successful companies missing the shift to new technologies.

On the other hand, it seems just as common that the providers of innovation are moving ahead while the customers are just not "there" yet. It took the banking industry many years to shift customers away from live tellers to automated teller machines. Adoption of broadband service has been slowed somewhat by technology challenges, but much more by reluctance of users to upgrade from their familiar dial-up services. Wireless companies in the United Kingdom recently paid billions to the government in an auction for new transmission frequencies that will support dramatically new capabilities—and then came to the realization it will be years before they can get any economic value from that expensive investment.

Paradigms can hold on to a market and technology long after they are relevant. The television industry in the United States is a good example, I think. For many years, the programming, production, and advertising activities of the major networks have followed an annual cycle: New shows planned for autumn are introduced in spring, mid-season "replacement" shows are introduced in January. A large portion of the advertising time is sold during a bargaining period in May known as the "up-fronts." Ratings are captured during special "sweeps" periods at several set times during the year. Even the TV critics' calendar is organized around two annual "Press Tours" where the networks show off their programs and tell their stories. But consider these facts:

- For nearly a decade, the major blockbuster shows have premiered in the spring or summer, not the fall (e.g., *Who Wants to Be a Millionaire?*—August 1999; *Survivor*—May 2000; *American Idol*—June 2002).
- The premiere dates for the fall programs, which all used to launch within a period of two or three weeks, now are staggered over a period of months.
- By sticking with the calendar (according to the folks I worked with at NBC a few years back) the competition for actors, writers, and studios becomes more intense as everyone is doing the same thing at the same time.
- Cable channels—while still having individually small shares of viewers compared to the large networks—are less beholden to the annual cycle and have a much more fluid programming approach.

As the old saying goes, "Imitation is the highest form of television." Clearly there are advantages to sticking with the traditional calendar, but there are also clear signs that the unity is falling apart and persists more out of industry habit and convenience. It's certainly of little relevance to viewers; time will tell if it remains.

This example, and many others, simply demonstrate that there is no single "truth" about change. Yes, it's fast. And it's slow. It's been proven time and again that the biggest breakthroughs—just as air travel, Xerography, personal computers, text messaging, or reality television have been in the past—won't make a blip on your annual customer surveys or trend analyses. And the things you *think* are going to be a hit could just as easily be a flop or take years to find a market.

So you have to listen to your customers intently—but also be prepared to ignore them completely, to take chances, and anticipate things they can't understand. And you have to be fast on your feet—because where you're standing might start turning tar-like—but also be careful not to start running headlong and find yourself stuck and sinking.

To summarize, avoiding extinction requires a Six Sigma Leader to adopt some fundamental survival practices (and then hope for the best!):

- Routinely ask: "Where are the possible tar pits where we could get stuck?"
- Take a broad view of your industry, supply chain, and customers' environment to spot warning signs: What changes are impacting our suppliers? What new needs or offerings are impacting customers? Is how our products or services being used changing?
- Use your detailed understanding of your customers—informed by greater empathy and awareness of their needs—to find hints about opportunities that even they may not recognize.
- Don't panic at every disturbing piece of news, or jump too quickly on every promising new thing. Question the assumptions behind staying where you are; give intense scrutiny to any plan to move elsewhere.
- Factor these threats and potential opportunities into your change portfolio management decisions: Invest in short- and mid-term efforts to defend current markets and grow organically; place ambitious but well-managed bets on the future with mid- and long-term efforts that enable adaptation to a changing world.

In all these practices of a Six Sigma Leader so far, the emphasis has been on managing *yourself* to improve how well you guide your organization. One critical dimension I've not yet touched on in detail is the primary focus of leadership: people. In the next chapter, we'll look at how a Six Sigma Leader turns the advantages of using smart habits into getting the best from the people you lead—and those with whom you share leadership.

Selling People, Telling People

Time makes more converts than reason.

—Thomas Paine

I PREVIOUSLY compared the role of a leader to that of an orchestra conductor. As a conductor, you establish the vision, set the tempo, guide people to ensure things are done well, provide energy to the enterprise, and take action when things are out of harmony.

The great music produced by your organization only comes to life through the collective effort of the musicians. In organizational terms, the musicians are the followers. Just as none of the instruments or pages of music are of any merit without people to play them, none of the assets—physical, financial, and intellectual—of the organization add any value until people, together, put them to work. People are the focal point of leadership.

Achieving Six Sigma Leadership therefore will require you to translate your improved habits and skills into actions taken *by your followers*. Otherwise you're just a conductor waving his or her arms while the orchestra pays no attention!

We have touched on people issues various times through the course of the book, but now that you have a thorough foundation in the methods of Six Sigma Leadership, we can focus on people and how they can respond to your improved way of conducting the organization.

WHAT DO FOLLOWERS WANT?

I began my organization-change career teaching and applying problem-solving and decision-making skills. It was a great experience, working with many different types of business functions, from marketing to HR to engineering, and many levels of a business as well. A lot of the concepts that we taught and applied in those workshops were actually elements of Six Sigma Leadership: defining priorities, using facts, identifying goals, managing risks, etc.

Easily the most frequent question I received from people in those workshops was: "Why don't our leaders/managers think this way?" My usual answers were:

- They probably do, but they may not communicate it to you very well.
- They probably do, but just not very consistently.
- They have so many pressures on them, it's easy for them to fall into bad habits.

I would not let people try to use "*They* don't do this, so why should I?" as an excuse not to examine and improve their *own* thinking skills. But it was not an easy question to answer. Not surprisingly, we get the same kinds of questions today when teaching Lean Six Sigma methods to people trying to improve their business performance—and the answers are about the same as they were 15 to 20 years ago.

Let's turn the question around. If you've gotten this far in this book and are still wondering why being a Six Sigma Leader would be a good idea, one emphatic answer I'd offer is "Because the people who work for and with you will welcome it enthusiastically!" Six Sigma Leadership is a huge benefit to the *followers* in your organization because it makes their work more meaningful, focused, empowered, and results-oriented. Here are some of the advantages they should notice, based on questions I've heard about, and from, leaders going back 20 years:

- Priorities and the rationale for them will be clearer; changes in priorities (which are inevitable) will be better understood.
- Links to and relationships with other groups will be smoother; mutual issues can be addressed collaboratively versus through finger pointing.
- The appropriate amount of time will more consistently be dedicated to tasks that need it; rush efforts will be better managed to avoid unforeseen problems; longer-term efforts will either make progress or be eliminated.
- Opinions—including the leader's—will have to be supported by facts; "usual suspect" solutions will be minimized in favor of determining the *best* solution.
- If we have to take action based on intuition, we know why and can prepare in case we're wrong.
- The connection between what we do, and how it supports or impacts our customers, will be clearer; we'll have less non-value-added work, and things will get done faster.

Of course, these remarkable changes won't appear overnight. In fact, it is not a smart idea to just go out and suddenly change your whole approach to leadership right after finishing this book. You will need time to learn and get comfortable with new habits (even ones that make good common sense). Just as critical, your *people* will need to make accommodations and adopt new habits to match yours, which will require a transition process as well. Rushing the change process on the front-end usually makes it harder to sustain in the long run. While a crisis—a "burning platform"—can no doubt be helpful in compelling change and building commitment around new behaviors, you will need a long-term view to sustain adoption of Six Sigma Leadership.

Nevertheless, the bottom line is that what people *want* and what Six Sigma Leadership offers match very closely. People seek a leader who is:

- Clear
- Consistent
- Honest
- Flexible
- Open minded
- Confident
- Interested
- Goal oriented
- Collaborative
- Principled
- Understanding
- Approachable
- Balanced

It's an ambitious list, to be sure, but as a true leader you should be ready to aspire to it. It's not critical that you achieve perfection in every one of these dimensions (though failure in some, such as honesty, are very hard to recover from). The more important thing is that your followers see you modeling the behaviors you have perfected, struggling with those you have not, and accepting responsibility when you fall short.

It's beyond the scope of this book to address the interpersonal or communication skills that are key to these characteristics. Clearly, your effectiveness in these so-called "soft" skills will have a bearing on your success. However, assuming you're already fairly decent as a communicator, the focus and balance of Six Sigma Leadership can have a significant positive effect on your interpersonal skills. Still, you should consider your own strengths and weaknesses and look for help if you find that those areas are individual opportunities for additional improvement.

With these notes of advice, let's look further at how you begin to be more of the kind of leader your "followers" want—as well as how to bring them around to accepting and adopting valuable elements of Six Sigma Leadership.

PULLING AND PUSHING THE OARS

The image of an eight-person racing boat is a common and apt analogy for an organization. There's direction, speed, coordination, skill, alignment, and environment, which all must be considered and managed if the vessel is going to move through the water smoothly. If we were to translate the efforts from an office, store, or plant to a boat, what you'd see might not make for a good training video. Some people—not all—would be rowing, but the coordination would be poor. Progress would be made, but some folks would almost certainly be steering in a different direction; some might even be trying to stop or go the opposite way. Each would probably claim "This is what I'm supposed to do!"—though others might argue, "No, you should be doing something else!"

Getting people oriented toward common goals may be one of your first priorities as you begin to bring them into alignment with your vision of Six Sigma Leadership. Of course, pointing a business in the right direction is more difficult than it is with a boat. With that in mind, here are some questions to help focus your efforts.

Process or Project?

Is there a greater need for enhanced alignment in your day-to-day operations, or among various special projects? (It may take a little time to decide; or you may have needs in both categories.)

Within or Outside Your Organization?

Are your "direct reports" on the same page, or do you see them working at cross purposes? Are there disconnects with other groups within or outside your company?

Source of the Misalignment?

If possible, can you determine what's created the crossed oars? Here are some common issues:

- Too many things on people's plates?
- Misinterpretation or unclear communication?
- Mixed messages from leadership (you, or you and other leaders)?
- Priority "churn"—people are unsure what's most important?
- Lack of "context" or big picture view?

Some basic ideas/options for improving alignment are presented in Table 8.1.

Fixing alignment issues is not the end of the race; you can use many of these same tactics to help *maintain* alignment as well. Like a boat, organizations tend to drift, and you need to remain a vigilant navigator.

SHARED RESPONSIBILITY

Aligning goals is the first step, but not enough to effectively engage your people in the improved habits of Six Sigma Leadership. Your followers need to understand an enhanced set of ground rules, or operating principles, that both you and they must adopt to build greater balance and flexibility in your organization. Here's the *Genius of the And* popping up again: It's not about you or your people working smarter, it's about *both*.

However, *you* have to take the lead in explaining and adopting the new shared responsibilities. Like a parent influencing a child, your *own* behavior has to be a model if you want to promote smarter habits among your followers, or peers. If you make snap decisions (and don't explain them), keep changing priorities willy-nilly, or throw solutions at problems without determining if they're the right ones, you can't expect your people to be any sharper or more focused than you are.

Table 8.2 presents examples of the reciprocal responsibilities of leaders and followers in bringing smarter business habits to life.

By now I hope you've picked up on the fact that Six Sigma Leadership is in a fundamental way *all about* dealing with and managing ambiguity. If you make the effort, you can eliminate a lot of ambiguity through better thought processes and smarter actions. On the other hand, I've often observed inflated expectations on the part of followers about how perfectly neatly and cleanly they think leaders should be able to spell things out. They complain about leaders not making priorities *crystal* clear or defining roles with *no* potential for overlap.

Part of your job as leader is therefore to help your people become more tolerant of ambiguity and understanding of the need to be disciplined, yet flexible. Instead of worrying or complaining about the inevitable unknowns, you can then turn your energies toward the question: How do we better prepare for the things we aren't sure about? By posing that question, you may begin looking at your business in ways that lead to some real breakthroughs.[1]

You can very likely apply *both* columns of the table to yourself. Everyone but the most senior executives in an organization play the role of "follower" at some point or another. Just as you must share responsibilities with your followers to build Six Sigma Leadership, you also should be a more effective follower to your *own* leaders.

RESULTS = QUALITY × ACCEPTANCE

Executing effective change is a central element of Six Sigma Leadership—so it follows that driving *acceptance* of change is among your most essential people-leadership responsibilities. Failure to pay adequate attention to change acceptance is far and away the most important cause of failed initiatives—far more than technical

---

1. The birth of Lean enterprise and "pull" systems was essentially a breakthrough posed by the inescapable ambiguity/inaccuracy of the traditional sales forecast. Since the forecast *can't* be perfect, apply Lean so you can respond rapidly and you don't *need* a forecast!

	Process	Project
Too many priorities	• Review key process outcomes and customer requirements. • Look for non-value-added activities that can be eliminated.	• Assess portfolio and identify efforts to put on hold. • Add resources, if warranted and available
Misinterpreted goals/unclear communication	• Check and clarify performance goals. • Review measures and operational definitions.	• Review and refine project charter. • Ensure goals have observable, measurable component and, if possible, a baseline.
Mixed messages from Leader(s)	• Convene leader meeting to review goals, meetrics, responsibilities. • Clarify responsibility and timing for communicating.	• Convene leader meeting to review goals, metrics, responsibilities. • Clarify responsibility and timing for communicating.
Constantly changing priorities	• Ensure customer needs are clearly defined and interpreted (in case priorities are changing unnecessarily).	• Review portfolio management process and establish ranking and clear time frames to reduce ambiguity.

	• Clarify nature of services and need to review and ensure goal alignment frequently (when nature of the process requires variable needs/priorities).
	• Coach people on the reality that priorities *have* to flex and that "focused but flexible" is a key objective/value.
Lack of "big picture" view	• Provide a "systems" view of the process.*
	• Explain relationships between key groups, including customers and suppliers.
	• Provide a summary to the organization on all key projects, their purpose, and priorities.
	• Clarify links and dependencies between different initiatives as needed.

* The most common technique to accomplish this is called a "SIPOC" (SYE-pahk) diagram, for: "Supplier, Input, Process, Output, Customer."

Table 8.1 Actions to Support Improved Goal Alignment and Task Coordination

Leader Responsibilities

- Provide a broader perspective on the organization, end customers, internal interdependencies.
- Develop and communicate a clear set of priorities for change/improvement.
- Review and revise priorities regularly.
- Avoid adding new efforts without rebalancing the portfolio.
- Define problems and engage support in finding solutions. Avoid jumping to solutions prematurely.
- Openly accept feedback on your ideas and proposed solutions.
- Encourage assumption busting and innovative ideas.
- Demonstrate and encourage use of facts to support decisions.
- Practice and encourage risk management.

Follower Responsibilities

- Take responsibility for and interest in looking beyond existing organizational boundaries.
- Manage time and focus on the priorities; avoid getting distracted by unimportant issues/projects.
- Be prepared for and accept that priorities *will* change.
- Raise questions if priorities are not clear or are shifting excessively.
- Provide data to validate suspected problems.
- Raise questions if leader is pushing a poorly thought-through solution.
- Challenge own assumptions and seek creative solutions when warranted.
- Demonstrate and encourage use of facts to support decisions.
- Practice and encourage risk management.

• Establish and communicate a vision to drive progress toward ambitious results.	• Embrace and strive to achieve ambitious results according to the business's vision.
• Remind people that some ambiguity will always exist and that *managing* it is a key to success.	• Accept ambiguity; avoid placing unrealistic expectations on leaders to make everything "black and white."
• In turn, be a good follower.	• In turn, be a good leader.

Table 8.2 Examples of Reciprocal Responsibilities of Leaders and Followers in Building Six Sigma Leadership Success

issues or even lack of resources. Fortunately the practices of Six Sigma Leadership—greater focus, improved use of facts, customer understanding, speed, and discipline—provide a huge advantage in achieving buy-in and enforcing compliance. (Both are needed!)

Breaking Down the Equation

The formula *Results = Quality × Acceptance*^{2} is commonly used to emphasize the impact of acceptance. Quality—meaning the effectiveness of the change solution—is where most leaders and followers on the "team" concentrate their efforts. Here are two imaginary cases where a "perfect" score for Quality and Acceptance would be 10 (i.e., optimal Results equal 100):

Case 1—Outstanding Solution, Weak Acceptance
Quality × Acceptance = Results
10   0.5   5

Case 2—Good Solution, Good Acceptance
Quality × Acceptance = Results
8   6   48

In other words, diverting some of your energies away from perfecting solutions and toward building support for change could be a very good investment.

In reality, these variables—*R*, *Q*, and *A*—are far more interdependent than this simple equation suggests. For example: your ability to describe *desired* Results (for example, through a well-defined Vision and/or Goal) will significantly impact both the ability to formulate a strong solution (*Q*) and to convince people that it's a worthwhile effort (*A*). Having a well-thought-out solution (a strong *Q*) can be a huge advantage in getting people to support and accept the change—so *Q* can drive the *A*, which boosts the *R*.

---

2. Adapted from GE's "Change Acceleration Process."

High levels of *resistance* (i.e., objections signaling low Acceptance) can provide valuable clues to strengthen the solution (if you and your change team keep an open mind)—meaning a low A can lead to an *improved Q*, which in turn will lead to improved results.

None of this, however, should happen by accident. A Six Sigma Leader must be proactive about achieving support, and you should make it a priority for the people to whom you've assigned responsibility to develop and implement changes. This is neither easy, nor really magical—but it certainly is often an area of unconscious incompetence.

Tips for Developing Acceptance

Here, then, are some key reminders on how to boost the *A*, as well as the *Q* and the *R* in your change equations.

Start at the beginning. Acceptance, or the likelihood of it, should be a factor in your choice of change investments. An attractive opportunity or critical issue that you know will be a "tough sell" may need to go lower on your priority list compared to others that will be more readily accepted. If you do decide to move forward with an effort that's likely to be highly controversial or difficult to gain support for, you'll need to invest more effort to gain buy-in.

Develop a plan. The message of *Results = Quality × Acceptance* is that attention to gaining support is far too often an afterthought. As soon as an effort is launched, you and/or the team responsible for it should begin your "acceptance" planning. That plan will usually evolve, especially over the course of a longer-range initiative, so it needs to be revisited regularly

Identify and target your audiences (stakeholders). Different individuals and groups will have differing levels of influence and impact on any operation or initiative. From the perspective of the business, process, or project, these are the stakeholders. We all know that "key" stakeholders—the CEO, senior managers, customers, and investors—must be factored into your plan if you hope to lead the effort to success. But we frequently give short shrift to other stakeholders, such as the employees who have to live with the project, or partners who must adjust their systems to it. And sometimes, with great peril, we actually fail to recognize a critical stakeholder. Early in my career I learned about this the hard way.

I was a young account executive with a PR agency. My assignment was to plan and organize the grand opening of Citicorp Center, a new high-rise office building in downtown Los Angeles. The 32nd floor of the still-empty building had been decked out with carpeting, lights, a piano, catering gear—with spectacular views all around—and a number of VIPs of the Los Angeles political, commercial, and real estate fields had been invited.

On the evening of the party, guests were starting to arrive. From the lobby window, out on the unfinished Plaza, I see my client, one of the development company managers, in a heated conversation with the LA City Fire Marshall. Bottom line: An occupancy permit has not yet been issued for the building. So there's no way the Fire Marshall will allow us to have a party on the 32nd floor of the building. Should I—a lowly PR account executive—have been expected to know about this particular stakeholder? Maybe. Even though no one blamed me, I still felt bad.

But it taught me an enduring lesson. For every significant project, I make a list of all potential stakeholders, paying particular attention to the invisible stakeholders who have a habit of showing up at the worst possible time. (By the way, the event worked out. After much pleading, the Fire Marshall gave us permission to hold the party in the lobby. We frantically moved the food, beverages, and most of the equipment down the 32 floors (we decided to forget the piano), and people seemed to have a good time, more or less. My clients did cringe every time they saw a canapé accidentally fall on the as-yet-unsealed granite floor.)

Practice change marketing. Citicorp was getting ready to consolidate its LA operations into its new Citicorp center. This meant shifting a lot of people who had occupied real offices in their previous buildings into cubicles (very nice cubicles, but cubicles nonetheless). Citicorp anticipated problems and objections. The company marketed the entire transition with a logo, a slogan (*It's Your Move!*), and a newsletter. They had tours of the new facility to let people see in advance the quality of the surroundings. They did not just *manage* change; Citicorp managed people. The company recognized that people would not jump for joy over the new arrangement and would need to be sold on the change—so the company carefully built a case for the change and presented it effectively to the key stakeholders: in this case, Citicorp's employees.

This is where having a good understanding of your stakeholders becomes so important. The effectiveness of marketing depends on how well you tailor and present your message to each key audience. Smart businesses understand that in selling their products. Pharmaceutical companies for years focused their marketing efforts on physicians, but in recent years have also become very effective at marketing to end users. While consumer-based pharmaceutical advertising remains controversial, it's a good model for the kind of campaign that may be needed to sell your most critical change efforts.

Following are some marketing pointers for your change initiatives.

Start with personal, targeted, or face-to-face sales. A mass approach launched too soon will just create resistance. Your initial goal should be to build support among the most influential or critical stakeholders—the ones with the greatest potential impact on your success. These may be regulators, for example (think Fire Marshal), or thought leaders (respected individuals who can help you sway others).

Work the entire hierarchy or supply chain. In Chapter 2 I referenced the challenge of the "frozen middle," where leaders market their initiatives directly to employees or customers while neglecting to drive acceptance/compliance from managers, supervisors, or others who make daily decisions on priorities and resources. While that's the most common gap, you also find plenty of cases where managers are briefed in detail, but nobody seems to raise questions such as, "How will this go over with the troops?" And then there's shock and dismay when the troops reject the change. The same effect can arise in selling exciting new products to consumers, but failing to prepare distributors for the challenges of your innovative new package.

Beware of sugar-coating or overselling. The one potential misgiving I have about campaigns like the *It's Your Move* program is that they can seem to gloss over or ignore tough issues or challenges that come with change. If your marketing message is 100 percent positive and does not confront some of the pain or unknowns head-on, you will likely lose credibility and may even risk dissipating all the good your marketing efforts might otherwise have done.

Avoid surprising people. A common problem for longer-term efforts is what I call "going underground." For example, a team at building-products company Fibreboard (now part of Owens Corning) had been developing a new point-of-sale ordering system for the company's vinyl siding division. After some thorough up-front work—interviewing key stakeholders and getting agreement on goals and specifications—they went thoroughly underground. Work proceeded for over a year, the new system was tested and perfected—but with no ongoing engagement of the managers or users in the field.

When the time was getting close to launch, the reaction from "customers" was shock, a high level of surprise, and immediate resistance. By going underground, the Fibreboard team allowed even the people they'd interviewed to forget about the whole effort. And instead of bring thrilled when the project came back to the surface, they needed to be mollified and convinced.

Listen to and learn from resistance. This does not mean giving an audience to every complaint. But as noted earlier, the misgivings of your stakeholders can be an extremely valuable reality check on your ideas and plans. Even if you know, through fact and/or conviction, that the change concept and execution are the best they can be, the objections you hear (and you should hope you hear them!) are indicators of where you need to refine your message, address concerns, pay more attention to certain stakeholders—in other words, improve your change marketing plan.

Provide and allow for time. The quotation at the start of this chapter—*Time makes more converts than reason*—is one of the most enlightening, appropriate, and in some ways ironic ones that I've ever run across. Here's the entire passage, the first paragraph in the pamphlet *Common Sense* by Thomas Paine:

> **Perhaps the sentiments contained in the following pages are not yet sufficiently fashionable to procure them general favor; a long habit of not thinking a thing *wrong*, gives it a superficial appearance of being *right*, and at first raises a formidable outcry in defence of custom. But the tumult soon subsides. Time makes more converts than reason.**[3]

Paine was about to present one of the most influential *reasoned* arguments and one that hugely influenced the founding of the United States. But the first thing he points out is, no matter how good an argument—or a "business case"—you have, people are going to need a while to let their initial discomfort, habit, and tumult subside.[4]

I would guess if you reflect on your own response to new ideas you'll find plenty of examples supporting Paine's comment. I could relate some revealing situations from my own career where I resisted very smart, practical observations and proposals, mostly because they did not fit my current set of assumptions. But over time, my frozen mind thawed enough to permit a belated enlightenment, and a certain embarrassment at having said "no way" to something that should have been obvious. Bottom line: You can argue, cajole, market, plead, PowerPoint, and threaten till you turn

3. Thomas Paine, *Common Sense*, New York: Dover Publications edition, 1997, p. 1. Pamphlet was first published in January 1776.

4. There's a clear parallel here to the concept of "paradigm shifts" and the psychology of resistance to change. But from a practical standpoint, I'm going to assume Paine pretty much nailed it and avoid going down that path.

blue, but if you are not prepared to give stakeholders *time* to think, reflect, and just let that conversion process happen, you're still likely to have a low acceptance in the change equation—and a much higher risk of failure.

In Table 8.3 you can see a guide to questions that can be applied over the course of an initiative to help optimize the three factors in the change equation. These are not just good change management questions, they're good things to consider as good *project* management. In other words, running the initiative and managing acceptance should *not* be seen as separate and distinct tasks—they are integral and essential.

CONSENSUS AND ENFORCEMENT

The emphasis on building acceptance for change is based on a practical reality: getting people to adopt smart leadership/followership methods, or to support value-adding change, is much smoother if they do it through their own initiative. But "selling" has its limits and effective Six Sigma Leadership is all about balance—in this case, between selling and *telling*. In this final section, we'll look at both.

Getting Everyone on the Same Page

It's helpful to remember that consensus is not about *unanimous* agreement. The goal of consensus is to get all key stakeholders to *accept* a choice or participate willingly in a change, whether or not they're in full accord with the plan. (It's typically much easier to get people to "go along" than to "agree.") Fortunately, the practices of Six Sigma Leadership can help you gain leverage when driving for consensus. Here's a review of some of the key factors that will work in your favor.

- *Better understanding of the "big picture."* Looking at the organization as a system—knowing how the pieces fit together to drive customer and economic value—enables you to frame goals and describe implications of your choices in a much more convincing or reassuring way. A "connected" view of the business lets you add comments along the lines of:

- ○ "I realize how this will affect several groups, and we're taking that into account."
- ○ "By coordinating these efforts, we'll be able to provide much better value to our customers."
- ○ "This will require a change in . . . that some of you may not yet welcome, but I know we can make it work by focusing on the real value-adding work that needs to be done."

- *Stronger facts to support your choices—and define results.* With better evidence and greater objectivity you can describe direction, decisions, and solutions more clearly. A Six Sigma Leader can more effectively differentiate *hypotheses* from facts, assuring others that you not only know what you know, but also what you *don't* know. Better facts also help you define the current state (baseline) and what the future state (goal or vision) can mean in more concrete, vivid terms.

- *More focused priorities that make best use of your resources and talent.* A typical source of skepticism from all levels of followers is the feeling that "this is just going to mean more work!" And well it may, but also being able to put a new initiative in the context of the broader portfolio—explaining how it will get done with current or even additional resources—will give you a big edge in reaching consensus.

- *Greater clarity around the strategy and time frame of the effort.* Managing your efforts by scale and time frame can give doubters a better understanding of the relationship between the various assignments and projects. A Six Sigma Leader more effectively distinguishes between the short-term/sure thing efforts and the longer-term "big bets" that are key to being competitive in a changing environment.

There are many ways to build consensus, and you may certainly rely on key people in your organization to help build support for

Acceptance

- Are the vision and business case compelling?
- Is the organization ready for the change?
- Who are the key stakeholders and what are their views?

- Have we engaged the right people at the right time?
- Are we using objections to adapt/refine the solution?
- Do our action and communication plans support the transition?

Quality

- Is the problem/opportunity well defined and understood?
- Is solution pre-determined? Should it be?
- What is the appropriate solution "strategy" (improvement, design, quick-fix) management?

- Is the action/solution supported by facts?
- Have we considered customer requirements?
- Are processes and systems aligned? How are we managing risks?

Results

- Have a vision and goal been developed?
- Are benefits measurable?
- Is this effort clearly a priority?

- Are we holding firm to the goal? Should it be adapted?
- Is the expected benefit still visible? Can we track it?
- Have priorities changed?

Prepare

Implement

Manage		
• Have anticipated results been met? Documented? • Can we quantify the gain or validate the benefit? • What new opportunities were uncovered?	• Is there clear ownership of the solution? • Will there be appropriate monitoring/measures? • What's the plan if results dissipate?	• Has the broader organization been engaged as needed? • Are performance criteria clear? • Are stakeholders happy?

Table 8.3 Key Questions to Drive Results, Quality, and Acceptance over the Course of a Change Initiative

important initiatives. One prerequisite, though: Consensus will never happen without a proposal or decision to focus on. Six Sigma Leaders recognize that deliberation can create more effective decisions, but also that nothing replaces *decisiveness*.

Compliance and Performance Management

Even your most effective efforts to engage followers and build consensus will not sway everyone. The smart leader uses a balance of carrot and stick to achieve sustainable results. (Even strong supporters of a change may have trouble adapting to it and need reminders/incentives to prevent backsliding.) The stick should not be a last resort either—consequences for noncompliance should be integrated into your planning and not added after the fact. (That would be like trying to install sprinklers in your office after fire's broken out.)

Here are some of the main considerations and recommendations as you plan for your change *enforcement* efforts.

Objectives/Focus

The first question is, "What am I trying to get done?" As you consider actions to promote compliance, focus on followers' actions that are most essential to success. The following phrases or questions can help:

> In order for us to achieve/sustain this goal, people will have to . . .
>
> Areas/activities that will be most difficult for people to adjust to would be . . .
>
> Tasks or approaches that look easy but would be subject to "backsliding" include . . .

Using a systems view—identifying critical results and the upstream actions that will drive them—can also help in your prioritization, especially in refining or aligning performance management criteria.

Timing

There's an understandable temptation to start by giving people direction, watching to see how well they respond, and then taking action if they're not getting things done as hoped. After all, you may be hurting yourself by appearing *too* forceful. On the other hand, there's another perspective reflected in a guideline I once heard recommended for schoolteachers: "Never smile before Thanksgiving."[5] This argues that it's more effective to start tough and then relax than it is to start by being nice and then having to enforce discipline on people when you aren't happy with their performance.

Audience

The kind of enforcement or rules you put in place will necessarily vary by the group and their role in the change or process. One of the earliest targets for the "tell" efforts is the team involved in developing and/or implementing the change initiative. In an ongoing operation, you should avoid what I've heard people call "skip level management"—where you impose performance criteria and monitoring on people in the trenches and fail to engage, or hold accountable, that group's direct supervision.

One possible strategy for gaining support among the frozen middle is to involve managers in developing the performance guidelines and evaluation methods that they will then be using to guide their own groups. This is a great example of where "telling" and "selling" can support one another.[6]

---

5. For readers outside the United States, the school year usually begins in August or September, Thanksgiving is in November—so that means two to three months before showing students you have a "nice" side.

6. A form of this approach that quite a few companies use, with varying effectiveness, is "policy deployment"—also known as "Hoshin Planning"—where high level goals are reviewed, interpreted, and then fed back to senior leaders as specific functional or departmental goals.

Consequences and Rewards

Generally, it seems the right approach would be to follow your organization's standard performance management policies and practices. The one caveat would be to stay away from giving people rewards simply for doing what their jobs require. Eventually you have to take away the rewards, and then your lose the power of your incentives.

Therefore, I'd encourage you to consider the following, even though it may be a new direction in encouraging/enforcing performance:

1. Identify the tasks, skills, or performance levels critical to achieving your goals, for each key role.
2. Define the appropriate measures or verification methods you will use to assess each role or individual.
3. Build those performance requirements and measures into job descriptions and performance management plans. Define consequences for not performing, as well as reasonable—but not special—positive incentives for meeting the new requirements.
4. Include additional incentives for collective success; for example, each function is rewarded if the entire process meets or exceeds goals, since each is critical to success.
5. Use it!

This is a perfectly logical and straightforward approach to integrating critical change goals into a performance management system. It's also pretty rare—the standard bad habit being to get around to adjusting performance criteria well after the fact, if at all. Making it a standard practice in promoting change should be a priority for a Six Sigma Leader. We'll return to this topic and expand on it somewhat in Chapter 9.

Sympathy . . . to a Point

Change can be frustrating, frightening, worrisome, and even personally costly for those who are left behind as a business adapts its strategy to meet changing customer needs, streamlines its operations, and/or boosts efficiency. A smart leader should not ignore the personal impact of change on the people in an organization, and should work to mitigate the negative effects. In my mind, that's both good business and good personal ethics.

On the other hand, change is necessary—and often is a necessary *good*, rather than an *evil*. It creates opportunity; adds energy; brings new products, services, and features to customers; provides for new learning; and, when done well, keeps an organization in business and accelerates growth.

So your compassion for the few must be tempered by compassion for, and responsibility to, the many. I get alarmed when I hear *change management* defined more as trauma counseling for victims than as a key business need. A Six Sigma Leader needs to remind people continually that "We either change and improve, or we fade away." And fading away is overall a lot more traumatic than getting on with the challenging but exciting work of making positive change a reality.

We've now seen most of the critical dimensions of balanced leadership that make up the new standard for 21st-century organizations. These are skills that, with practice, every leader can master. There's no magic here. All success requires is a diligent, dedicated, and never-ceasing effort to fold these disciplines into your conscious competence. And over time, if possible, to make them your unconscious habits.

CHAPTER

Bringing Six Sigma Leadership to Life

Success is something you attract by the person you become.

—Jim Roan

I F YOU HAVE persisted this far, you have realized that my goal in writing this book is nothing less than prescribing a new, compelling standard for guiding a 21st-century organization. The value you glean from these pages, of course, will only be determined by how well you can *apply* Six Sigma Leadership to enhance the success of your organization and your own career. In this chapter, we'll take a realistic look at the incentives and challenges—the "thrills and spills" as I like to call them—of sustaining these smarter leadership skills

Included here will be some recommended actions to help you get traction on these important concepts. However, remember that these smarter methods start with how you *think*—and there's no simple menu to make you a better leader. It will require commitment, self-awareness, discipline, and your own compelling vision of what kind of leader you want to be.

POSITIVE AND LIMITING FORCES
FOR SIX SIGMA LEADERSHIP

The first thing to explore will be some of the factors that make improving leadership easy as well as difficult. These are not "pros and cons" but rather forces that pull you toward, or push you away from, balanced, flexible leadership.

Positive Forces (Some Factors Favoring Your Succes in Applying Six Sigma Leadership)

Six Sigma Leadership is based in common sense. The "Good Habits" are intuitively accepted by most people, even if not consistently practiced.

You can begin applying many of these principles with only a small up-front investment (see "The 10-Second Rule"). Because it ties so closely to actions and approaches you take to improve your organization, you can simultaneously be a smarter leader and see the benefits in improved performance.

The skills of Six Sigma Leadership provide appealing benefits to any leader. These include:

- Greater understanding of the factors impacting your and your organization's success. You can ask better questions and make better decisions.
- More effective balance between short- and long-term goals.
- Improved ability to link your needs to those of your customer, while keeping a long-term view on changes.
- Greater respect from your people because you can see various perspectives more clearly and guide them more effectively. (And even empower them more, and with greater confidence.)
- Enhanced return on the investment you and your organization make in change and improvement efforts. (Better "portfolio management.")

The costs of failing to apply Six Sigma Leadership are visible in everyday organizational pains, as well as most leader and business failures.

Six Sigma Leader practices are *flexible* to the situation and objectives. In fact, the goal is to seek a balance in many critical success factors, such as:

- Fact-based *and* intuition-guided decision making.
- Dramatic change and innovation *and* stable, effective execution.
- Managing and mitigating risk *and* pushing to learn from failure.
- Total customer satisfaction *and* ignoring the customer completely.

You almost certainly *already* apply some elements of Six Sigma Leadership—but not thoroughly or consistently. Even an incremental improvement will make a meaningful impact!

Limiting Forces (Obstacles to Becoming a Successful Six Sigma Leader)

The "Bad Habits" are powerful and very hard to break. For example, purely gut-based decision making often *seems* faster and easier than looking for facts.

There may not be *enough* motivation to change. Complacency and inertia have their supporting structures, including:

- The leadership skills you've used have gotten you this far—why change?
- Six Sigma Leadership requires you not just to admit, but even *look*, for evidence that you may be wrong. That seems like weakness.
- Having a *lot* of change efforts happening at once—so hopefully something will get done—just feels better. Focusing and prioritizing seems like it'll slow you down.

- Looking beyond and even stepping outside your defined area of responsibility—a key to Six Sigma Leadership—is uncomfortable, risky, and not likely to be welcome by others.
- You feel the business is going really well and customers love your products and services. Just delivering takes all your time and energy. *Or* You're going through some tough times now and need to concentrate on solving your problems and making a turnaround, not enhancing leadership.
- Life's complicated enough as it is!
- The notion that change needs to be managed and marketed—that you can't "just do it"—can be hard to accept or take necessary time to do.

In a hierarchical organization, you may feel *your* leadership role does not provide you enough influence or authority to impact the things that are key to Six Sigma Leadership (e.g., the change portfolio, how your business thinks about and interacts with customers, or how well your leaders work as a team).

Changing leadership practices requires vigilance: you can never be completely satisfied. As soon as you think "I've perfected my leadership skills" you become highly vulnerable to unconscious incompetence.

A good hint when trying to promote change is to focus attention on both sets of forces. We'll look at strategies to address both elements shortly.

WHOSE MEDICINE *IS* THIS?

Another important obstacle to building smarter leadership practices is what I term the "other people's medicine" problem. Many leaders unfortunately view the ailments that plague their organizations as a malady of the followers, other leaders, or the business itself, but not themselves. So they expect *others* to take the cure. The best leaders, of course, *do* look at their own skills and behaviors as a key to how successful their organizations will be. I've worked with several leaders who've understood that the *questions* asked based on Six Sigma principles are fundamental to smarter leadership. But that's really a minority; most prefer to prescribe the cure for others who, they assume, badly need it. As for themselves, they assume the cure is not necessary.

A related implication of the medicine problem seems to arise from the way business improvement solutions are packaged and sold. Some common ways these cures are presented, with examples, include:

- A *theme* (innovation, customer focus)
- A *method* (reengineering, *kaizen*)
- A *model* (Plan-Do-Check-Act, DMAIC)
- A *toolkit* (statistical process control, balanced scorecard)
- A *program* (Six Sigma, TQM, Lean)
- An *application* (Enterprise resource planning, CRM)

Positioned like this, the leader's role is akin to being a physician *to* the business: he or she provides the appropriate medicine and makes sure it's applied consistently. That's implied whenever people say of an effort that "You have to have top management support"—it means leaders need to be good doctors and encourage people to take their medicine.

Once an approach or cure is perceived as something leaders *give* to their businesses, it's hard to change that positioning. I'm well aware, for example, that some people with preconceived notions about Six Sigma are likely to have trouble understanding it as a vision/process for *Leadership*. If that happens, it won't be the first time: For example, one of the most famous and influential business gurus of the 20th century, the late W. Edwards Deming, claimed to be advocating for new behaviors of management and *leadership*. But Deming was never able to have his ideas consistently embraced outside the realm of "Total Quality." He still has many disciples, of course, but not many who apply his teachings in the executive suite.[1]

However, it seems there's a simpler, more important reason for the "other people's medicine" challenge: that's the reluctance of leaders, and those of us who advise them, to confront the frank reality that none of the business/organizational cures on the market will be as effective, or lasting, without improving the overall health of *leadership* itself. In other words, if you keep *giving out* medicine and never *take any yourself*, things may feel better, but the risks of a relapse will be high.

The bestselling book, *Good to Great*, resonates with the theme of leaders taking responsibility. The first essential for an organization to make the transition from "good" to "great" is to have what's called "Level 5" leadership. The parallels between Level 5 and Six Sigma Leadership are striking. For example, Jim Collins writes: "Level 5 leaders embody a paradoxical mix of personal humility and professional will. They are ambitious, to be sure, but ambitious first and foremost for the company, not themselves." Further, they "display a workmanlike diligence" and also "look out the window to attribute success to factors other than themselves. When things go poorly, however, they look in the mirror and . . . [take] full responsibility."[2]

But Level 5 leadership is about personal traits more than specific skills of leadership, and Collins shies away from offering tips on *how* to do so, other than to follow the rest of the "Good to Great" steps. Still missing, then, is the prescription for stronger, healthier Six Sigma Leadership.

ADOPTING SIX SIGMA LEADERSHIP YOURSELF

Bringing Six Sigma Leadership to life requires applying the treatment first of all to yourself. These are recommended actions, but you should *not* view them as "steps." This is not a linear process,

1. This was partly Deming's own doing. For one, he spent a lot of time in his lectures and writings talking about applying statistical process control—a valuable tool, but not hugely applicable in day-to-day leadership. He also identified *fallacies* of leadership, but did not offer much in the way of *how* leaders should change.
2. Collins, pp. 17–40.

and each activity is one you can do independently of the others, even though they can complement one another. (The order in which they're presented is deliberate and you may follow it, but again these are not steps, so the order is totally up to you.)

Personal Action One: Apply the 10-Second Rule

I've stressed this simple technique/concept because the first step in thinking smarter is to *think*. As a leader, you are paid for the quality of your thought and the actions that arise from it, so investing in thinking makes sense. These valuable extra moments give you a window of opportunity to pose one or two relevant questions that may make all the difference between the thrill of smart leadership and plain old bad habits, confusion, and misery. For hints on what to ask in this brief window of opportunity, read on.

Personal Action Two: Check Your Priorities

You might think a key question would be "What's the goal?" But having a clear goal is deceptive if you're working on the *wrong thing*. It's *so* easy to get your attention diverted by an exciting idea, a new problem, or even a random comment from a customer, that priorities *have* to come before goals, and you have to use your first 10 seconds to ask: Is this really what we/I ought to be working on? This may well lead you to establish more formal means of tracking and reviewing priorities—but even the formal processes are vulnerable without constant vigilance and reflection.

Priorities will be important in your own "transformation" to a Six Sigma Leader. As you'll see in my final words below, you'll need to decide what elements should be your *personal* starting point for change.

Personal Action Three: Question Your Assumptions

This may be the most important single action for a Six Sigma Leader to adopt. Reviewing your assumptions does not mean your view of things, facts, or goals are *wrong*—it just is a way of reminding you they *might* be wrong. From there, a whole world of opportunities arises, for example:

- If you're confident in your assumptions, you can move ahead more aggressively
- If you need to better validate or sell your assumptions, you may look for more facts
- If you need to move ahead without solid validation, you may identify ways to guard against the risks of being wrong

It's okay, of course, to question *other people's* assumptions. But starting with your own will make you a more effective and credible "devil's advocate."

Personal Action Four: Look, and Reach, "Up and Out"

This is where *initiative* and *teamwork* join forces. When you see an opportunity, confront a problem, establish a critical priority, you should not—to borrow a line from my favorite band Steely Dan—"quake in your respective hidey-hole." In fact, one of the best ways to validate your priorities and test your assumptions is by exposing them to other people's views. Just as importantly, any meaningful challenge you confront will very likely require a collaborative effort; your independent efforts will have limited impact. Ask: Whose help do we need? Who else is dealing with this? Who are the key stakeholders?

Again, establishing more regular, formal "teaming" opportunities can support this action, but nothing will take the place of your willingness to reach out.

Personal Action Five: Calibrate Your Speed

Reviewing priorities, testing assumptions, and engaging the right people can help put you on a much faster path to getting results, but it's still an important "10-Second" question to ask whether you've established the right pace and are making appropriate progress on the critical opportunities in your organization. And while "Six Sigma" is sometimes equated with moving more deliberately, your job as a leader is to push for *more* speed when it's needed, and less when it's not, or when speed risks mistakes.

More rigorous portfolio management—which you may elect to initiate as part of your Six Sigma Leadership effort—can add a forum to check the timing of your investments. But "speed control" should be a *daily* concern for a smart leader!

Personal Action Six: Fight Complacency

It's great, even essential, to celebrate successes, have a positive outlook, and to be proud of your people and your achievements. But you can't let the glow of success or the comfort of a good period in your business let things become *too* comfortable.

One of the things I say from time to time is, "Life's not worth living if you don't have something to complain about." It's partly a joke, but when complaining is done as a sign of wanting things to be *better*, it has its positive side too. My advice would be, You should *always* be looking for things that could be better, and recognize also that as soon as you believe everything's great, you're probably in for a surprise or two.

One essential requirement: You have to look for things about *yourself* that could be better, too. Otherwise you revert back to giving medicine to everyone *else* and never taking the responsibility to cure your own shortcomings as a leader.

These questions can help you achieve that all-important balance as you strive to enhance both your own and your organization's success. Of course, the more you can bring other people in your organization into that same balance, the greater the potential impact of your new leadership.

BUILDING SIX SIGMA LEADERSHIP
IN YOUR ORGANIZATION

Here's a key recommendation: take the medicine yourself before you prescribe it to others. Eventually you'll share Six Sigma Leadership habits with your followers, and perhaps your peers and those who lead you as well. Because this is about organizational and not just personal success, your ability to advocate for smarter leadership will definitely have a bearing on what you can accomplish.

These are some simple suggestions, some easy and some requiring more planning and effort. Since your own path to Six Sigma Leadership will take time—and you will really never "be there"—you should have patience and persistence in building these approaches.

Organizational Action One: Explain What You're Doing

As you examine opportunities to apply smart leadership—for example, to clarify impact on the customer, review and tighten priorities, check assumptions, etc.—it's smart to briefly share the rationale for your actions. Over time, as you get more comfortable with these better habits, you will probably want to be more thorough in your explanation, even going so far as to establish new practices in your organization (see below). But my advice is to be clear but subtle in your approach at first; as you learn, followers will be learning, too.

Also be careful of inflating others' expectations. Replacing old habits with new ones usually involves some setbacks. *Not* recommended: announcing "I've decided to become a Six Sigma Leader!" (If you announce such a thing, you have to prove it. And if you can prove it, you don't need to announce it.)

Organizational Action Two: Present/Encourage a Systems View

Providing your people with a "big picture" understanding of your organization, and their place in it, is fundamental to your success in building smarter behaviors. Seeing beyond their immediate environment can keep people better connected with customers, enable them to work more collaboratively, and promote more effective decisions. It also provides the context for better understanding impacts and risks, and for developing more effective measures.

A good approach to building the business-as-a-system view is to identify your critical or "core" processes, including how they connect with external customers, partners, suppliers, etc. Keeping it at a high level, so the *essence* of how the pieces fit together, is key. Too much detail becomes distracting and buries the benefit of the end-to-end view. Whether on paper or online (as a graphic), or just in your mind, this view can help when you or your people ask, What's really going on here?

Organizational Action Three: Establish a Leadership/Management Vision

A vision for your *organization* is essential to define and prioritize initiatives for change and growth. Here, however, I'm talking about a vision for the leadership and management "best practices" you see as critical to your organization. Interestingly, I've not run across this type of "leadership vision" definition that I can recall—it's really different from company values, ethics, policies, or management competencies, which are fairly common. Instead, this would describe accepted approaches and characteristics of your desired "leadership culture." An example, in part, would look like this:

> **"We expect our leaders to . . .**
> **. . . consistently ask how their actions and operations impact our customers.**
> **. . . have a clear and focused set of improvement priorities that are managed as an investment.**
> **. . . critically assess ideas and assumptions and support decisions with facts.**
> **. . . reach out to other parts of the business to address issues/opportunities that demand a broader approach.**

> . . . fight complacency by constantly challenging the status quo
> and looking for opportunities to do better.
> . . . accept responsibility for problems and share credit for suc-
> cesses.

I would not endeavor to *tell* you what your leadership vision ought to be. While the principles of Six Sigma Leadership have consistent themes, there is also a good deal of flexibility and the vision for *your* business should fit your strategy and goals, as well as be informed by the current culture and history of the organization.

Organizational Action Four: Upgrade Performance Management Systems

This is the action to consider when you're ready to get serious. Raising the standard of leadership across your organization can happen through advocacy and your good example, but current habits are deeply ingrained. To make smarter leadership a *consistent* advantage for your business, it should be part of how you assess people. I've long since lost count of the times (dozens at least) I've heard the comment, from senior managers as well as folks in the trenches: "People around here are rewarded for firefighting." Or "We have way more projects than we handle." If people are rewarded for heroism instead of preventing problems, or never see consequences of their bad habits, you won't be able to sustain Six Sigma Leadership.

This task is *not* to be undertaken lightly. Adjusting how you evaluate leaders, and followers, is one of most challenging changes you can engineer. There are many reasons *not* to do it—people are trying, they do a pretty good job, business is good. On the other hand, *not* upgrading your performance management criteria means you are very likely *not* going to see meaningful change in your organization's standard of leadership for any extended period.

Please note, in light of the "taking your own medicine" princi-ple, that the most important group whose evaluation criteria ought to be upgraded is *leaders*—very likely including yourself.

Organizational Action Five: Link Leadership
Improvement to Business Results

There are many *personal* traits and abilities—charisma, great speaking skills, passion, courage—that can contribute to the effectiveness of a leader. But those are very challenging to quantify, difficult to develop (they tend to be inherent to the individual), and especially hard to tie to meaningful business benefits. Six Sigma Leadership, on the other hand, is observable, learnable, and relatively easy to link to achievement of critical results. Working on the right things, asking the right questions, gaining insights to customers—all these are practices you can assess and connect to real organizational objectives. In doing so, you can avoid making "Leadership" and "business results" two important but disconnected variables in your success equation.

This action may be tied to *Action Four*, performance management criteria. However, it can also be incorporated into routine, informal "coaching" efforts. Sample questions/comments to use with your team include:

- When you investigate this opportunity, be sure to assess how it will impact our customers.
- We don't want to bite off more than we can chew. Get with your team and review your priorities before determining how best to meet our goal.
- There need to be some clear, measurable benefits to tie to this initiative. Define some metrics and financial impact before going too far.
- This looks like a big issue that we can turn to our advantage. But first we need to challenge and validate our assumptions.
- We can't solve this on our own. Contact Sully and see about getting an interdepartmental team together.

Hopefully these "coaching comments" help you see that Six Sigma Leader practices really have the greatest impact, and show up clearly as common sense methods, when linked to the right business opportunities. Leadership aims for results; the opportunity for results provides a context for smarter leadership.

STRIVING FOR A NEW STANDARD

In the Quality field, before Six Sigma came along, there was a program that went by the initials "ZD," for "zero defects." People were encouraged to strive for the standard of zero defects on the job. A lot of posters were printed and training was delivered urging people to get behind the Zero Defects goal. With hindsight, I think most ZD programs were somewhat misguided. For one thing, few of us want to be judged by a zero defects standard; second, almost no one really accepts it can be done. As noted in Chapter 7, it's often difficult to even agree what a defect *is*.

The Six Sigma measure changed that standard in a subtle but very important way: it acknowledges that there's no such thing as perfect (or Zero Defects). But it strives for something as increasingly near to perfect as the business can achieve. By understanding a customer's needs, the process for creating value, the causes that inhibit success, and the measures that track performance you can narrow the likelihood of defects substantially. Similarly, by intelligently linking customer or market needs to critical decision points in a streamlined process, you can turn a slow, dumb, costly business into a lean, responsive powerhouse.

As you reflect on what you can learn and apply from *The Six Sigma Leader*, one of the most important things to remember is that the standard for leadership in the 21st-century is *not* perfection: it's the continual striving to become a better, smarter, more balanced leader. It would be easy to say it's "too hard" or "I don't have time"—but those excuses only work if you assume the expectation is to suddenly upgrade yourself into some super-leader. That's neither realistic nor necessary.

The real key to Six Sigma Leadership is to accept the standard of *approaching* perfection, knowing you will not achieve it (there *is* no perfect leader), but knowing also that by adopting that standard you have the potential to be a *much* more successful leader than you would otherwise be. The same, of course, is true of the organization you lead. Holding its achievements to a higher standard—knowing it won't be any more perfect than you are—gives you a context for exercising and measuring your own skills as a leader.

In presenting principles of Six Sigma Leadership, I've tried to avoid making it formulaic, inhibiting, or theoretical. That leaves you with the opportunity to now interpret and decide which elements—which smart habits—you want to work on first. And that's just where I invite you to start the journey. Having clear priorities is a principle of Six Sigma Leadership, so it makes sense to focus your own effort to achieve that higher standard. It then becomes a process of reviewing, redefining, and evaluating your own performance against the new standard.

So, in closing, these are the most important actions you can take to achieve your return from having invested in reading these pages:

1. Accept and enthusiastically welcome the challenge of striving to become the best leader you can be.
2. Identify your personal "starting point" for upgrading your habits; continually work on all your habits over time.
3. Tie your identity and success criteria as a leader to the effectiveness and performance of your organization.
4. Don't expect Zero Defects, but try to be as close to perfect as you can.

I believe if you accept the standard and recognize your own capacity to improve, you can indeed be a Six Sigma Leader. By deciding to open this book and reaching this point, you have demonstrated all the discipline and commitment that will be required. Congratulations. Welcome to the journey.

Life under Six Sigma Leadership

The first responsibility of a leader is to define reality. The last is to say thank you.

—Max DePree

Let's END the book by putting the pieces together: examining the opportunities and challenges of Six Sigma Leadership in action through a story of a leader and business under the real pressure of change, competition, and the need to replace old habits with new, smarter ones.

This scenario is fictional, but is based on real-life observations and situations distilled from over 20 years of consulting experience. You will note that adhering to a higher standard of leadership performance is *not* a quick and easy thing even in fictional situations. At the same time, I hope you'll also notice that the ability to be a much smarter leader is already present in most individuals in leadership roles today, *if* they begin to assess their own actions more objectively and honestly. From there, the impact can be impressive.

SETTING THE SCENE

Sam Lee is vice president and head of the Door-Lock Division at Global Lock & Security Corporation, a 52-year-old business that has become a worldwide manufacturer and distributor of all kinds of locks, safes, and other equipment to protect homes, businesses, and other property.

Sam's career at Global Lock began when he was in his mid-20s. He'd started his career in marketing for a high-tech company and enjoyed it for a while, but the opportunities and challenges he saw at Global Lock were very appealing, and when he was offered a spot in their international management development program 15 years ago he jumped at it. There have been no regrets.

Sam has worked in a variety of jobs at Global Lock, including sales and operations, and has worked in several countries. His ability to get things done—even by himself, if necessary—caught the eye of senior management and he was put on a leadership succession plan. He was named head of the Door-Lock Division 18 months ago, moving from the Portable Security division where he ran marketing.

Door-Lock's specialty is locksets for homes and offices. The division is not the biggest in the company; that prize goes to the Commercial group, which serves industrial and construction markets. Portable Security, where Sam came from, is also larger than Door-Lock and sells padlocks and other smaller locking mechanisms for equipment, vehicles, guns, and bicycles.

ALL SYSTEMS GO?

When Sam took over the Door-Lock Division, his boss, Global Lock COO Steve Langdorff, told him it was critical to hit the ground running. "There are a lot of issues with this division," Langdorff commented, "and if we aren't taking action quickly there may be some problems keeping the operation in the black." It took Sam a while to get a handle on what those issues were (Langdorff had not provided a lot of details). In talking with directors of the different business units and functions, he was able to glean some facts:

- The Door-Lock Division was making a good profit, but margins were getting thinner, especially in the booming Asia markets.
- To meet demand in Asia, the firm was investing in new capacity, but it was taking time to bring the new production on line.
- A couple of Global's competitors had recently introduced locksets with special identity recognition features that were threatening to make a dent in the Division's revenues; however, it seems there were technical problems with some of those new products.
- Some salespeople had reported that distributors were unhappy about the unreliable delivery of Global door lock products.
- Each member of the division leadership seemed to have a different view of the group's major issues. Some mentioned costs being too high, others complained about lack of innovation. Others said marketing was not effectively presenting the company's advantages to distributors.
- Everyone agreed that Global's design flair was one of the most important keys (pun intended!) to the Doors division's success and was still a passion of many old-timers in the company.

Sam put some immediate changes in place. He knew it would be important to get the Division's attention by swift action—and after all, that's what his boss had recommended. "I'm very concerned about this new technology that's hitting the market," he announced to his first management team all-hands meeting. "I've been told it will take a year to get our entry into the personal ID market in production—I want us to cut that to 8 months!" To lead the effort, Sam was able to convince Stella LoBianco, his right-hand person back at Portable Security, to join Door-Lock; Stella brought two of her best people to work with her.

Sam also issued a stern warning about the thinning margins: "I'm counting on each of you to help boost our profitability. I want each department head to identify 7 percent in budget cuts for the remainder of this year, along with another 7 percent for next fiscal year." (Sam noticed a few people looking a bit dismayed at that challenge, but he knew it was important to be forceful and in command. And to deal with the price pressures the company was facing.)

"I'm confident if we all put our heads down and get on with meeting these challenges, we'll be able to deliver on the targets Steve Langdorff has given me."

Some of the feedback he got after the meeting bothered Sam a bit. His director of Logistics, Sanji Lata, made an appointment to see him the following week and complained about the budget cuts. "I have people working overtime constantly dealing with correcting messed up and late shipments and now you're saying I have to give some of them up! How are we going to get products out if we don't have people to handle these problems?" Lata complained.

Sam thought Sanji had a point, so he told him to aim for a 3 percent cut. "I don't want to make this too painful," he explained to Lata. "And you're right about getting the shipments fixed." Sam also reminded Lata of the new order management software system that was in the works. "Once you have that, I'm pretty sure you'll be able to cut even more than 7 percent!" Sam exclaimed optimistically. Lata looked both relieved and a bit uncertain as he thanked Sam and left.

Over the following months, Sam remained positive about the new direction and discipline he was instilling in the Door-Lock division. He had utmost confidence in Stella LoBianco to develop the new technology; he knew the budget cuts would help the financial picture; and he felt he'd set a tone where the group would respect him. He was a bit surprised to find out the bonus plan for Door-Lock was different from the one in his old division; that each manager was given a fairly small incentive payment at the end of the year based on department goals being met and not on performance of the division as a whole. He argued about it with Sy Lowe, the division HR manager, but Sy convinced him that Door-Lock had been very successful with that kind of plan for quite a few years.

"Wouldn't want to shake things up," Lowe explained, "when folks are used to something like that."

Still, the monthly management meetings were reassuring. He asked each BU and department head to make a brief 10-minute presentation on his or her area and to focus on the achievements each had made. "I want results, not problems," was how he defined the objectives of the meeting. And that was what he got! Each manager had good things to say about progress and accomplishments.

On a couple of occasions, some arguments broke out when one manager challenged something in one of the presentations. For example, the head of sales for the office lock business unit seemed a bit upset when Sanji Lata of Logistics claimed success in cutting order errors by 26 percent, which he estimated was about 2,000 fewer bad shipments per quarter. "But that still leaves us with about 7,500 messed-up shipments, right?!" the salesperson challenged. Sanji noted that the data was only an estimate and his 26 percent reduction was a conservative number.

"Really, it's hard to pin down the exact number of bad shipments," Sanji explained, "because it changes a lot from week to week. We're doing our best with the data and the staff we have available." Sam told the group that he did not think anyone could criticize Logistics when they had made some big strides in improvement. He heard someone from the back of the room remark that Logistics had gotten a break on budget cuts, but other than that, Sam's comment ended the debate.

UNRAVELING IN THE DOOR-LOCK DIVISION

About seven months into his tenure, Sam began to get some signs that made him uncomfortable. The first alarm came when one of the largest office lock distributors in Europe sent a terse letter saying that it would stop carrying Global Lock's products. The letter mentioned issues with unreliability of shipments and the impact that was having with design and construction firms that were the distributor's customers. Sam brought in the Sales head for office locks, Sarah Lightfoot, and Sanji Lata from Logistics. "What the heck happened?" Sam demanded.

"I'm not sure," Sanji answered first. "I know we'd reduced the problem, but I guess not enough."

"Well, this is why I raised the question two months ago!" reacted Sarah. "Losing this distribution is going to knock out 20 percent of our sales in the EU and it could have been avoided."

"I can only do so much," Sanji responded. "We have to deal with the production group and they are very hard to get coopera-tion from. We're just one division and so my team has to deal with the shipment issues on the back end of the process."

Sam was aware that Global Lock's centralized manufacturing operations were a thorn in the side of the Divisions; he'd had issues with it while at Portable Security, though as a larger division it had more clout—plus its customers were much less picky than the dis-tributors Doors had to deal with. (They could be a pain!) He'd been relying on Logistics to deal with the issues and spending his time making sure the budget cuts were being made as ordered. Sam had not felt a need to get involved in any production issue. . . .

Sam was keeping in close touch with Stella LoBianco, his long-time colleague from the Portable days, and the new technology development effort she'd been brought in to lead. It had taken Stella a while to get things moving. The existing new products people in Doors were not willing to cooperate with her at first. They kept making excuses about not having time to meet with Stella or the other people she'd brought with her from Portables. There were already six fairly significant new product development programs under way when Sam announced the major new initia-tive. He did not want his boss, Steve Langdorff, to think he was backing off on any of the existing efforts, so he challenged Stella and the current development leader to keep all the initiatives on track. He realized that would be a stretch, but he also had faith in Stella's hard-charging style to keep people working at top speed.

But things improved after these initial struggles. Stella and her team had pulled some of the better development people off the existing projects and gotten them going on the new technology effort. Sam was able to get extra funds to bring in experts in personal recognition systems to help in the development. They had a prototype ready in four months and, though the costs were high and the price they would have to charge would be a steep premium, Sam green-lighted the first two products—one for home and one for office—to go into full-scale production.

Then Stella came to his office one day looking worried. "I've been so focused on getting this product ready, and I'm really proud of what we've done. But now I'm starting to think we may have made a mistake." Sam sat up and asked her what the problem was.

"It's really several things. We've done an outstanding job avoiding the technical problems our competitors had with their high-tech locks. We thought their low initial sales were tied to the quality problems—except our salespeople are starting to think it was a deeper issue."

"What?" Sam asked impatiently. Stella was usually quicker at getting to the point.

"There's not much demand for personal recognition locks for homes. Certainly not at the premium prices we're charging. That may be what *really* caused the other firms to scale back their technology offerings."

"What about the office market?" Sam asked, looking for a bright side.

"There's *definitely* demand for enhanced technology in the office arena," she replied.

Sam felt his spirits jump. "Except we can't tap into it—and I'll tell you why." (She knew Sam was starting to get nervous and wanted to get it all out.) "We have two obstacles: First, integrated security system companies have a better connection with the people who are ready to invest in these more sophisticated products, and some already are selling products like ours. Second, even though our new products have advantages over those existing ones—ours are less expensive, believe it or not—our reputation for unreliable delivery keeps coming up."

"How did you find all this out?"

"Well, I started meeting with the sales guys in the office and home business units about a month ago." Stella hesitated before continuing. "I'm sorry, Sam, I should have told you sooner. I'd been so focused on getting the development work done, but when we'd have our management meetings I could see a lot of the people looking very uncomfortable; either that or just zoning out. And I felt like I was isolated, and you were isolated, and that maybe we hadn't paid close enough attention to what was happening in the division. Plus I knew pretty soon we were going to have to start *selling* this new stuff and wanted to see what the salespeople were thinking." She looked at Sam intensely. "What I started to hear was worse than I expected."

Sam felt blindsided. But he knew Stella, despite her tough reputation, was a very smart manager and always more interested in the company's success than her own, which was why they had seen eye-to-eye so many times. At Portable, they'd had to fight against the short-term view more than once. Now he began to suspect he might have fallen into that same trap himself—though he knew Steve Langdorff seemed satisfied with how he'd gotten started at Door-Lock.

"What do you think we ought to do?" Sam asked.

"Probably think things over a bit, first," Stella replied. "I know I agreed with how you set a strong tone and aggressive goals when you came here and that's one reason I agreed to move to Doors. But maybe we let ourselves get a little overconfident? The sales guys have shared some feedback about how the whole division has been very upset and even afraid to say much. Most folks are just doing their jobs and keeping their heads down—especially with the budget cuts still being decided on."

"How come I've not heard about this?" Sam was still doubting Stella's unsettling picture of the division.

"I know you'd have been open to hearing about issues in the past, but the other folks here don't know you that well. And you set an expectation through the managers' meeting agendas when you asked for results and not problems. So you *didn't* hear about problems. Neither did I, until I started to ask."

"I've talked a lot to Sanji about the Logistics issues with delivery errors!"

"Well, that really reflects a bigger problem," Stella commented. "We dealt with the production group back at the Portable division and it was always an adversarial thing. But we could get away with more order troubles than the Doors distributors will tolerate.

"So Sanji and his team are just cleaning up problems that have already happened and he can't get any help from the production side. Apparently he's given up trying. Since the production people are only rewarded for meeting quota and cutting costs from suppliers, and because they're in a corporate role, they've come to see themselves as the lynchpin of the company—but not really responsible to the divisions."

At this point, Stella left to attend a conference call. Alone in his office, Sam began reflecting on how he'd handled the division up to that point. He began to see some points where, as head of Door-Lock, he'd made mistakes or taken action he would probably not have done earlier in his career. He found it very hard to come to grips with not being the totally on-target leader he'd imagined himself to be.

Sam decided to follow Stella's lead in getting more input from "the troops."

TESTING SOME ASSUMPTIONS

Sam's first step was to talk to Sanji in Logistics. "Sanji, I know your team is working very hard to solve delivery problems, but is that really possible?"

Sanji hesitated. "Do you really want the truth?"

"Maybe not," Sam said with a half-smile. "But try me."

Sanji decided to go for it. "Frankly, I don't know if it is possible. It feels like we're working all by ourselves on issues that ought to be an enterprise concern. For example, sales doesn't always tell us about problems until weeks later—so we don't really know what's going on. And we get less input now because other departments are angry we got a break on the budget cuts."

"What about dealing with Production?" Sam inquired.

"I'm sure there are some very good people there, but we get so little cooperation from them. Because much of our data is anecdotal and comes after shipments are on the way they don't give us much credibility."

Sam next talked to each of his sales chiefs: Sarah Lightfoot from the office business unit and Sebastian Leverovsky in the home group. He asked their frank opinions about the state of the division. Sarah spoke up first: "Sam, you've tried, I realize, but I just think you missed some of our inherent problems when you took over, and actually have made a lot of them worse."

Sam turned to Sebastian: "Honestly, when you took over the division I thought, 'This is the kind of kick in the butt people need around here.' We've had a good comfortable run of success and we're not near death yet, but we need to be smarter and tougher. And you're definitely smart and tough, Sam. At first I really liked our management meetings; I was tired of people complaining about their problems." Sebastian paused and sighed before continuing. "But I've begun to think we're just *hiding* problems. We need to be a different kind of smart and tough to make Door-Locks what it can be."

Sam nodded. He appreciated the candor of the sales chiefs, even though the message was not what he'd have hoped for. Their comments were fresh on his mind when Sam called Suki Lehto, the bright head of the Door-Lock R&D team into his office. R&D handled new product development efforts for both the home and office divisions. Suki took a while to open up, but when she did, it was a bit like a dam breaking. "I've had to cut back on staff and materials, taken on a huge new development effort with technology that's already been developed by *other divisions* [this was news to Sam], and still been pushed to finish six other projects that were already under way. The result is that not much is getting done and my team is totally burned out!"

He hoped to get some relief after hearing from Suki by talking with division IT manager, Sigmund London. No such luck. Sigmund had his own perspective, but much of it fit with comments from the other managers: too many demands, too little direction, not enough understanding of the real problems, and little coordination among the various groups, both within the division and with other parts of Global Lock.

"Did Sanji mention this new order management application we're about to launch?" Sigmund asked. Sam shook his head, inviting Sigmund to continue. "Okay, the order management system will work just fine, *but* it's not going to do anything to address the high number of bad shipments. It took the Logistics folks a while to realize this, even though my people had told them that simply having an easier way to *fix* errors will not reduce the errors themselves."

These chats took place over a span of a couple of weeks. Meantime, Sam reflected a lot on the way the division had been run before he came on board and how he'd handled these first several months. He realized that his approach was pretty "by the book" in terms of the way he'd seen other leaders at Global operate when they took over a division. But somehow it was not working out as he'd hoped. . . .

SAM TAKES SOME FIRST STEPS

Having made a "big splash" when he'd taken the helm in the Door-Lock division, Sam was wary of over-reacting. Luckily the division was still making money and not in immediate danger, though icebergs were on the horizon. He also knew that as a leader he could not make the necessary changes in the division on his own.

Nothing could be undone overnight, and it would take a team effort for any change to really stick.

He decided to start with a simple, but meaningful step. For the next managers' meeting he asked each group to leave their "accomplishments" slides in their offices. Instead, he asked them to come with a "short list" of two top issues or concerns that the group saw in the Door-Lock Division. He asked only for a short description and some facts to validate the problem or issue. Other groups would only be allowed to ask clarification questions, but not to object or make any other comments about whether the issue was real or not, or whose fault it was.

Sam led off the meeting with some remarks: "Through my conversations with all of you, it's become obvious we need to clear the air, and get ourselves aligned and focused. For today at least, please do your best to listen and not judge. There will be time to evaluate. For right now, I think everyone needs a bit of time to process where we are, or think we are."

The group stuck to the meeting ground rules for the most part; they'd become used to sitting and listening anyway. There were a few discussions that went astray and threatened to get heated, but Stella and some of the others reminded the group that the main objective was just to listen. Sam himself was about to throw out a suggested solution once, but thought twice and realized his idea was premature.

That first meeting began a process of identifying the division's challenges, as well as the needed improvements in how the division was being run. Sam definitely took the lead, but he found it surprising how many of the management team were willing to talk openly, once they became confident that he was open to new ideas.

It was not all smooth, happy conversation either—the management meetings got pretty heated at times as some long-held assumptions were tested and past problems finally got an airing. In some cases, Sam had to make some proposals when an argument seemed to reach an impasse. He was able to get people to "agree to disagree," but move forward.

After a few weeks, Sam held a special meeting where he presented the managers a summary of the critical issues affecting the Door-Lock division. "I think by now most all of us have come to terms with these challenges," Sam noted. First he addressed the high priority business challenges; these included:

- *High rates of delivery errors*. Sam commented, "Even without really accurate data we know this is an issue for both BUs. We've tried to address them through constant *fixing*, but we need to address the causes. We need to get the Production group involved, but we can't assume they are causing the issues either—after all, we take the orders.
- *New product portfolio and resources*. "I pushed us to leap too quickly into developing products based on new personal identification technologies. We need to look at this area strategically to understand how we can become competitive, build success in the home market, and deal with our shortcomings in the office market. We also need to work with other divisions to leverage our work in these technologies— there's a huge need for better collaboration across Global Lock. We also have to review the new products on the drawing board. Some look suspiciously like ideas we think are cool, but that no customer will ever care about. We may not be investing our resources in the right place."
- *Address margin pressures*. "Every new boss I've had, both before I came to Global and since, has started out by asking people to tighten their belts. When I saw how tough things are getting in Asia it seemed like I ought to do the same. Well, that was not smart. I thought it would challenge people to be more efficient, but it did not offer a solution any more subtle than a chainsaw. 'How do we salvage our margins?' Frankly, I don't know. I have quite a few *ideas* and I know you all do, too. We need to look at value all across our supply chain to determine how we can combine innovation, flexibility, and efficiency to be the best *and most profitable* provider in our markets."

After reviewing these business issues—and pledging to put his entire focus as head of the division on those priorities—Sam turned to the management and leadership issues facing the division.

- *Teamwork.* "The good news is, this is already starting. We have to keep working and progressing as a team, and soon (but not yet) start reaching outside of the division to work with our partners within Global as well as our distributors. This is a problem that was here before I took over and it's going to take time to get us operating like a well-oiled machine."
- *Alignment.* "This is a really big one, so I'll break it into two areas: One is setting our sights on customers—*especially* our end users. Our distributors carry many products besides door locks; we need to get closer to the people who *install* and *use* our locks so we can better meet their needs. If we can show distributors how to make more money on door locks by helping them understand *their* customers, we may discover one of the answers to our margin challenges. Second is my responsibility: how we assess our performance. The things we need to do—for example, working more as a team, or preventing problems—are not really evaluated in our current review process. And too often departments are given incentives that don't mesh with our overall goals. I've asked Sy Lowe in his role as our HR expert to start helping upgrade our performance review process. He'll be asking for your help. The vision is for a plan that recognizes and rewards contributions to the overall cause as well as individual achievement."
- *Priorities.* "When I came to Door-Lock, I knew your plates were full—but that didn't stop me from piling on *more* priorities, even while asking you to cut resources. I used to complain about that when I was an employee and even a manager—and now I've learned a lesson we all need to take to heart: If we don't figure out and focus on the *important*

stuff, it'll be *much* harder to achieve our goals. I hope the list of business priorities I've just reviewed reinforces the point: we have to be ambitious, aggressive, and bold, but not foolish about it by trying to do too much. We will have to be advocates for this new focus. The eager people in our offices around the world will want to take initiative on their own. Our job will be to guide their energy toward the things that are critical to the division. And we'll need to listen to their concerns, because they may see problems and opportunities we would miss."

- *Facts and assumptions.* "The progress we've already made on this one is very encouraging. I think we at Global have tended to operate with the attitude I heard Jack Welch of GE describe once: 'If we're going to base this on opinion, I'd prefer to use my *own*.' But by challenging our assumptions openly and looking for facts more consistently, we have a big opportunity to make our decisions and solutions much stronger. I've also been using something called the '10-Second Rule.' I'm trying to add a few extra seconds before I speak or act, to check my own thoughts and opinions. It's quick . . . and it works!"

At that point, Sebastian Leverovsky from home sales asked if opinions didn't count any more.

"Opinions and intuition will *always* count, Sebastian. We can't expect conclusive proof for everything we do; our gut will sometimes be our guide. However, we do have to be more disciplined about checking our beliefs with facts. And over time, we need to develop and use better measures so we can really see the impact of our actions."

Sam realized he'd spoken for a long time, but knew his messages were important *and* well received by most of the managers. There were a couple he was concerned about—one long-term person who seemed unable to accept change in the division, and other young "star" who was convinced he had the answer no matter what. He wondered if they'd be able to keep up with the rest of the group.

SMART LEADERSHIP PAYS OFF AT GLOBAL LOCK

The following weeks brought a mix of excitement and progress along with several lessons learned. Sam and his team found that in some ways it was easier to address the business problems than to adapt their own leadership approaches. But all agreed that either one on its own would have been much less beneficial; and in reality they were working hand-in-hand.

One of the big, immediate benefits was the improving collaboration across the different departments. For example, Sales and Logistics started to together work on the problem of order errors, making some important discoveries. They learned, for instance, that Sales was not spending adequate time with Distributors to determine their optimal inventory levels. That contributed to shipment problems that could be corrected with better communication across the supply chain.

Instances of departments or country offices working on their own "pet projects" did not cease overnight, of course. Sam instituted a regular "portfolio review" for the division, and asked each manager to do the same in his or her own department. The division's employees began to see a real difference when managers actually *reduced* the list of current priorities, redirecting people to focus on opportunities aligned with division initiatives. Learning to reach out to other groups took time, but it was definitely a positive change for the division

As Sam had expected, it was not always easy for the leaders to stay on the right path. They had a long history of reacting to problems as if they *knew* the answers. But they began to keep one another in check. For example, when Sam sat in on a meeting and kept pushing one of his own ideas, the entire room practically stopped and stared at him. "Oh, sorry," he said. "Guess I'm breaking my own rule about not falling in love with our own assumptions."

Fortunately, the benefit of *validating* assumptions helped them to avoid taking some unneeded actions in some cases, and to develop *better* solutions in others. It was that process that led to identifying some product features that were especially popular in the tough Asia market; this led to both higher margins and increased sales volume.

The new performance management plan was taking shape and would go into effect in the following quarter. The team found it extremely helpful to use a diagram or map of the whole division—not too detailed, but just enough to see the basic flow of critical work and responsibilities—to give Sy in HR a much better starting point for ways to align performance goals and criteria.

After a couple of months, Sam started to turn his attention toward expanding the scope of change, both inward and outward in the organization. Seeing how other levels of the organization were still wrestling with an unfamiliar beast—leaders asking for more facts, more focus, and more teamwork—he began a series of informal meetings with Door-Lock people around the world to share the vision and the key business priorities. It meant a lot of traveling, but Sam felt it was worthwhile and received very positive feedback. He also asked Sy to review how performance management criteria could be upgraded for other levels of the organization to better reward smarter thinking and results for every associate.

The second area of focus for Sam—outward—involved other groups within Global Lock. Knowing that his team might lack the clout to tackle the delivery issues on an "end-to-end" basis, he made initial contact with the heads of Production and Purchasing to engage them in an effort to explore the problems, both short- and longer-term. He also got in touch with other division heads and convened a meeting to discuss *corporate* strategies for new technology development. Despite some old-fashioned "not-invented-here" skepticism, that first meeting surfaced some immediate opportunities for the divisions to share knowledge and resources.

Sam couldn't help feeling fortunate about how things had played out. He mentioned it to Stella when they were reviewing progress (she had taken on a special, part-time role of Change Champion in the division). "I probably shouldn't admit this," Sam confessed, "but it seems like if I hadn't come on so strong when I took over the division I might not have realized the need to change. I can look back and see many cases where we should have looked more closely at our leadership approach, but we always had some excuse—we don't have time, business is good, business is bad, whatever—and we just ignored it."

Stella agreed. As they looked over some of the promising sales numbers (up 14 percent worldwide) and reviewed the new insights their "voice of the customer" research was gleaning about *users* of Door-Lock products, Stella had an insight: "You know, it's usually one or the other. A business can try to improve processes or improve leadership. Like, you fix leadership one day, and you work on the business the next. This feels right, and is working for us, because we're doing both *together*!"

"Hope we can keep it up!" Sam responded.

"No kidding!" Stella laughed.

We leave Sam, Stella, and the Global Lock team with the story upbeat, promising, and yet unfinished. Because as any smart Leader knows, an inescapable challenge—and thrill—of leadership is that the story is really never complete. And for the 21st-century leader, the only way to ensure a consistently positive story is to stay close to customers, maintain balance and flexibility, and continually set and demand a higher standard for yourself and others. That is the essence of Six Sigma Leadership.

Index

About the Author

Peter S. Pande is president of Pivotal Resources, a global change leadership consulting firm. In a 20-year career supporting all types of business and process change efforts, he has worked with many leading companies including Cisco, GE, Starwood Hotels, BP, American Express, and adidas. He is coauthor of the bestselling *The Six Sigma Way*, *The Six Sigma Way Team Fieldbook*, and *What Is Six Sigma?*, all available from McGraw-Hill.

For additional background see www.pivotalresources.com or address comments to ssl@pivotalresources.com.